Hesiod's Ascra

Hesiod's Ascra

ANTHONY T. EDWARDS

University of California Press

BERKELEY   LOS ANGELES   LONDON

University of California Press
Berkeley and Los Angeles, California

University of California Press, Ltd.
London, England

Library of Congress Cataloging-in-Publication Data

Edwards, Anthony T.
  Hesiod's Ascra / Anthony T. Edwards.
    p.   cm.
  Includes bibliographical references and index.
  ISBN 0-520-23658-0 (cloth : alk. paper)
  1. Hesiod. Works and days. 2. Hesiod—Homes and haunts—
Greece—Ascra. 3. Didactic poetry, Greek—History and criticism.
4. Hesiod—Knowledge—Ascra (Greece). 5. Boeotia (Greece)—In
literature. 6. Ascra (Greece)—In literature. 7. Farmers—Greece—
Biography. 8. Poets, Greek—Biography. 9. Agriculture in literature.
10. Farm life in literature. 11. Villages in literature. I. Title.

PA4009.07 E39   2004
881'.01—dc21

                                    2003003877

Manufactured in the United States of America
13 12 11 10 09 08 07 06 05 04
10 9 8 7 6 5 4 3 2 1

For Leslie

Contents

Illustrations

Preface

The origins of the present study lie in another project, still under way, dealing with the representation of the countryside in the literature of Archaic and Classical Greece. In the course of writing a chapter on *Works and Days* for that study I became increasingly dissatisfied with accounts of the historical context of the poem. As I devoted more space to that issue, the topic took on a life of its own and ultimately has itself grown into a book. This enterprise has led me, a literary scholar, into the unfamiliar terrain of writing about history. The upshot is a book that risks appearing inadequately historical to historians, inadequately archaeological to archaeologists, and not very literary to literary scholars. In my defense I would argue that such a chimerical quality is an unavoidable result when one attempts to squeeze history out of a poem. Adding to the difficulty is the slender amount of information otherwise available about Ascra, Hesiod, Thespiae, Boeotia, and the period of the late eighth and early seventh centuries in Greece generally.

I must also confess to having dipped my hand into the cookie jar of anthropological theory, although I have tried to be judicious in my reference to sociocultural evolution. In particular I have striven not to fetishize models by using them deductively, to predict the presence of institutions or practices to which Hesiod does not explicitly attest. It is my intention that such models and their analytic categories serve rather as a guide to productive questions and as a framework for evaluating evidence and arranging it in sensible patterns. In the face of the generalizing force of theoretical descriptions and ideal types, which threaten to efface all that is unique to a specific time and place, I have tried to keep my nose securely anchored in the text of *Works and Days* and to insist that my claims are supported there first. It is my assumption here, however, that the particulars that make ancient Greece exceptional inhabit larger-scale commonalities that make comparisons among societies of different times and places both possible and fruitful.

I hope that this study will revise accepted views of the community that *Works and Days* takes for granted and that provides for us the historical context of the poem. I believe that the poem speaks of the village, not of the city, and looks back to the Dark Age and its modes of social organization more than it looks ahead to the Archaic period and the emerging polis system. If my argument is successful, it will cut the established link between *Works and Days* and the history of the polis, or, perhaps better, it will reorient our understanding of the poem's testimony on the rise of that peculiar social formation. The world described in *Works and Days* is at best only marginally connected to the most significant features of the Archaic period, namely its economic development and the rise of complex political structures. It is my hope that my picture of Ascra, as it straddles the end of the Dark Age and the beginning of the Archaic, contributes to a richer, more varied, and more nuanced vision of the early Archaic period.

First among those to whom I owe a debt for assistance is David Tandy, who not only shared with me his own *Warriors into Traders: The Power of the Market in Early Greece* when it was yet in manuscript, but also shared his considerable expertise by generously and constructively criticizing various versions of this book. I thank him here and hope that the relationship between our work will continue to be that of the good *eris*. I wish to express my gratitude as well to Walter Donlan, whose comments have substantially improved my argument, and to Ian Morris and Irad Malkin, the reviewers for the University of California Press, whose suggestions and criticisms were invaluable to me. Victor Magagna has provided me with a wealth of useful bibliography and valuable commentary on a presentation to his seminar on political theory. Finally, I remain indebted, as ever, to Leslie Collins for her acute criticisms and her patience. To thank these individuals, of course, does not suggest that they agree with what I have to say, and the mistakes and inconsistencies that remain are all mine. I also wish to thank Kate Toll, Cindy Fulton, Betsy Ditmars, and all the other staff members of the University of California Press whose expertise and effort have done so much to improve this book.

I express here my gratitude to Robin Osborne and to the editors of *Antiquity* for their generous permission to reprint material for which they hold copyright. The *Thesaurus Linguae Graecae* of the University of California at Irvine has been a valuable resource for this project. I refer unless otherwise noted to M. L. West's texts of *Works and Days* and *Theogony*.

1 Introduction

HESIOD'S ASCRA: BACKGROUND TO THE PROBLEM

Works and Days presents a double social dynamic. On the one hand the poem is animated by a contrast between village and city, Ascra and Thespiae—or so I assume—built around the figures of Hesiod and the *basilēes,* or "kings." This opposition structures the opening appeal to Perses (*W&D* 27–41) in which Hesiod advises that he stick to the farm and avoid the *agorē,* where the kings preside over disputes. On the other, the opposition between the poor and the prosperous—a slender difference, as I shall argue, for Hesiod's small world—has also left a deep imprint upon the poem, foremost in the contrast between Perses and Hesiod. This contrast is introduced by the good *eris,* "strife" (*W&D* 11–26), who stirs the shiftless and needy farmer to follow the example of his prosperous neighbor and get to work on his farm. Each of these two oppositions occupies a central place in the thematics of *Works and Days,* but there are competing accounts of their mutual relationship.

The current consensus is founded on Édouard Will's 1957 article "Aux origines du régime foncier grec. Homère, Hésiode, et l'arrière-plan Mycénien." Will explicitly employs Solon's depiction of the situation in Attica as much as a century after *Works and Days* was composed to illuminate the historical setting of *Works and Days.* The key elements of Will's account—an inheritance system leading to debt and loss of land for small holders, oppression by wealthy aristocrats, and the relationship of Hesiod's account in *Works and Days* to Solon's—reappear regularly in later discussions of the historical context of *Works and Days.*[1] Ernest Will (1965) subsequently

---

1. Detienne 1963, 15–27; Austin and Vidal-Naquet 1977, 58–59; Spahn 1980, 537–39, 544–45; Jajlenko 1988, 95–97, 108–9. Trever's article of 1924 can be added to this list as can David Tandy's recent book (1997, see especially 125–38 and

made a direct assault upon Édouard Will's central theses but nonetheless does not abandon the basic opposition of village small holders versus the city's aristocratic large holders, arguing simply that it is rather the aristocrats who are in retreat because of the inception of hoplite infantry tactics and the consequent rise in the political power of the class serving in the infantry (549–50).

Recently Victor Hanson (1995, 95–126) has argued that Hesiod represents in *Works and Days* a new breed of independent yeoman introducing intensive agriculture into previously marginal grazing land, but he sees much the same historical dynamic at work as does Ernest Will. Hanson, like Will, assumes that Ascra has already been incorporated within a discrete territory subject to the power of an aristocratic elite. Both read *Works and Days* in terms of independent small farmers locked in struggle over land and political rights with an entrenched elite of the town. Both view Hesiod as prototype of the hoplite farmer familiar from the Classical period. Indeed, Hanson observes a clear continuity between the community described by Hesiod and Solon's Athens or Theognis's Megara (1995, 120–26).

In the latest discussion of the historical setting of *Works and Days* David Tandy (1997) resumes the position that Hesiod describes in Ascra a peasant community under the authority of the *basilees* of Thespiae. The role assigned by Édouard Will to the inheritance system, however, is filled in Tandy's reconstruction by a new set of economic relations imposed by elites of cities like Thespiae upon surrounding rural zones. As with Édouard Will's scenario, the result is debt for peasants such as Perses and the alienation of their land (1997, 203–34).[2] In Tandy's view (1997, 133–34), the situation outlined by Hesiod leads directly towards that presented by Solon. All of these accounts offer scenarios for which the contrast between village and city functions as the dominant opposition in *Works and Days*, controlling a subordinate contrast between the poor and the prosperous.

208–14), though Tandy differs at points that I will discuss below. Bravo (1977, 10–24) assimilates *Works and Days* rather to Theognis's Megara, arguing that Hesiod and Perses represent impoverished aristocrats. Mele (1979, 47, 57) also has Solon and Attica in mind though Ionia perhaps looms larger as a frame of reference (40–52, passim). Thomas and Conant (1999, 144–61) present a somewhat more primitive Ascra, yet nevertheless take most of the traditional assumptions for granted.

2. Strictly speaking, Édouard Will and Detienne both argue that land was at this time inalienable but that cultivators lost control of it because of debt. Tandy (1997, 134) believes that private property has come into being and land is alienable. Bravo's (1977, 7) suggestion that the alienability of land came under tighter regulation only later, in the Classical period, when the polis system had crystallized—and land was in shorter supply, I might add—seems attractive.

As Tandy's analysis shows, this scenario of rural, small-scale cultivators exploited by an outside elite through some such mechanism as debt or rent is easily accommodated in comparative terms to the model of the peasant community. Already in 1945 an article authored by E. K. L. Francis appeared in the journal *Rural Sociology* with the title "The Personality Type of the Peasant According to Hesiod's *Works and Days*" More valuable, however, for its comparative approach is Robert Redfield's use of Hesiod's *Works and Days* as a case study alongside the examples of the rural people of nineteenth-century Surrey, England, and of a Mayan village of twentieth-century Yucatan. In this section of his 1956 study *Peasant Society and Culture* (105–42) Redfield argues that Hesiod in *Works and Days* expresses as much as the other two cultures studied what he considers to be the coherent and consistent outlook of the peasant society. Peter Walcot in his *Greek Peasants, Ancient and Modern* likewise argues on the basis of extensive parallels he sees between the life of modern Greek peasants and *Works and Days* that Hesiod does indeed portray there a peasant community.

Essential to the definition of the peasant is the relationship between rural cultivators and an external, usually urban, elite able to claim a share of the cultivators' produce. Redfield (1953, 30–31) states this clearly in a discussion of the origins of the peasant: "The developing city required economic support from a wider and wider area of production, and so affected, at first only in terms of labor, tribute, and sale, peoples as yet not civilized, or only partly civilized. . . . It required the city to bring [the peasant] into existence. There were no peasants before the first cities." Essential to Redfield's definition of the peasant as developed in the first two chapters of his *Peasant Society and Culture* (1956) are the hierarchy of city and country and the influence and control exercised over the rural domain by an urban elite. Peasant societies exist in a symbiosis of urban and rural in which they are dependent politically, economically, and culturally upon the city. The ability of the peasant community to organize and regulate itself is truncated at a certain point by the intervention of an external elite incorporating that community within a larger system of political, social, and economic relationships. It is this dynamic, organizing relations between rural community and outside elite, that Redfield refers to when he designates peasantries as "part-societies with part-cultures."[3] Walcot's discussion of

3. Redfield's implicit bias in favor of "civilization," the culture of the city, is discussed formally in Redfield 1953, 139–65. Redfield assumes that Hesiod's Ascra was indeed dependent upon the neighboring city of Thespiae. Francis (1945, 282), whose article Redfield refers to frequently, likewise takes this for granted. Francis, for his part, is also familiar with Redfield's views on peasant societies: 277 n. 4.

relations between Hesiod's village and the world beyond takes Redfield's discussion as an explicit starting point to argue for the dependence of Ascra upon the "kings" of the city (Walcot 1970, 94–117).

The peasant's values and traditional way of life cannot be separated from the subservient status of peasant communities upon which Redfield insists, an element in its essentials has persisted in the definition of the peasant.[4] As regards this issue in the relation of Hesiod's Ascra to the kings of Thespiae, the analysis of *Works and Days* on the basis of comparative ethnographic models corresponds closely to the results of historical studies working back from Solon to Hesiod. Both analyses turn on the political and economic power exercised by an outside elite over the cultivators of Ascra. The use of the ethnographic model of the peasant society is attractive not only because some have tied it explicitly to the community depicted by Hesiod in *Works and Days* but also since, in a more general way, it makes it possible to evaluate Hesiod's testimony against a broad set of features that ought to accompany the most prominent institutions and relations in his account. That is, the peasant model enables us to ask whether *Works and Days* exhibits the full range of characteristics typical of communities of small cultivators that have come under the power of an outside elite.

It is from this perspective that I wish to comment upon the work of Paul Millett. Millett (1984) has, in my view, shed considerable light on this issue of the customs and institutions of *Works and Days* by jettisoning Solon and relations with the city in exchange for comparative ethnographic data on peasant societies. Millett argues—quite rightly, I think—that in fact the city occupies a place altogether peripheral to Hesiod's experience as it is portrayed in *Works and Days*.[5] Yet this assertion has its costs. In a detailed consideration of the criteria employed to define the peasant (Millett 1984, 90–93) Millett zeroes in on the status of peasant communities as "part societies," "subject to demands and sanctions of power-holders," with explicit reference to Redfield's work, but he does so only to disqualify this criterion as inappropriate to the analysis of ancient societies. This, of

4. On this point see Victor Magagna's discussion of the "forces of constraint" in Magagna 1991, 25–46. See also, e.g., Ellis 1993, 5–7; Johnson and Earle 1987, 297–301; Shanin 1987, 2–5; Thorner 1987, 62–65; Scott 1976, 44–55, 157, 180–92; Wolf 1966, 10–12, 48–59. All of these discussions include the criterion of exploitation by an outside elite. As Wolf points out, this elite does not always live in a city, but such is normally the case.

5. "So, far from living 'in terms of the city' Hesiod has dealings with the πόλις only when things go wrong in his own village community (κώμη, 639). It is argued in the following section that links beyond the individual οἶκος normally extend no further than the local community" (Millett 1984, 90–91).

course, is to cut the heart out of the concept of peasant. It is worth noting in this connection that peasant societies share with other social formations many of the features focused upon by Millett—agriculture, reciprocity, primacy of the single household, for example. What really distinguishes the peasant society is the fact of subordination to an elite along with these other features.[6] Millett thus places himself in a contradictory position: on the one hand he dismisses as inadequate a central criterion by which anthropologists have identified and described peasant communities since that criterion does not characterize *Works and Days*, but he embraces, on the other hand, the body of knowledge amassed within the limits of this faulty definition as something indispensable to understanding the society portrayed by Hesiod in that poem (1984, 92–92).[7] It is my contention that instead of attempting to argue away this fundamental discrepancy between Hesiod's Ascra and the peasant society, Millett should rather have pursued its implication that Hesiod describes a community more primitive and more autonomous than a peasantry.

One upshot of this position—that Hesiod portrays a peasant society but it is not subject to domination by an outside elite—is Millett's uncertainty about the specific historical setting of *Works and Days*. According to Millett, *Works and Days* does not represent a limited, evolutionary step away from Homer towards the tyrannies of the late Archaic but it does not testify either to a deep structural transformation of the Homeric world. Millett approves of Édouard Will's agrarian crisis theory but accepts as well

6. Cf. the progression of social formations detailed by Johnson and Earle 1987. In their characterization of the peasant society (297–301) they point to the characteristically impersonal nature of relations between peasant and elite and the lack of reciprocal responsibility obligating the elite to the peasantry, contrasting with the relations between a chief or Big Man and his followers. Cf. Sahlins 1972, 139–48.

7. See the astute comments of Whitley (1991, 362–63), who is skeptical of the characterization of Hesiod as a peasant. Hanson (1995, 95–105), who offers an unjustifiably dismal caricature of the peasant, argues emphatically that Hesiod is not a peasant but nonetheless contextualizes *Works and Days* within the familiar historical scenario of rural small holder struggling against an elite of the city and its legal and political apparatus. Although Thomas and Conant (1999, 144–61) liken Ascra more closely to the Dark Age village of Nichoria than to early Archaic Corinth (140) or Mycenae of the late Bronze Age (158–59), still they characterize Ascra and Hesiod as peasant. Burford (1993, 82–85) argues that the concept of peasant is not applicable to the ancient Greek world at all (but cf. the various forms of dependent labor described at 193–207) while T. W. Gallant (1991, 4, passim) considers that "the vast majority of ancient Greeks" were peasants. I am in general agreement with Ste. Croix (1981, 210–14), who considers the peasant farmer a common phenomenon in antiquity, distinct from slaves as well as from the propertied classes, who are supported in large part by the labor of peasants.

Ernest Will's refutation of that approach (Millett 1984, 103–7). But to make a decision about where to place Hesiod on the continuum extending from Homer to Solon and beyond would of course reopen the troubling issue of the relation of Hesiod's community to other communities and the influence, or lack thereof, of external elites in local village affairs. For once *Works and Days* is firmly anchored on the time line, the institutions and communal patterns it testifies to will need to be brought into conformity with the trajectory of Greek history from Homer to Solon. So Hesiod's community, outside the influence of the kings of Thespiae, is left floating outside the chronology as well.

This difficulty in Millett's argument points to a theoretical problem in the way historians have approached *Works and Days*. In order to grasp the place occupied within Greek history by the community that Hesiod reveals to us, it is crucial to distinguish the issue of social complexity from that of a historical chronology. Together the two produce the concept of social evolution, the process by which a society becomes more (or less) complex over time.[8] It is on the basis of this concept that *Works and Days* has been identified as a way station between Homer and Solon within the narrative of Greek historiography. It must be admitted, however, that the rudimentary chiefdoms of the Homeric polis must have emerged from simpler, less hierarchized forms of community; that the transformation of Greek society did not move relentlessly in the direction of ever more complex forms without divagation or reversal; and that the evolutionary process that the movement from the Dark Age to the Classical period describes did not progress at the same pace or follow the same itinerary in all regions of Greece. There is no compelling reason to maintain a priori that Hesiod's Ascra must occupy a location on a linear, evolutionary path between the Homeric polis and the Athens of Solon.[9] While Hesiod's *Works and Days* may as a *text* be later than Homer's epics and earlier than Solon's poems, this temporal relationship among texts does not entail that Hesiod's Ascra stand midway between the Homeric polis and Solon's Athens on an evolutionary continuum connecting the distinct forms of community attested to by those two

8. Tainter (1988, 22–37) offers a useful discussion of the concept of complexity. Sanderson (1990, 141–42, 190–95) takes issue with this criterion, which he associates particularly with the work of Robert Carneiro. See also Trigger 1998, 8–14, 167.

9. Mele (1979, 18–19 and passim) exemplifies the logic I am questioning here. There is no good reason to assume that conditions in Boeotia at the time when we assume Hesiod to be composing are so similar to what will occur in Attica a century later, during Solon's time. See Burford 1993, 17–20; Coldstream 1977, 314–15; Morris 1997, 545–48; Trever 1924, 165 and 168; and Whitley 1991, 341–46.

witnesses. The relative dates among these texts entail no necessity that Hesiod's Ascra represent a less complex form of community than Solon's Athens or a more complex form than Homer's polis. Chronology and complexity do not necessarily advance *pari passu*—decline and stagnation are also possibilities as the Greek Dark Age, for example, makes glaringly clear. Nor can the character of a social formation be deduced from its place in a temporal sequence since such an inference leaves out of account the spatial field of history, regional variations in the pace of change. In my view the Ascra of *Works and Days* represents a much less complex form of community than Homer's polis, a form that preexisted the Homeric polis and its *basilēes* and that continued to coexist alongside the newer polis well into the Archaic period in many parts of Greece. Only the advance of the process incorporating virtually all regions of Greece within the territory of one polis or another could destroy the type of community represented by Ascra, turning their inhabitants into citizens, exiles, or peasants.

These two essentially congruent approaches to *Works and Days*—that interpreting the poem in light of Solon and that assimilating Ascra to a peasant society—merge the pair of contrasting terms, village/city and poor/prosperous, according to a specific logic: poor villagers are exploited by the wealthy elite of the city. The controlling contrast in this scenario is the geographic division between village and city, since this defines the inequitable distribution of power resulting in the specific distribution of wealth. This account of *Works and Days* produces, in my view, a picture of a community far more hierarchized and far more complex internally than the evidence warrants. I do not deny the thematic centrality to *Works and Days* of the opposition of village and city. Indeed, I will discuss its role in Hesiod's persuasive program in some detail later. But my position nevertheless will be that the organizing contrast is rather that of the poor with the prosperous and that this is entirely enclosed within the limits of the village. The contrast of village and city is in fact opened only as a side effect of the conflict between villagers, namely Hesiod and Perses, and it is specific to that circumstance. It is the good *eris*, which arouses the poor to emulate their well-to-do neighbors, that dominates the poem and controls the contrast between the village and the polis. Accordingly I consider the village of Ascra as depicted in *Works and Days* to remain as yet autonomous and independent of Thespiae and its kings, and Hesiod in my view is no peasant.

As I have argued, the model of the peasant society is able to subsume the agrarian crisis approach to the historical context of *Works and Days*. The question of the validity of this description turns in the first place upon the relationship between Ascra and Thespiae. Did the kings of Thespiae exercise economic and political control over the cultivators of Ascra? Second, what is the internal organization of the community depicted by Hesiod? This is especially pertinent to arguments that Hesiod portrays a peasant community, but it is implicitly so to the claims of the agrarian crisis approach. Does Hesiod's Ascra exhibit the interdependence and hierarchy, the complexity characteristic of peasant communities? In my view the answer to these questions is no.

I do not raise this question of whether or not Hesiod is a "peasant" as a narrow debate over the appropriate usage of a theoretical label. Rather I hope to explore through this problem Ascra's nature as a social, political, and economic entity. If my case is often cast as refutation, this merely responds to the accumulation of opinion against which I argue. Out of this, however, there emerges, I believe, a positive characterization of a form of settlement otherwise unknown to us, a glimpse of the institutions and values of a small-scale Greek community at the dawn of the Archaic period. Hesiod attests in this setting to resistance to the spread of the polis system as well as to the roots of Greek egalitarianism. The larger questions that I wish to address, then, beyond Hesiod's status as a peasant, are how was Ascra organized as a community and how does it fit into the narrative of Greek history.

MODELS AND THEORIES

These questions about Ascra's relationship to Thespiae and its internal organization must be posed for the simple reason that Hesiod does not tell us in *Works and Days* everything that we would like to know about the historical context of his poem. I attribute this silence about so many facets of community life to his assumption that his audience was already perfectly familiar with the necessary background. This assumption, reasonable enough for Hesiod, constrains us, however, to do a fair amount of guessing. The process of moving from what Hesiod does tell us to conjectures about what he does not has relied on models and comparative data. This reliance is explicit in the case of those viewing Hesiod as a peasant—Millett, Walcot, Redfield, and Tandy. Those arguing, like Édouard Will, for an agrarian crisis precipitated by overpopulation and debt utilize, I believe, European feudalism, focused through the lens of Solon's poetry, as at least an implicit model for their reconstructions of the historical dynamic at work in Hesiod's Ascra. The validity of these models is confirmed or rejected by their coherence with the evidence that Hesiod does supply directly in *Works and Days*. As I have already suggested, I find these reconstructions at many points inconsistent with that evidence. In my attempt to provide a more satisfying account I likewise rely upon models derived from theories of sociocultural evolution. I use evolutionary theory in the first place to provide a set of reference points by which I can gauge the degree of social complexity exhibited by Ascra. Evolutionary theory also supplies models of social organization that as ideal types can illuminate the institutions and mode of social organization to which *Works and Days* attests.

My use of evolutionary theory requires if not justification at least some acknowledgment of its complexities and risks. This is especially so since I am not trained as a social scientist. For, judging from its apologists, evolutionism as a theory is hardly the majority report among anthropologists.[10] The present project could be described at least in part as an attempt to see how far one can get in reconstructing the outlines of Ascra as a community by placing the evidence available directly from *Works and Days* itself within the framework primarily of Johnson and Earle's (1987) evolutionary scheme. This approach, however, entails certain dangers. It is possible, as their critics think, that the sociocultural evolutionists have got it fundamentally wrong. Or perhaps their work is simply not applicable to ancient Greece. And there is the ever-present temptation in analyzing what *Works and Days* tells us to lay Hesiod upon an evolutionary bed of Procrustes. I do my best throughout my argument to avoid the trap of distorting the evidence from *Works and Days* in order to preserve the integrity of the model. In pursuing this line of inquiry in the way that I have, I have already made my decision about the viability of sociocultural evolution as a theory and about its power to shed light on ancient Greece. I believe that comparisons with similar societies can illuminate at a general level the dynamic and inner logic animating ancient social formations. The claim that there are broad similarities between the societies of antiquity and societies from other times and places, however, in no way diminishes the unique features of Greek civilization. In fact, though it is not the focus of this study, such comparative work can serve precisely to highlight the distinctive elements of Greek culture.[11]

10. See Johnson and Earle 1987, vii–viii; Sanderson 1990, 209–22; Trigger 1998, 1–14, 152–85.

11. It is worth noting just for the record that Johnson and Earle, Boserup, and Magagna (discussed below) all use historical examples among their case studies. Regarding the problem of the modern orientation of ethnographic studies, see Tandy 1997, 30–34.

The fundamental assumption of sociocultural evolutionism is that there is a common direction to historical change and that this directionality produces patterns in the way societies change.[12] As Trigger (1998, 10–11) states, "Evolution is concerned primarily with understanding directionality as a major characteristic of human history. This directionality involves an overall tendency towards creating larger, more internally differentiated, and more complexly articulated structures. . . ." Or, to quote Sanderson (1990, 216), "evolutionary theories are those that discern and attempt to explain patterns of historical change that are common to a large number of societies." This, of course, is not to claim that such change only moves in one direction, is continuous, always occurs at the same pace, or results from properties inherent to nature or to the human species. Trigger conceptualizes this process of change in terms of complexity, the tendency for societies to become more heterogeneous in terms of hierarchy, division of labor, and systems of knowledge.

The recognition of patterns that is central to the construction of evolutionary theories is necessarily an exercise in abstraction. The more varied and rich the data, the more the observer must smooth out inconsistencies and trim away the outliers in order to produce a recognizable trend. The greater the degree of detail and idiosyncrasy that is tolerated, the less potential there is for comparison among cultures. Yet greater abstraction diminishes the descriptive power of a model when confronted with a real society in all its specificity. The extreme anti-evolutionary position maintains that any society is too deeply embedded in its own internal dynamics to permit the emergence of significant common patterns among distinct societies. At the opposite extreme lies what Sanderson (1990, 41–42) refers to as the "strong" unilinearist position, claiming that all societies must move through precisely the same developmental stages in the same order, with no skipping, regression, or stalling permitted. The "weak" form of the hypothesis, however, asserts that "cultural development generally moves along broadly similar (but not rigidly uniform) lines" (Sanderson 1990, 42). This formulation, if applied to evolutionism generally, allows for the unique eccentricities and anomalies of specific societies while at the same time preserving the possibility of comparison on the basis of larger-scale features. In a discussion of criticisms of the concept of directionality, Sanderson (1990, 218–19), relying upon the work of Marvin Harris, presents a continuum of degrees of abstraction. At the lowest level of abstraction it is easy to identify unique and unparalleled features of specific soci-

12. See Trigger 1998, 8–14 and Sanderson 1990, 5–6, 216–19.

eties. At the highest level are found universal features, such as the taboo against nuclear family incest. In between these extremes occurs a middle ground where a few significant similarities can be emphasized at the expense of myriad insignificant differences. It is in this intermediate zone that such indispensable categories as egalitarian society or feudalism operate. At this level of abstraction and generalization distinct societies can be meaningfully compared and sorted.

If the notion of change defines the temporal axis of evolutionism, then the patterning posited by evolutionary theory comprises a synchronic taxonomy of social formations. While I discuss at various points the direction and motives of change in Hesiod's Ascra, it is apparent from what I have already said that the chief attraction that evolutionary theory holds for me is its taxonomy of social formations. The continuum provided by evolutionary theory of modes of social organization sorted according to complexity offers a valuable tool for answering questions about the form of historical communities. These classificatory categories are useful for ordering large numbers of cases for broad comparisons, moreover, precisely because they are abstract. There arise, however, certain dangers when such schemes are narrowly focused upon a single case. Heterogeneous, incomplete, and conflicting evidence from a specific society can fail to comply with the smooth continuities of an abstract and rationalized model. There is a clear temptation to introduce teleological lines of reasoning by fetishizing analytic categories, which are themselves derived inductively, as something more real than the empirical data they are called upon to order and account for. The directionality evident in historical change at a general level of abstraction does not translate into a destiny at the level of the specific case nor does the logical coherence of a model in itself authorize filling in an apparent lacuna in an empirical account.[13]

I am asking whether Hesiod's Ascra is comparable as a community to the Homeric polis or Athens of Solon's time, is it in fact a peasant society, or is Hesiod describing a community that is fundamentally different from these. Evolutionary theory provides a framework within which this set of questions can be productively posed. It details a sequence of social formations of increasing complexity that can serve as points of comparison for the attempt to construct a picture of Ascra based upon what Hesiod tells us. My goal is not to pigeonhole Ascra within a specific slot in an evolutionary tax-

13. Regarding these issues, see the debate between Morris and Small over the use of evolutionary theory to account for the Athenian democracy: Morris 1997b and 1998 and Small 1997, 1998, and 1998b.

onomy so much as to distinguish a range on the evolutionary continuum where Ascra seems to fit. As a consequence, though, I necessarily remain focused upon broad similarities exhibited between Ascra and certain ideal types as well as broad differences exhibited between Ascra and others. This seems to me a reasonable approach to reconstructing a picture of Ascra as a community and highlighting its considerable differences from what we encounter in Homer's or Solon's poetry. My preoccupation with the relationship between Ascra and certain models, however, does not presuppose that such models are adequate to account for all the myriad possibilities of human social organization or especially that general similarities preclude the existence of unique and distinctive features of ancient Greek culture.[14]

Let me focus now on specific aspects of the approach I am adopting. Allen W. Johnson and Timothy Earle, in their *The Evolution of Human Societies* (Stanford, 1987), construct an evolutionary model composed of three stages of development, each subdivided into a less complex and a more complex form.[15] The family-level group designates the simplest societies, including the family/camp and the family/hamlet forms of organization. Next in complexity is the local group, including the acephalous local group and the Big Man collectivity. The level of highest complexity is that of the regional polity, including the chiefdom and the state. It is not necessary at this point to summarize the characteristics of each individual form identified by Johnson and Earle. The chief criteria on which these various formations differ are: population density; size and stability of habitation group; territoriality and warfare; use of wild versus domestic food sources and intensity of cultivation; mode of food storage; and development of the political economy (trade, dispute settlement, ceremony, diplomacy, community infrastructure, public offices, etc.).

The development from less to more complex forms of social organization occurs through interrelated processes of subsistence intensification, political integration, and social stratification. In their own words, "foragers diversify and gradually adopt agriculture; villages form and integrate into regional polities; leaders come to dominate and transform social relationships" (Johnson and Earle 1987, 4). In their view population growth is the independent variable that propels a community along the path to greater complexity. Although they acknowledge the self-reinforcing spiral of pop-

14. In spite of this orientation, I believe that my argument's grounding in the minutiae of *Works and Days* insulates it from the sort of criticisms leveled by Morris against Small (note 13 above).

15. For what follows, see Johnson and Earle 1987, 1–25.

ulation growth leading to technical improvements in the subsistence economy that lead in turn to further population growth, they nevertheless regard population growth as the starting point for this evolutionary process.

Evolution of a community towards more complex forms involves a shift in the balance between what Johnson and Earle term the subsistence economy and the political economy. The former is the household economy, composed of a self-sufficient household and aiming solely at providing for its own needs at the minimum expenditure of effort. It is a principle of the household economy that as the total amount of food produced rises, the labor costs per unit of food also rise—or, as more labor is devoted to food production, the marginal gains in production per unit of labor decline. The political economy is comprised of the exchange of goods and services among families (subsistence economies) within a community. While every community participates in at least some minimal level of political economy, a true political economy comes into existence only when a certain threshold in social development has been reached. A political economy, in contrast to the aims of the subsistence economy, is mobilized to transfer a surplus from the subsistence economy—something that households resist producing except in limited amounts as individual subsistence insurance— into the hands of a non-producing elite to finance social, political, and religious institutions. The subsistence economy is organized by the family itself and looks only to the satisfaction of the family's needs while the political economy is organized by outsiders interested in extending the boundaries of their influence. Expansion of the political economy depends in large degree upon the willingness of families to participate in it, which in turn depends upon the balance of costs and benefits that the political economy entails. Johnson and Earle argue that population growth, exerting pressure on the resources available to subsistence economies, produces a balance of costs and benefits favorable to the political economy's expansion. Under such conditions of heightened competition for resources families face problems beyond their capacity to solve on their own, making group action and leadership attractive especially in the areas of risk management, warfare, technology, and trade. Johnson and Earle liken the political economy to an expanding bubble: those within find the balance of costs and benefits favorable while those who remain outside do not.

At a certain point a community must respond to rising population by intensifying its subsistence economy. Intensification, however, brings with it a new set of complications. Production risks increase as the best land and crops are depleted and what once served only as buffers against famine become primary food sources, increasing the risk of food shortages. Forms of

communal food storage (pooling, or social storage) serve as a frequent response to this problem. Such storage includes not only some sort of centralized facility in which food from different households is kept, perhaps as
the property of a community leader, but also systems of intangible obligations or of non-food tokens provide their possessors with a claim against
the output of other households at a future date. As good land becomes less
plentiful, it must be defended, and cooperative defense measures become
necessary as does a war leader. Intensification of production itself requires
increased capital investment in infrastructure that is generally beyond the
means of the individual family. This too requires the resources and organi-
zational guidance of a leader. Depletion of local resources necessitates trade
in order to replace them from outside. Large-scale trade requires a head
trader, a leader able to exercise control. All of these effects of subsistence
intensification—risk management, trade, technology, and warfare—entail
political integration and social stratification, or, in a word, hierarchy.
Within Johnson and Earle's multi-linear evolutionary theory, any one of
these four factors is sufficient to fuel the movement toward greater
complexity.

　　According to Johnson and Earle, population, the subsistence regime, and
hierarchy all interact in mutual determination. The movement, moreover,
toward a more complex social formation continuously shifts the balance
between the subsistence and the political economies as the household progressively surrenders autonomy over its own resources to an elite in exchange for risk-sharing, for participation in pooling or social storage, under the umbrella of the political economy. This process of progressive
intensification of the subsistence regime, integration of political institutions, and stratification of society results eventually in what can be described as a peasant society, but there are many preliminary stages on the
way to that outcome.

　　Johnson and Earle's view of the rise of the political economy as a solution to population growth and subsistence crisis comprises, as Sanderson
(1995, 82–83) points out, an at least implicit functionalism. That is, although Johnson and Earle are well aware of the costs imposed upon households by increasing levels of social complexity, their emphasis upon the
common benefits of an elite's managerial role leads them to underestimate
the presence of conflict and elite self-interest in the growth of complexity.
The advancement of centralization and stratification creates conflicts of interest for a community even as they serve to manage the process of subsistence intensification. I believe that it is important to an understanding of
Works and Days, especially regarding the contrasts between the prosper-

ous and the poor and between village and polis, to recognize that the political economy invariably carries a price tag and that individual households and even whole communities will resist its demands at least indirectly even if it is believed to be indispensable to the community's well-being.[16]

In Marshall Sahlins' classic study *Stone Age Economics*, the balance between what Johnson and Earle term the subsistence and political economies is analyzed in terms of forms of reciprocity (Sahlins 1972, 191–96).[17] Generalized reciprocity is the mode of sharing characteristic of the household according to which resources are pooled and made available to all members more or less equally. Such sharing entails a counterobligation, but it is not stipulated by time, quantity, or quality. Such pooling comprises a system of reciprocities organized by a movement of goods from the many to one and then of redistribution from the one to the many. Its operation defines a center and a social boundary as well as a hierarchy between the agent of distribution and his clients—within the family, between the head of the household and its other members. Balanced reciprocity, reciprocation in equal value without delay, governs amicable relations outside the circle of generalized reciprocity. This can include transactions under the headings of trade, buying and selling, alliances, and contracts. The extension of relations of generalized reciprocity beyond the limits of the household marks the emergence of what Johnson and Earle term the "political economy."

The agent of a widening circle of generalized reciprocity is in its minimal form the so-called "Big Man," who embarks upon a career of self-exploitation and generosity in order to build up a network of influence and obligation. The successful Big Man functions as an agent of redistribution within his community, exacting a surplus from households of the community the Big Man then recirculates within the community as his largesse. Through the obligations that his generosity accumulates, the Big Man succeeds in constraining the households of the community to produce a surplus beyond their own immediate needs. Because he is able to organize and control the production of a surplus by the households of the community, the Big Man is able to provide the essential service of social storage, pooling, and so to spread out the risks of subsistence failure across all the households of the community. The web of obligations organized through

16. Scott 1976 and Magagna 1991 offer detailed analyses of precisely these sorts of conflicts and the forms of resistance they spawn within peasant societies. See Tainter's (1988, 127–92) analysis of this balance of the costs and benefits of complexity across a series of state-level societies and Sanderson's (1995, 82–86) summary.

17. For what follows, see Sahlins 1972, 101–48 and 185–275.

generalized reciprocity comprises a mechanism of social storage, a convention through which individual households surrender some control over their own labor and their own output in exchange for a claim against the output of other households in the community in time of need. Thus, within Sahlins' account the extension of generalized reciprocity beyond the limits of the individual household is accompanied by the appearance of hierarchy, in the person of the Big Man or chief, and of subsistence intensification under his influence.[18]

I suggested above that at the heart of the present inquiry lies the question of which opposition is dominant in *Works and Days:* that between village and city or that between prosperous and poor. If it is the first, village opposed to city, then we can speak of a conflict between competing political economies—that of Ascra and that of Thespiae. If it is the latter, however, then we must speak of a conflict between the subsistence economy and the political economy—will Hesiod acknowledge an obligation to another household, will the subsistence economy of the individual household permit the emergence and strengthening of a political economy able to link households together in relationships of mutual obligation and reliance? As I shall argue, Hesiod and Perses are negotiating through their conflict the relationship between the subsistence and political economies, or, in other words, where the boundary of generalized reciprocity is to be set.

The relationship between population growth and intensity of cultivation lies at the center of Ester Boserup's fundamental study, *The Conditions of Agricultural Growth* (Chicago, 1965).[19] Boserup outlines there a sequence of five agricultural regimes of increasing intensity that are distinguished

18. Cf. Schusky 1989, 79–97. This summary is, of course, oversimplified. See Earle's (1997) extended discussion of the acquisition of power in the more complex social form of the chiefdom. Within the logic of this argument, Mele's (1979, 12–13) assertion that reciprocity in Ascra is evolving from generalized in the direction of balanced, even as the social formation becomes more complex, makes no sense. See Donlan's (1982, 137–41, 171–74) discussion of the relation of forms of reciprocity to the level of social complexity in the world of the Homeric epics.

19. For what follows see Boserup 1965, 11–34. See also the more recent *Population and Technological Change* (Chicago, 1981), 15–90. Boserup's work has provoked substantial criticism since its appearance. See the references in Stone and Downum 1999 and Lee 1986. Wood 1998 and Lee 1986 defend Boserup's theory but argue that a more coherent account of the relationship between population and economic intensification can be achieved through a synthesis of the work of Boserup and Malthus. Stone and Downum 1999 and Lele and Stone 1989 argue for limitations to Boserup's theory while accepting her basic principles. See as well Cohen's (1977, 1–70) defense and elaboration of Boserup's work. Livi-Bacci (1997, 80–111) provides a general discussion of the issues.

by their fallowing cycles, the frequency with which agricultural land is worked. The fallowing periods in this progression vary between decades for forest fallow cultivation (swidden or shifting cultivation) and bare weeks for multi-cropping, which define between them the regimes of least and greatest intensity. Boserup demonstrates, however, that as fallowing periods are curtailed and intensity increases, not only do crop yields rise but the cost in labor per unit of produce rises as well. That is, more intensive regimes do produce more food in absolute terms, but the increase in the amount of food is outstripped by the increase in the amount of labor required to produce it. As cultivation is intensified, the productivity of labor falls. This unfavorable ratio of labor to produce makes intensification an unattractive option for farmers.

The factor that compels farmers to turn to intensification is rising population density. Once a population has expanded to the point that all available land is already being farmed, except for emigration there is no alternative to intensifying cultivation in order to meet growing demand.[20] As Boserup shows, moreover, rising population and intensification bring with them hierarchy and increasingly complex social formations.

Victor Magagna in his *Communities of Grain* (Ithaca and London, 1991) analyzes the distinctive features of the internal organization of peasant communities. Magagna focuses particularly upon the territoriality of the village, the sense of boundaries and membership, upon hierarchy, and upon the moral obligation among villagers to cooperate and share. Within the framework provided by Johnson and Earle, we recognize here the criteria of political integration and social stratification. Cooperation and sharing raise again the issue of the articulation of the subsistence economy with the political economy. Magagna's work provides a set of criteria against which to evaluate the level of complexity exhibited by Hesiod's Ascra strictly in terms of internal organization.

Based upon what I have said about the role of population density, it would be sound methodology to begin my investigation of *Works and Days* at that point and move forward from there. Both Johnson and Earle and Boserup provide specific guidelines for population density as a criterion for distinguishing different levels of complexity or of subsistence intensity respectively. Bintliff and Snodgrass (1985, 140–43; cf. Bintliff 1996, 197 and Bintliff 1997b), relying on earlier work, estimate a population of 165,000 for Boeotia in the late fifth century and on the basis of their own research propose as a conservative figure a population density of

---

20. See, however, Sanderson's (1995, 36–42) qualifications of this principle.

70 people per square kilometer. Snodgrass (1985, 94) claims that Ascra exceeded in area the size of the neighboring polis of Haliartos and must have possessed a population numbering in the thousands. Bintliff (1996, 197) suggests a population for Ascra of approximately 1,300 at its climax in the Classical period. A density of 70 persons per square kilometer would place Classical Boeotia at the bottom of Boserup's (1981, 8–11) density group 8 and under the designation "dense." We would expect a population at this density to practice the most intensive agricultural regime. A settlement with a population in the thousands, especially a secondary settlement as Ascra is regarded by Bintliff and Snodgrass, is diagnostic of a developed chiefdom or a state-level social formation within Johnson and Earle's model (Johnson and Earle 1987, 20–21, 314).

These estimates characterize Ascra in a later, far more populous period than Hesiod's, however, and at the very best can serve to establish a benchmark from which we must work back a considerable distance in order to reach conditions in Ascra within the time range of 725–675 B.C when the population was, of course, much sparser. On Bintliff and Snodgrass's (1988) plan of Ascra, the Archaic settlement occupies only a fraction of the area of the Classical site, around ten or fifteen percent (see map 2 below, p. 90). Our knowledge in any case about population levels in the ancient world is notoriously uncertain, and to use population estimates as a starting point for my argument would amount to building upon a foundation of sand. While I certainly intend to use what information we possess about population levels and trends in Boeotia, I consider what is known about this topic inadequate to serve as a major piece of scaffolding for my argument.[21] I prefer, therefore, to work from the other side of the equation. *Works and Days* offers considerable, if lacunose, information about the farming regime and gives more information by far about the community's social organization than about its population density.[22] Within the framework laid out above,

---

21. Tandy (1997, 19–43) offers an excellent, up-to-date discussion of the population of Greece in the Dark Age and the Archaic period. Sallares' (1991, 42–107) discussion of the population of Greece, focused upon the population of Attica in the Classical period, is also quite informative. Morris (1987, 72–109), who likewise focuses on Attica, gives good reason, however, to be cautious about moving directly from mortuary evidence to population estimates. For Boeotia specifically, see pp. 32–33 below. The specific population densities that Johnson and Earle (1987, 18–22), for example, are able to provide for different social formations and modes of subsistence, however, are beyond our reach. Cf. Boserup (1981) 9–14, 43–75.

22. I am very skeptical of the position that *Works and Days* could have served as an agricultural instruction manual not because what the poem tells us about farming is inaccurate but because it is incomplete. So, I assume that what Hesiod

I propose to focus especially, though not exclusively, on the criteria of the agricultural regime and of storage since Hesiod's interest in these topics allows some generalizations to be made. It will be a working principle for me that the lower the intensity of cultivation and the more decentralized storage is, the lower the population density, the less stratified the community, and the less complex is the social formation generally.

WORKS AND DAYS AS HISTORY

To what extent can *Works and Days* reliably be used as a witness to history?[23] This question arose the instant Hesiod opened his mouth to recite the poem. After all, simply to speak at all of an event or experience strips it to some degree of its uniqueness and specificity by incorporating it within the finite and conventionalized system of language. This problem becomes significant, however, in the case of poetic diction. For it is well established that Hesiod's poems, as part of the larger phenomenon of oral poetry, rely on highly traditional subject matter and a comprehensive set of narrative conventions extending from the words themselves to the patterns organizing entire poems.[24] In order to be incorporated within the system of poetic representation, any historical entity must undergo distortion and transformation in accordance with the conventions governing literary representation.

This is not simply a matter, moreover, of the technicalities of poetic craftsmanship. Representation encompasses as well the issues of moral value and point of view. *Works and Days*, like any piece of verbal representation, especially literary representation, is constructed as much from what it does not say as from what it does say and from the particular way in which it says it. It conveys a vision of the world made up of lacunae, deformations, structured absences. In David Tandy's words it both reflects and refracts the social world to which it refers. For example, Hesiod's treatment of the themes of labor and of justice in the poem and the manner in which he intertwines them are heavily influenced by his own social posi-

---

does bother to tell us about farming practice is basically accurate. Isager and Skydsgaard 1992 frequently note the lacunae in Hesiod's account (see p. 7 e.g.). See also Burford 1993, 104; Heath 1985, 255–56; Nelson 1996, 45–48 and 1998, 48–58.

23. The historical value of literary sources in general is now under debate. See, for example, Small 1998 and Osborne 1996, 4–17.

24. Regarding the conventional character of the poem as a whole, see G. P. Edwards 1971 and Peabody 1975.

tion. These themes are manipulated to lend credibility and prestige to the successful farmer, implying that his prosperity is all his own and that he has merited it by living in accordance with the divine will. Similarly, the integration of the farmer's life with the seasonal cycle and with astral and nature signs in *Works and Days* endows that way of life with an apparent rightness and naturalness in a manner that must be seen as heavily ideological. The life of toil on the land that Hesiod recommends to Perses conforms with the laws of nature and the will of the gods as life in the town square of the kings does not. Simultaneously, however, the perspective that Perses might take on his conflict with Hesiod—the arbitrary factors that can bring a farmer to ruin, the rationale behind his requests for aid, his motives for turning to the kings—is simply not represented in the poem. It inhabits *Works and Days* only as an absence.[25]

We must also confront the status of our poet. That is, how do we know that the author and the narrator of *Works and Days* are the same person? To speak of "Hesiod" is to speak of at least two different phenomena. One is the historical poet who composed *Works and Days*, a real person whose existence can be deduced at a minimum from the fact of the poem itself, and the other is the persona of the poem, the voice that emerges from the fabric of the poem's verses, a textual effect, if you will, not a real person. These two are irreducibly distinct, although that does not preclude close similarities and parallels between poet and persona. At a minimum we encounter here the difference between a real person with a complaint against his brother and the self-representation of that same person through the conventions of literature. Beyond that, however, we must allow for the poet's conscious fashioning in his poetry of a self-image for persuasive purposes. In my final chapter, where I address *Works and Days* as a piece of persuasion, I analyze this problem of how Hesiod (the poet) seeks to invest his voice as persona with moral authority. Finally, how can we verify that Hesiod really had a brother named Perses at all, or that he ever walked behind a plow? It must be conceded that Hesiod the poet, the composer of *Works and Days*, may really have little or nothing in common with the persona of his poem.[26]

25. I discuss briefly the issue of the relationship between history and literary representation in A. Edwards 1993, 92–93; on this matter see also Tandy 1997, 11–13 and Morris 1986.
26. The interplay between persona and poet is explored by Nagy at Nagy 1982, 43–49, Nagy 1990, 47–51, 67–79 and Nagy 1996, 5–103; by Griffith 1983, 37–65; by Martin 1992, 11–33; and by Lamberton 1988, 1–37.

I have outlined here a series of barriers that might stand between the world recounted in *Works and Days* and the historical context within which the poem was composed and performed. The conventions of verbal representation, the ideological bias of the poem, and finally the distance separating the poet from the persona within the narrative all serve to distance the text from its narrative context. These are factors that affect any text to some degree. But the question for me, obviously, is their impact upon *Works and Days* as a historical source. Where, if anywhere, can we locate the historical element in this poem?

Some of the differences between *Works and Days* and Homer's poetry serve to highlight the relationship between Hesiod's poem and its historical context. First, Homer formulates his narrative in the third, not first person, and does not enter into it himself in any way. Second, Homer places the events he recounts in a distant past that even he knows only through the agency of the Muses. Indeed Homer openly acknowledges that many feats of strength, for example, are beyond the abilities of men such as live nowadays. Finally, Homer's audience fully expects discrepancies between the historical reality they experience directly and the reality conjured up within the narrative—monsters, talking horses, magic boats, exotic armor. Homer's narrative is distanced existentially, temporally, and ontologically from poet and audience, who, as a consequence, expect systematic ruptures of verisimilitude in certain aspects of the narrated world. Much the same can be argued of *Theogony*. Yet this can hardly be said of *Works and Days*. The poem does not comprise an objective, third-person account of events from various perspectives but an interested, first-person piece of persuasion presented as if it aimed overtly to alter the course of present events. *Works and Days* has not only an audience whom it seeks to entertain but an addressee whom it harangues. While Hesiod refers to events from a distant past, the action of the poem occurs within an immediate and incomplete present in which the narrator is intimately engaged. There are, moreover, no elements in the poem to defamiliarize its action and signal to its audience that it portrays a reality somehow removed or different from that which they experience every day. *Works and Days* hardly qualifies as *klea andrōn*. These features do not require that *Works and Days* directly render a historical event or even that it be based upon a kernel of truth, but they do at a minimum establish a specific form of verisimilitude mediating between the narrative and the lived reality of its audience.

These observations suggest that *Works and Days*, which is perhaps best thought of as representing a genre distinct from Homer's poetry, is more

closely anchored in its historical context than is Homer, that it is more realistic. This is interesting in view of the generally accepted notion that
Homer offers an accurate and realistic representation if not of specific
events and persons at least of the institutions and values of a historical society.[27] There are essentially two sorts of argument adduced to support
claims for Homer's historicity. It is argued in the first place that the ensemble of institutions and values presented in the poem is paralleled by
what we know of other, historical societies, and in the second place that
even an audience expecting the fantastic to predominate in certain story
elements would nevertheless find either distasteful or simply incompre-
hensible a society portrayed through unfamiliar institutions and values. It
remains true today that the world revealed by real social history is generally regarded as far stranger than that created by various forms of historical fiction. The case I am arguing for *Works and Days* is precisely that the
evidence from the poem does not cohere with the models of social institutions so far offered to account for it. So that test of the historicity of *Works
and Days*, its coherence with comparative models, will have to be put on
hold, for the moment at any rate.

The argument from verisimilitude, however, seems to me to require se-
rious consideration. Verisimilitude as a property of literary representation
would require a degree of likeness, of semblance between the world as depicted and the world as experienced. Suffice it to acknowledge here that
such similitude is itself conventional, a matter of the forms of artifice regarded by a particular audience as realistic and of the relation between the
structure of cognition and the conventions of representation. For my purposes it is necessary to posit only that some texts mimic reality as it is experienced more closely and others less so. A composition such as *Works
and Days* that claims for itself the immediacy of the moment, that harangues and attempts to persuade an addressee, and that is formulated in
the first person implies in its own conventions an audience who expect a
high level of verisimilitude.

If we assume a high degree of faithfulness of *Works and Days* to its historical context, this could suggest for the poem a basis in a real dispute between the poet and a brother over the family farm. Such a composition
would have served to sway the brother directly but, perhaps more impor-
tantly, also to win over public opinion to the poet's side. We need not imagine that the brother was present when *Works and Days* was performed in

27. See, e.g., Morris 1986, 86–91; Donlan 1989, 5–7, 1998, 52–54; Whitley
1991, 363–64; and especially Raaflaub 1998.

order for it to serve that purpose. Perhaps, though, to assume that the scenario of Hesiod's dispute with Perses is true in a simple and literal sense demands too much of a poetic text. But even if the name Perses is the product of mythic associations and designates a fictional character, and even if Hesiod the poet is neither an Ascran himself nor a farmer but an itinerant singer, nevertheless *Works and Days* in its unique details is tailored to fit into and interact with a specific and real historical context, one emerging from the general relations between the prosperous and the needy within the village of Ascra and between the inhabitants of that village and those of the neighboring city of Thespiae. The scenario of Hesiod's dispute with his brother Perses is anchored in real tensions and conflicts at work within the village, and this close engagement with the moment of its composition gives the poem an intense verisimilitude cast in scenarios, character types, and anxieties that bore a palpable immediacy for its audience.[28] The poem's celebration of work and its condemnation of idleness, its injunctions to perform one's tasks in season and to store away the land's produce, and its admonitions about the justice of the city and outside interference in village matters were all formulated for villagers who would have found the dispute between Perses and Hesiod realistic even if they knew it was not literally real. In fact, if verisimilitude comprises a convention or mode of literary representation, then it should make no difference to the historicity of the final product whether what is represented actually happened or is fictional from the outset.

Verisimilitude as an element of literary representation serving to preserve historical detail varies in importance with genre and style. I have already suggested, for example, that it may operate with less force in the Homeric epics than it does in *Works and Days*. Certainly, it cannot be denied that in spite of the mask of the persona and the generic force of narrative conventions, Hesiod nevertheless incorporates into *Works and Days* a wealth of specific detail that he need not have included simply to sing of the farmer's life. In order to produce a composition rooted in the life of the village and constructed out of the mythology and the seasonal tasks of that region, the poet did not need to introduce Perses, drag in the kings and their town square, launder the family's dirty linen in public, or mention the name of Ascra. If the generic themes of farming, justice, or labor are the main content of the poem, there is little advantage in encumbering them

28. Millett (1984, 84–86) and Tandy (1997, 13–14) both argue that Hesiod represents accurately in *Works and Days* contemporary social institutions and customary practices. See also the brief but insightful comments of Sihvola (1989, 8–10).

with obscure, confusing, and unnecessary detail about Perses and Ascra. Such ornamentation adds less color and texture to the poem than obscurity. But it is precisely the more specific themes of a quarrel in the family, a dispute over land, the arrogance of the city, or the hardships of farming that would capture the interest of an audience because of their immediacy and relevance to lived experience. It is in fact far likelier to suppose that the more generic elements of the poem—the myths of the origins of labor, the contrast between the city of justice and the city of *hubris*, the calendar— have been incorporated into the poem to serve the needs of the specific scenario rather than the reverse.[29] These traditional elements provide the moral framework within which Hesiod evaluates the more specific and historical elements.

If such specific details do cohere with the patterns and hierarchies of narrative convention, such coherence means only that Hesiod was competent to select from the vast array of conventional elements those that best served as vehicles for the topic at hand, that he employed the tradition to invest the particular scenario of *Works and Days* with the ethical values and paradigms encoded in that tradition. Thus even as there is a process by which the particular is made conventional through incorporation within the narrative tradition of hexameter poetry, there is a simultaneous countermovement through which conventional elements of the tradition are localized to the demands of a particular narrative. Thus, to take an example, even though the agricultural calendar of *Works and Days* exhibits all the features of poetic discourse from its diction through its thematic development, this quality of the language does not require that there be no basis for the calendar in historical practice, that it is unrelated to what farmers really did. We confront in this example, moreover, an instance where there must have been a fairly direct movement from historical practice into poetic representation since it is prima facie unlikely that the influence moved in the reverse direction. Even those who believe that *Works and Days* could have served as an instructional handbook for novice Greek farmers would agree that the lessons propounded there must have originated with practicing cultivators rather than with poets. *Works and Days* displays its connections to a specific, contemporary historical setting in a way that Homer's poems, for example, do not, and this connection cannot be dismissed simply by demonstrating that the setting has been assimilated to traditional patterns of representation.

29. See Raaflaub 1998, 177–88 and Nelson 1998, 31–33, 36–39.

The link between any text and lived reality is mediated by conventions of verbal representation that vary with genre, period, and style. *Works and Days* is neither a work of historiography nor a documentary text such as a memoir or an autobiography, and it cannot be treated as such. It is, rather, a harangue, a piece of persuasive exhortation, a moral diatribe. The exempla Hesiod employs to argue his case are mythic, the values and motives he utilizes as touchstones are idealized, and his representation of the social world is selective. Hesiod interweaves in his presentation the mythic with the historical, the individual with the generic, the immediate with the cosmic so that they merge in the flow of his narrative. But persuasion must be rooted in a shared vision of reality, of how things work, of what people must do, and of what they ought to do. Such a vision comprises the viewpoint of a historically rooted and real group, prosperous village farmers in this case. It does not make sense to exhort someone to mend his ways by reference to a whole range of unreal or unfamiliar institutions, practices, and beliefs. We must assume that for Hesiod's audience the village, farm life, daily work, the progress of the seasons, saving and storing, dealing with neighbors and relatives, and so forth were a familiar reality that was recognizably depicted in *Works and Days*. If Hesiod (the poet) does not really belong to this group, then he has successfully fashioned a persona for *Works and Days* able to voice their perspective on the world.

WORKS AND DAYS AND HISTORIOGRAPHY

Works and Days demands our attention as a historical witness for a number of reasons. Hesiod is certainly the earliest Greek author to express the resistance to the power of an elite that is perhaps a uniquely Greek response to the rise of the state. In recent discussions this orientation of Hesiod's has been associated with his status as a *metrios*, a "middling" man between the impoverished and the elite.[30] As I shall argue, though, Hesiod rejects more than simply the centralized authority of an elite. Additionally, *Works and Days*, in my view at any rate, offers detailed evidence for the different rates of economic, political, and social development in various regions of the Greek world over the course of the Dark Age. What is true of contemporary Athens and Attica does not characterize Boeotia and certainly not Ascra. Hesiod is our sole witness to a world that the more ad-

---

30. See Hanson 1995, 91–126 and Morris 2000, 109–95, esp. 163–68.

vanced communities in Greece are rapidly leaving behind. *Works and Days,* in fact, provides perhaps the clearest articulation in ancient Greek literature of what I elsewhere term the voice of the *agros,* the expression of the values and experiences of the rural population.[31] Hesiod provides powerful testimony for a view of life that is rooted in agriculture and the village, not in the city. As I've already acknowledged, we cannot be certain about the nature of Hesiod's connection to Ascra since we are unable to penetrate the persona created within *Works and Days* in order to see beyond to the historical author. Yet, even allowing for this uncertainty, what Hesiod provides in *Works and Days* seems far less a case of ventriloquizing than do that poem's nearest competitors, the old farmers of Aristophanes' comedies— Dicaeopolis or Trygaeus, for example.

This aspect of *Works and Days,* that it contemplates the world from the perspective of the rural village, puts it somewhat at odds not only with Greek literature generally but with the modern historiography of ancient Greece as well. While it is a generalization too large to substantiate with a few citations, I think it is safe to say that the ancient Greek institution that has claimed the focus of modern attention has been the polis. The work of Mogens Hansen's Polis Centre, or Victor Hanson's preoccupation with the polis in *The Other Greeks,* a book devoted to the farmers of Classical Greece, are only recent examples of this. Understanding the Greek city-state has been seen as the key to understanding the political institutions, the artistic productions, and philosophical speculations to which it was host—in a word, the entire achievement of the Classical period. I can add that this is not an assumption with which I wish to quarrel. The desire to understand the origins of this social formation, so distinct from the earlier flowering of Greek civilization in the palaces of the Mycenean age, has fueled interest in the Archaic period and then in the Dark Age. The growing consensus that most of the institutions and values of the Classical period show a clear continuity with the world of the Archaic period puts the focus of this search for origins on the Dark Age. The massive transformation occurring between Mycenean and Classical Greece had to be located in this least well known of periods—and that we know anything at all about the Dark Age must be largely credited to the enormous progress made by archaeologists working on the period.

Robin Osborne, in his recent *Greece in the Making* (1996, 29–32), characterizes the Dark Age as a "slate rubbed clean," a complete break with the preceding Bronze Age that left Greece ready for an entirely new set of in-

31. Edwards 1993, 54–77.

stitutions.[32] Yet Carol Thomas and Craig Conant (1999, xviii–xxi), though acknowledging the view of the Dark Age as a "trough" into which Mycenean Greece disappeared and out of which Classical Greece miraculously emerged, prefer to view the period as one of continuity between what preceded and what came after. These different approaches to the Dark Age really only point up the fundamental problem with which the period confronts us: we know that the Mycenean civilization disintegrated into it and that Archaic and then Classical Greece arose out of it, but it remains difficult to figure out how that occurred.

From the middle of the second millennium B.C. down to the end of the first, the tenth century represents the nadir for evidence of human habitation in Greece. By the end of the ninth mainland sites such as Lefkandi and Athens, which was inhabited continuously throughout the Dark Age, have begun to give evidence through grave goods of hierarchy and trade as well as of the higher level of social organization implied by the regulation of cemeteries in terms of admission, placement, family divisions, and wealth. Yet Greece remains sparsely populated during this period and at a low level of cultural development. The eighth century, however, exhibits a substantial rise in the number of settlements and in their size. This population growth is accompanied by the commencement of long-distance trade, the foundation of colonies in the Black Sea and Italy, the reappearance of figurative art, and the establishment of temples (Osborne 1996, 19–136). Yet in spite of the new developments gathering steam in the eighth century, the huge transformation that has occurred by the time of the seventh remains hard to explain. That century witnesses the appearance of the hoplite phalanx, state-level organization with regular civic offices, law codes and constitutions, synoecism, fixed and defensible territories, the institution of tyranny, and writing. The problem facing students of the period is the absence of a well-articulated and documentable transition between the ninth and the eighth and the eighth and the seventh centuries. Snodgrass's "The

---

32. It might be helpful at this point to outline the dates as they are conventionally given for the periods of early Greek history relevant to this discussion. The Bronze Age as a whole runs from 3200 to 1150 B.C.; the Late Bronze Age, 1600–1150, is also referred to as the Mycenean Period. The Dark Age lasts from 1150 till 700, and the Archaic Period from 700 till 500. Because our knowledge of the Dark Age is so dependent upon archaeological data, it is frequently subdivided by reference to pottery sequences: Submycenean: 1125–1050; Protogeometric: 1050–900; Early Geometric: 900–850; Middle Geometric: 850–750; Late Geometric: 750–700. These dates are approximate since the chronology of pottery sequences tends to be localized. The period from 1100 to 700, roughly the Dark Age, is also sometimes referred to as the Early Iron Age.

Rise of the Polis" (Snodgrass 1993) is largely devoted to this problem of, in effect, how Greece of the ninth century managed to evolve into Greece of the seventh century. Snodgrass concludes that the archaeological evidence does not make it easy to see how the tiny population of the ninth century, inhabiting small, widely separated settlements, could have transformed itself into the "rapidly changing and feverishly active world of later eighth-century Greece" (37), and that although the second half of the eighth century is the only place to seek the genesis of the institutions characteristic of the seventh, the attempt to do so "takes us out of the area of consensus" (35).

If the generally accepted dating of Hesiod's lifetime to the late eighth and early seventh centuries is correct, then Hesiod witnessed first hand that transitional period between the end of the Dark Age and the onset of the Archaic. Hesiod, primarily through *Works and Days*, has regularly been summoned as a witness to how that transition took place. Does Hesiod look ahead to the hard times of Solon's Athens, or back to the simpler Homeric polis, or does he present Ascra as something entirely different from either? The question at issue is not, of course, whether Greece really changed in the way it did between the ninth and seventh centuries, whether the polis system actually came to dominate Greece, but about what part of this change *Works and Days* illuminates.

What I perceive as inaccuracies and distortions in reconstructions of the historical context of *Works and Days* stem largely from its having been read precisely from the perspective of the city, more as a source for information about the polis than about the *agros*. I will argue that *Works and Days* at any rate hasn't much to offer on that score. In order to view the world depicted by Hesiod in *Works and Days* clearly, we must discard the models of the peasant community and of Solon's Athens. Hesiod presents rather a picture of an autonomous village with its own local hierarchy, little concerned with the city except to resist its encroachments into village affairs. In my view it is in fact worth considering whether attempts to place Hesiod historically between Homer and Solon have not led scholars to map out chronologically what are rather to a large extent regional differences. That is to say, it may be the case that Hesiod's orientation towards the "kings" and the city does not reflect the march of time past Homer's historical moment and on towards Solon's so much as the differences between the countryside's perspective upon the city (Hesiod) and the city's upon the countryside (Homer). The strong parallels between Hesiod's outlook in *Works and Days* and Eumaeus's attitude in the *Odyssey* toward the polis of Ithaca and the suitors who control it, all of them "kings," would support such a suggestion.[33] My contention here is that Hesiod's hostility towards the "kings" of Thespiae and their *agorē* does not need to reflect an agrarian crisis or a struggle with an entrenched aristocracy of the polis. Rural Greece always possessed reason enough to be suspicious of and somewhat hostile towards its urban counterpart.

My reading of *Works and Days* departs, I believe, from the majority opinion in that I do not regard Hesiod as pointing the way forward out of the Dark Age and on to the birth of the polis. Hesiod, of course, knows full well what a polis is, and this rising institution leaves its imprint upon *Works and Days*, but the poem's real focus is upon a village world that is more closely connected to the Dark Age than to the Archaic. My argument supports the view that we must be cautious regarding the rate of change in various areas of Greece. It cannot be assumed that what is observed in some areas of Greece at the dawn of the Archaic period—generally those leaving behind the most durable material remains—can be generalized to account for all of Greece. And if, moreover, the testimony of *Works and Days* can no longer be understood to illuminate what we regard as the central development of the Archaic period—the rise of the polis—still, it does offer a unique window onto the values and organization of an autonomous village at a moment when that social formation was becoming a thing of the past.

33. Regarding Eumaeus and *Works and Days* see A. Edwards 1993b, 66–70.

2 External Relations

Ascra and Thespiae

THE ARGUMENTS OF WILL AND TANDY

In this section of my argument I wish to cover four topics, the conflict between Perses and Hesiod, trade between Ascra and the outside world, arrangements for pooling of village resources, and general relations between Ascra and Thespiae. As a starting point, however, it will be useful to examine the main points of the arguments of Édouard Will, whose work has been so influential, and of David Tandy, who offers a recent and powerful development of this approach, since these focus especially upon the relations of Hesiod and Ascra with Thespiae.

Explaining Hesiod's situation from Solon's diagnosis of the situation in Attica as much as a century later, Édouard Will (1957, 9–10, 20–22) assumes a preexisting inequity between small holders such as Hesiod and aristocratic large holders as the context for an agrarian crisis induced by an inheritance system that divided the family farm among male heirs (1957, 9–10, 16–22; cf. W&D 37). The plots of small holders were divided and divided again as they passed from one generation to the next until they were no longer viable. The end result for these small farmers was debt to their wealthy neighbors and hence loss of control of their land, forfeited as collateral for unrepaid loans, and a permanent state of dependency. In support of this scenario Will (1957, 16–20) cites *Works and Days* 376, recommending only a single heir, and references to debt at *Works and Days* 349–50 and 394–401. Central to Will's argument is *Works and Days* 341 where, capping an injunction to avoid impious deeds and to worship the gods, Hesiod offers as the reward for such goodness that "you might acquire the plot of others and not somebody else yours" (ὄφρ' ἄλλων ὠνῇ κλῆρον, μὴ τὸν τεὸν ἄλλος). Here Will discerns a reference if not to the transfer of formal land ownership, at least to loss of control of the family plot, which the farmer then continues to cultivate in semi-servile status (1957, 12–20). It is this process of expropriation that provokes Hesiod's impassioned out-bursts against the "gift-eating kings." Hesiod thus bears witness to the on-set of the agrarian economy that Solon confronts in its grim maturity: a landed aristocracy, on the one hand, able to defend its position through control of the legal apparatus and, on the other, impoverished cultivators reduced to the status of serfs on their own land.

Tandy's argument (1997 and 2001) follows a similar trajectory though it is more sophisticated theoretically and draws upon a wealth of archaeo-logical data unavailable to Will. Tandy argues that Ascra is swept up as a peripheral community in a transition affecting the larger settlements of Greece as a result of a rising population and expanding trade. Greek soci-ety is moving from a rank society with a redistributive economy based on reciprocity to a stratified society in which wealth acquired by elites through participation in a "limited market" economy is no longer subject to the traditional bonds of reciprocity. Under the conditions ushered in by this "great transformation"—private property, debt, alienation of land, status a function of wealth, economic relations disembedded from social relations— the emergent elite abandons its ties to the periphery of the community, leaving it bereft of forms of aid that were available within the redistribu-tive economy. Rather assistance now brings with it debt and debt in turn brings alienation of land. Tandy does, then, see behind *Works and Days* an elite of the "center," the polis, who are able to control the movement of goods as well as public space and who exploit a politically and socially ex-cluded agrarian population primarily by means of debt. This scenario fits the classic pattern of peasants and lords. At the heart of Tandy's argument stand the *basilēes*, a new elite drawing wealth from the limited market economy, changing the rules for exchange within the community, and wielding power over cultivators. Like Édouard Will, Tandy places the op-position of rich and poor in *Works and Days* in the shadow of that between city and village.

Will's chief points concern the inheritance system, debt, land tenure, and the kings, who stand behind all this as the creditors benefiting from the failure of the small holders. Tandy's analysis revolves around the issues of trade, debt, land tenure, and the kings. I will deal with the more complicated topics of trade and the kings in separate discussions later (pp. 44–62, 64–73, 118–23) but I would like to confront the role played by the inheritance system, land tenure, and debt in the arguments of Will and of Tandy now.

1.   Hesiod does mention dividing his father's land with Perses (*W&D* 37) and may advise limiting children as a means of preventing divi-

sion of the paternal *klēros* (*W&D* 376; this line, however, may simply refer to the expense of raising more than one child). Will's argument from the inheritance system leaves out of account, however, the tendency of patrilines in ancient Greece to die out or leave a female as sole heir.[1] This process counters the tendency towards declining land holdings since it leads to concentration of holdings even as division among heirs leads to fragmentation. Thus this argument from partible inheritance works only if two conditions are met: one, a trend towards a larger population is already well under way; and two, there is a shortage of unimproved land available to be taken under cultivation. Under such circumstances, of course, a shortage of land will inevitably occur, which the inheritance system can only exacerbate. But are such conditions likely for Boeotia in the late eighth or early seventh centuries?

Sallares (1991, 84–95), focusing on Attica, argues that a sharp demographic upturn beginning in the ninth century reached its peak rate of increase in the eighth century, but population continued to grow thereafter steadily until into the fourth century. Tandy (1997, 19–43, 203–5) argues from evidence from Attica and the Argolid for a similar demographic trajectory. Morris (1987, 72–109), however, has reinterpreted the evidence from Attic burials and scales back the size of this population explosion considerably. Osborne (1996, 70–81), taking Morris's work into account and again relying on evidence from Attica, maintains that there was steady population growth in Greece beginning in the tenth century rather than an explosion in the eighth. Yet evidence for these regions does not necessarily give an accurate picture of contemporary Boeotia. Buck (1979, 92) speculates that there was no land shortage in Ascra until after the time of Hesiod, whom he dates to around 700 B.C. Snodgrass (1990, 130–31) states that for the period 800–600 Thespiae and Ascra were the only occupied sites in the region. He generalizes about Boeotia that "the 'take-off' of population-growth, which in

1. Sallares 1991, 194–95 and 204–8, suggests that the number of patrilines in a given generation leaving no heir or a female heir might run from 30 percent to 40 percent. The land controlled by these families would inevitably be distributed among the holdings of other families. Whether Hesiod's Ascra practiced the epiklerate (requiring an heiress to marry her paternal next-of-kin) familiar from Classical Athens is anybody's guess. Dowries, too, would in any case have served to redistribute land among families (Buck 1979, 92; cf. Burford 1993, 71; Sallares 1991, 217–19).

many parts of Greece leads to a sudden access of new rural sites, and signs of rapid growth at the major centres, within the eighth century BC, simply did not happen here" (131). Bintliff and Snodgrass (1989, 287) state similar findings, claiming that the populations of Ascra and Thespiae were quite thin for the period 900–600 B.C. and that the population of Boeotia lagged behind that of Attica or the Argolid, for example. Recently Bintliff (1997, 1–16) has placed Attica and the Argolid at the center of the first phase of post-Dark Age population expansion in Greece, in the Geometric and Archaic periods, and Boeotia in the second, for which population take-off occurs in the full Classical and early Hellenistic periods. Snodgrass in fact refers to "the small village of Hesiod's lifetime" (1990, 133) but elsewhere, apparently in reference to its Classical climax, claims that the site of Ascra was larger than that of the neighboring polis of Haliartos and that it must have had a population in the thousands (1985, 94).[2] Such a contrast in size must indicate that Ascra at the dawn of the Archaic period was sparsely populated. There is no question that such a demographic upsurge occurred in the eighth century in many parts of Greece, but available data also suggest that Boeotia lagged behind neighboring regions. Even if we allow for some population growth in Ascra during this period—the arrival of Hesiod's father, for example, might represent an influx from outside the region, it appears to fall short of the surge posited for other regions. This circumstance makes Ascra in Hesiod's time an unlikely candidate for the sort of crisis proposed by Will.

2. Will's sole piece of evidence for a crisis in land tenure is *Works and Days* 341: "in order that you might acquire *(ōnēi)* the plot *(klēron)* of others and not somebody else yours" (ὄφρ' ἄλλων ὠνῇ κλῆρον, μὴ τὸν τεὸν ἄλλος), which he explains in the context of peasants indebted to the elite of the town. The line clearly refers to some sort of transfer of land title though not necessarily to alienation—sale,

---

2. Cf. Snodgrass and Bintliff 1991, 91. See also van Andel and Runnels 1987, 107–9 and the discussion at 157–69 of the pattern of nucleated and dispersed sites in the southern Argolid. The proliferation of what appear to be homesteads from late in the Archaic through the Classical period in the areas of Boeotia surveyed by Bintliff and Snodgrass provides the first indication of a land shortage. This phenomenon can be explained as the interlocking effects of higher population and less available land coming into play during that time period. As population goes up, demand for food makes formerly marginal land viable at the same time as the resulting shortage of land makes it more desirable.

willing or forced. What does the passage tell us, then? It serves as the cap to an exhortation that Perses worship the gods devoutly and punctually. The sense of the passage would seem to be that the gods will pay back failure to give them their due with ill fortune culminating, I infer, in the necessity to exchange one's allotment of land for the means of survival. It is clear from *Works and Days* 341 that the sort of misfortune that Hesiod attributes here to slighted gods could compel a farmer to relinquish control of his land presumably in exchange for food, perhaps for shelter and work as well. We may infer from this with Tandy the existence of some mechanism for transferring title to land though, as Will argues, this is not necessary. The line does not entail that landless destitution awaits the man who has lost his *klēros,* since unimproved land was probably still available to be brought under cultivation. The line only requires that one plot could have more value than another because of such features, presumably, as location, soil, water, drainage, clearing, leveling, buildings, walls, orchards and vineyards, as well perhaps as the livestock, tools, and slaves found on it. As Halstead and Jones (1989, 52) point out, farmers will turn to many lesser measures in the face of shortage—eating animal fodder, appealing to relatives, working for a neighbor, trading—before taking the final step of exchanging land for food. The point of this line is not that land was sold all the time, that Ascrans constantly looked for opportunities to acquire each other's land, or that the land-tenure system was undergoing a fundamental transformation. The point is rather that angry gods could force a man to this final extremity.

The reciprocity of this formulation, moreover, leaving it open that either party might acquire the land of the other depending only on the gods' favor, precludes precisely the sort of imbalance of wealth and power between an elite and a peasantry that Will takes for granted in interpreting the verse. That is, if we accept Will's scenario of conflict between a failing peasantry and an ambitious aristocracy, then the line leads to this absurdity: a pious peasant is just as likely to acquire the estates of his landlord as a pious landlord is to acquire the two-acre plot of his irreverent peasant. Line 341 tells us nothing about hierarchy or class relations, but only about the advisability of piety. I will explain below (no. 3) why I think that this line also has nothing to do with debt.

Tandy (1977, 132–35) bases his claim that Perses has lost his land, his *klēros,* on *W&D* 405: "first get a house *(oikos),* a woman, and a plow ox." This is the "escape from debt and evasion of hunger" referred to in the line preceding. As Tandy (1997, 134) concludes, "Perses has no *oikos,* and so no *kleros.*" This argument presents several problems. In the first place the word *oikos* in Hesiod generally refers to a building (so Hofinger s.v. takes it here), located in Hesiod's case within a village (*W&D* 639–40) and so at best adjacent to his fields rather than in their midst. While there occur a handful of usages referring broadly to household or "house" in the sense of a descent group, Hesiod nowhere uses *oikos* with the meaning "farm" or "plot," for which he reserves the word *kleros,* unless it is so used here. Tandy understands this recommendation to start with a house, a woman, and an ox to mean that Perses literally has no house, from which he infers that the nobles must have taken it away. But Perses is told also to get a wife and an ox in this line. Even if we grant that the *basilees* got the ox too, do we assume the same for the wife, whom Hesiod now urges Perses also to replace?[3] On a reading both literal and specific to Perses, moreover, it strikes me as an interpretation at least as likely as Tandy's to reason that when Hesiod and Perses divided their father's *kleros,* Hesiod got the paternal *oikos* as part of his share, but Perses has yet to put up a house for himself to go along with his *kleros.* It may be relevant in this connection that *Odyssey* 14.208–209 shows heirs casting lots to decide what parts of an estate will be the portion of each. But perhaps the line is instead a maxim and more generic in force as West (ad loc.) takes it, and so not so much a comment on Perses' specific circumstances as a proverbial list of what is required for success in life. This view of the line is supported by the movement of the passage as a whole (381–413): it proceeds from a generic level to a personal focus at 396, marked by the aorist indicative *ēlthes,* and then back towards the generic almost immediately as is signaled by the futures at 396–97 and the general condition at 401–3. The passage continues at this hypothetical level of expression, culminating in the gnomic advice about procrastination at lines 410–13. If, moreover, 405 is not understood as a traditional adage, then Hesiod becomes mired in an obvious contradiction, as Tandy (1977, 222) acknowledges. What sense does it make for Hesiod to urge Perses that in order to get out of debt he must go out and acquire the very thing

---

3. The reference to the "wife" in this line is, of course, made problematic by the line following. See p. 83, no. 4.

he was unable to hang onto and has consequently just lost because of debt? Why does Hesiod repeatedly stress that Perses should get down to work (*W&D* 381–82, 392–94, 397–98, 410–13) if Perses cannot get back to work for want of a farm?

3. Both Ernest Will (1965, 542–45) and Millett (1984, 106) have pointed out that the debt Hesiod describes in *Works and Days* stems from informal lending and borrowing within the context of a small village community, not between hard-pressed farmers and their wealthy, aristocratic creditors. *Chreos,* "debt," occurs only twice in *Works and Days* and the related *chraomai,* "to need," and *chreïzō,* "to be in need of," appear four and three times respectively, spread over six different contexts. *Chreos* at *W&D* 404 is associated with borrowing food from neighbors and relatives. At 647 *chreos* occurs in the same context as *kechrēmenos* at 634, in reference to going to sea in order to avoid hunger. The attestations of *chreïzō* at 351 and 367 also appear in a context joining borrowing food from neighbors with debt and hunger. *Kechrēmenos* at 478 describes the need of the man whose harvest has failed, with the implication of the necessity of borrowing from a successful neighbor, and its occurrences at 317 and 500 (in tandem with *chreïzōn* at 499) suggest this same scenario. As we see, *chreos* and the state of need that leads to borrowing are associated with food and neighbors. There is mention neither of the *basilēes* nor of alienation of land as the outcome of unpaid debts. Hesiod does not present hunger, which is so frequently paired with debt, as the outcome of expropriation but rather as the effect of shiftlessness. Beyond that, failure to repay debt merely results in loss of further credit (*W&D* 349–51, 394–403; see pp. 98–100). There is simply no textual evidence, direct or by implication, that "debt" as Hesiod conceives of it comprises a lien against property, can lead to seizure of assets, or connects the village to the polis. It is for this reason that *W&D* 341 ("you might acquire [*ōnēi*] the plot [*klēron*] of others and not somebody else yours") can have nothing to do with *chreos.* A farmer must abandon his *klēros* not to pay off formal debts but in exchange for subsistence when his relatives and neighbors have become unwilling to continue sharing their own resources with him.

I have tried briefly here to compare several of the chief points in the arguments of Édouard Will and of Tandy with what I understand Hesiod to be saying in *Works and Days*. Hesiod does not complain in *Works and Days* of a land shortage; he does not complain of conflicts over land with local grandees; he does not protest debts, rents, taxes, corvée, interest, or unfavorable trading terms; nor, finally, does he fulminate against the oppression of a powerful aristocracy. Hesiod rather complains about litigation and false-swearing, of Perses' gifts to the kings in the polis, and above all he complains of shiftlessness. In Hesiod's mind, moreover, none of these ills is simply a fact of life, imposed from above by an unassailable elite, but rather all represent poor choices made by individuals who could act otherwise. When Hesiod's rhetoric is placed within the explanatory frames constructed by Édouard Will and by Tandy, it degenerates into irrational ranting, losing its force and its connection with his historical circumstances. If, as both argue, Hesiod is himself hard pressed by the same forces that have ruined Perses, then why does Hesiod attack Perses with such vehemence for shiftlessness and avoiding his responsibilities on his farm rather than commiserating with him over the ruthlessness of their common oppressor? Why is Hesiod so much harsher with Perses than with the elite of the polis, whom he never blames for Perses' failure? For his part, Hesiod appears to be far more preoccupied with what separates the prosperous from the poor within his own village than he is with relations between Ascra and Thespiae.

As I will argue, the ills confronted by Hesiod are not the effects of an elite, of hierarchy, so much as the result of its absence. Hesiod describes a less integrated, less hierarchized, and less complex form of community than even that depicted by Homer. Hesiod's Ascra is a community lacking kings, has not coalesced into a polis, practices a small-scale extensive agriculture, and perhaps resembles rather closely the communities of the Dark Age that preceded the appearance of the polis. In my view, the attempt to contextualize *Works and Days* historically by placing the poem on a time line of regular social evolution at some point between Homer and Solon has been mistaken. Peasant communities may well have preexisted Hesiod's time in the Greek world, quite probably coexisted with him, and certainly existed subsequently. But there is no reason to assume that every community of rural cultivators in Greece was a peasant community strictly defined. It is certainly possible that Hesiod depicts in *Works and Days* a community that is neither a polis itself nor a settlement within the territory of a polis. That is, the community of *Works and Days*—neither kingdom, nor city-state, nor *ethnos*—may stand outside the major evolutionary stages within which we are accustomed to think the history of ancient Greece.

THE DISPUTE WITH PERSES

Hesiod is not entirely clear in setting forth the details of his relationship with his brother Perses. Can it be assumed, as most do, that Perses has already taken Hesiod before the kings, that the kings have already exerted their authority over the dispute with a decision in Perses' favor, and that Hesiod as a consequence may even have lost some of his land? Beyond that, what does this dispute between Hesiod and Perses tell us about the balance between the subsistence economy of the individual household and the political economy of the village and about the extent to which Thespiae has succeeded in drawing Ascra within the boundaries of its own political economy? Does Hesiod suggest that the kings, as the magistrates of the city and representatives of an elite class, can settle this dispute with a free hand and in their own interests? As the event that provokes Hesiod's harangue, the quarrel between him and Perses comprises the flash point in *Works and Days* where the conflicting interests of the prosperous and the poor intersect with the opposition between the city and the village. As a consequence any investigation of the relation between Ascra and Thespiae must begin here.

The questions that I just posed are fundamental to our understanding of the world Hesiod describes for us, yet to provide them with answers we are dependent upon only thirteen lines of text. The passage in which Hesiod introduces his quarrel with Perses and gives most of the pertinent information about it runs from *Works and Days* 27 to 39:

ὦ Πέρση, σὺ δὲ ταῦτα τεῷ ἐνικάτθεο θυμῷ,
μηδέ σ' Ἔρις κακόχαρτος ἀπ' ἔργου θυμὸν ἐρύκοι
νείκε' ὀπιπεύοντ' ἀγορῆς ἐπακουὸν ἐόντα.
ὥρη γάρ τ' ὀλίγη πέλεται νεικέων τ' ἀγορέων τε,   30
ᾧτινι μὴ βίος ἔνδον ἐπηετανὸς κατάκειται
ὡραῖος, τὸν γαῖα φέρει, Δημήτερος ἀκτήν.
τοῦ κε κορεσσάμενος νείκεα καὶ δῆριν ὀφέλλοις
κτήμασ' ἐπ' ἀλλοτρίοις. σοὶ δ' οὐκέτι δεύτερον ἔσται
ὧδ' ἔρδειν, ἀλλ' αὖθι διακρινώμεθα νεῖκος   35
ἰθείῃσι δίκῃς, αἵ τ' ἐκ Διός εἰσιν ἄρισται.
ἤδη μὲν γὰρ κλῆρον ἐδασσάμεθ', ἄλλά τε πολλὰ
ἀρπάζων ἐφόρεις, μέγα κυδαίνων βασιλῆας
δωροφάγους, οἳ τήνδε δίκην ἐθέλουσι δικάσσαι,

Perses, store these words away in your heart:
do not let trouble-loving Strife keep you from your farm,
watching quarrels and attentive to the town square.
For there is scant leisure for quarrels and speeches   30

if a man does not have stored away enough of the season's livelihood,
which the earth brings forth, the grain of Demeter.
When you have a surplus of this, then you can start provoking quarrels
    and disputes
over other men's possessions. But it will not be possible for you
to do thus a second time—rather let us decide our quarrel right here   35
with straight judgments, which are from Zeus and are the best—
for we already divided our plot, though seizing many other things
you have been taking them to honor the gift-eating
kings, who like to render such justice.[4]

Hesiod announces this dispute in a passage opening with an appeal to Perses that he not permit the wicked Strife to force him from his farm into the town square, the site of litigation (27–29). Hesiod develops this topic further with a subordinate thought explaining (*gar:* 30) that a man without a year's supply of grain put away has no leisure for quarrels and litigation (30–32). He lingers here with an inversion of that same topos: when Perses has a surfeit of grain, then he might pursue the possessions of others through quarrels and contention (33–34). Hesiod then asserts, in a statement linked by the particle *de* (34b) to what has gone before, that it will not be possible for Perses to "act in this way" (*hōd' erdein:* 35) again.

The lines at 34b–35 are generally taken to cap the lines preceding: Perses cannot take Hesiod to court again (*ouketi deuteron:* 34) because he now lacks the necessary resources, the year's worth of grain, needed to finance a lawsuit.[5] Van Groningen (1957, 2–3) points out that up until lines 34b–35 there is no indication that Perses has actually undertaken a litigation against Hesiod, and it is in my view prima facie unlikely that a community organized along such simple lines as that depicted by Hesiod would routinely submit the inheritance process to authorities outside the family let alone to those of Thespiae. There is no justification simply to assume that the dispute has already been judged by the kings without good textual evidence to support that view. Fundamental to the generally accepted in-

---

4. There is not much consensus on how to construe line 39 (οἳ τήνδε δίκην ἐθέλουσι δικάσσαι). There is some tension between *ethelousi*, which implies a future action, and *tēnde*, which suggests something already known. Needless to say, how to negotiate this dilemma turns on a general interpretation of the passage as a whole. See Sinclair 1966, West 1978, and Verdenius 1985, ad loc.

5. See, e.g., van Groningen 1957, 2–3, 7–8, 12–13; Wilamowitz 1962, ad 34; Rowe 1978, ad 33–36; Verdenius 1985, ad 34. *Eti* of *ouketi* reinforces *deuteron*, stressing the unrepeatability of the action. The phrase does not mean that, while it was once possible to do so a second time, it is no longer permitted. Cf. *Iliad* 23.45–47 cited by West 1978, ad 34.

terpretation is a very literal reading of lines 30–34a: litigation is not for Perses since he has not stored away a year's supply of grain and, as a consequence, simply cannot afford to go to court. This understanding of the lines must, however, be taken to imply that if Perses did have a surplus put away, he might freely devote his energies to designs on the possessions of others. Yet is it likely that Hesiod endorses trumped-up lawsuits aiming to swindle another man out of his possessions as long as the plaintiff has brought in a successful harvest beforehand? Do we imagine that Hesiod would welcome the same suit from which he now dissuades Perses with such vehemence as long as Perses finances it by his hard work?

Presumably the "kings" have achieved this recommended level of prosperity, but Hesiod hardly seems prepared to commend their injustice. At 214–15 ff., following encouragement to hearken to justice and not to strengthen *hubris* (*mēd' hubrin ophelle*: 213; cf. *neikea kai dērin ophellois* at line 33), Hesiod elaborates the theme that *hubris* is bad for a *deilos* and even an *esthlos* cannot bear it easily but becomes mired down in calamities on its account. *Deilos* and *esthlos* designate social status here, but an individual's place within the social hierarchy of Hesiod's village is determined chiefly by his success at farming and possession of a surplus (see pp. 86–89, 102–18). Hesiod seems here to rule out such pursuits even for the prosperous. Indeed Hesiod explicitly equates "pillaging [wealth] with the tongue" (i.e., false testimony) with seizing it by outright violence, and he predicts for both the same divine retribution *(W&D* 320–26). One could cite further passages, but assuming, as we must, that in the present context Hesiod thinks of Perses' claims against himself as unjust and without merit, it appears highly unlikely that Hesiod approves in lines 30–34 of going after another's possessions as long as one has achieved a sufficient prosperity of one's own. If, finally, for nothing more than a lack of resources Perses is simply unable to undertake further litigation, as this interpretation insists, then the pretext and motivation for the entire first section of the poem extending to line 381—the present passage, the etiologies of labor, the exhortations to justice and then to labor—collapse. On this understanding of the passage why does Hesiod bother with the warning of 28–29, the qualifications of 30–31 and 33–34, the invitation at 35–36? There is no reason to dissuade Perses from a course of action he cannot afford to undertake to begin with.

As I have noted, the argument that Perses is a helpless victim of the kings of Thespiae or that he has been left homeless and landless by debt leads into the same sort of contradiction. Why would Hesiod bother to exhort Perses to get back to work and blame his failure on laziness if his brother's predicament is the result of forces beyond his control and too strong to resist? To attribute Perses' troubles to any reasons besides his personal, ethical shortcomings destroys the moral underpinnings of the poem. This is not a case of a rural conservative vainly explaining broad historical forces in terms of personal morality or making unreasonable criticisms of a despised relative. Hesiod's argument presupposes that Perses has access to land and that working it would lead to an immediate relief from his misery.

Gagarin (1974, 104–10) attaches no moral significance to these lines but sees them as a purely practical reference to the need to pay "court fees," honorific gifts bestowed equally by both litigants upon a judge, a necessity he infers from *Iliad* 18.508. So at lines 37–39, in which Hesiod states that Perses kept seizing and carrying off many other things with which to honor the "gift-eating kings," Gagarin sees only a reference to court fees. Yet the lines do not describe gifts that Hesiod and Perses have both rendered to the king in gratitude for a judgment. Rather they are a rebuke specifically to Perses for what he alone has offered in order to curry favor with these kings. If the reference is to the enrichment of the kings by court fees, then Hesiod must equally rebuke himself since by Gagarin's argument both litigants must render gifts. To posit "court fees" in the form of honorific gifts on the basis of *Iliad* 18.508 is in itself plausible enough, but there is no clear support for it in the text of *Works and Days*, and it produces a contradictory interpretation of these lines.

I believe that lines 30–34 must be understood within Hesiod's view of what brings success. It is first, Hesiod claims, the product of unremitting toil (e.g., *W&D* 20–24, 311–16, 382–83, 397–400); the only respite Hesiod allows his farmer is the brief pause of midsummer when it is simply too hot to work (*W&D* 582–96). Second, prosperity is the reward of justice (e.g., *W&D* 280–81, 225–37, and 158 with 172–73) while wealth acquired unjustly brings ruin (*W&D* 320–36, 352, 356; cf. 230–31). I think Hesiod's implicit point at lines 30–34 is that the prosperous have no leisure for litigation since they are too busy working, nor do they feel any desire to pursue the wealth of others through litigation since they have satisfied their wants and live in accordance with justice. That is, once Perses has satisfied Hesiod's prerequisites for engaging in litigation, he would no longer need or wish to do so.[6] In my view this passage must be understood

---

6. Jones (1984, 311–12) understands lines 33–34 to mean that farmers simply have no reason under any circumstances for being in the agora instead of on the farm. Perhaps this invitation to pursue litigation once he has a supply of grain in

in the context of the broader moral landscape of the poem. In that setting the interpretation of lines 34–35 that Perses simply lacks the wealth necessary for any further litigation must be judged unconvincing.

If, as I have argued, Hesiod's point is not that Perses will be unable to pursue further litigation simply for want of resources, then 34b–35 ("But it will not be possible for you to do thus a second time") cannot be taken to apply to the preceding lines, since Perses, even in his insolvency, remains perfectly capable of dragging Hesiod in front of the "kings." Indeed, if *hōd'* ("thus," "in this way") does not refer to the lawsuits and disputes of the preceding lines, the probable meaning of the passage is that Perses has yet to take his complaint to the "kings" of Thespiae in the first place. But, if *hōd' erdein* ("to do thus") does not refer to the lines preceding, then to what? The opening *d' ouketi deuteron* ("not a second time": 34b) might anticipate *all' authi* ("rather here/now": 35), with *all'* ("rather," "but") signaling the second branch of an antithesis in correlation with *ouk* ("not"), or else *d' ouketi deuteron* might await *ēdē men gar* ("for already") in line 37.[7] An antithesis of *ouketi deuteron* and *all' authi* does not advance our inquiry very far, however, since its "not X but Y" logical structure contradicts the analogical link that the word *hōd'* requires. The logical relationship expressed by *ouk . . . all'* precludes the possibility that *hōd' erdein*, governed by *ouk*, could refer to *diakrinōmetha neikos* ("let us decide our quarrel"), introduced by *all'*. That is, in an utterance structured "don't do thus but do this," the word "thus" (i.e., *hōd'*) is blocked from referring to "do this" (i.e., *diakrinōmetha neikos*) by the force of the conjunction "but" *(all')*. In the statement "But it will not be possible for you to do thus a second time—rather let us decide our quarrel right here with straight judgments," "thus" cannot look forward to the verb "decide" because of the force of "rather," which presents "decide" as an alternative to whatever "thus" is meant to specify. *Hōd' erdein* must, as a consequence, refer to something else.

Ēdē men gar ("for already") is a more likely candidate. *Gar* ("for": 37) points to another clause that it explains in the same way that *hōde* (35) points to another action that it describes, and *ēdē* ("already") links up nicely with *ouketi deuteron*. In this case I take *all'* (35) to mark a disjunc-

---

storage is offered with the same irony as is the description *phrenas aphneios* at 455 (cf. *nēpios* at 456) or, in my view, the troublesome *dion genos* at 299.

7. Verdenius 1985, ad 35, though considering *hōd' erdein* to be retrospective here, notes passages where it is used proleptically. So West 1978, ad 35 seems to take it, though I remain unable to figure out exactly what West means to say in that note. He appears, however, to associate the phrase with line 37 as do I.

tion almost parenthetical in force.[8] Hesiod argues, then, "It will not be possible for you to do so again—rather let us settle our dispute here (i.e., and now, not later in the *agorē* and before the "kings")—since *(gar)* we have already divided the farm." *Hōd' erdein* (35) thus points ahead to *klēron edassameth'* ("we have already divided the farm": 37) while *gar* (37) offers to explain the somewhat proleptic clause at 34–35 in which *hōd' erdein* occurs. Hesiod thus argues that since their inheritance has already been divided, it is impossible as a consequence to divide it a second time. So, let them try to work out their dispute between themselves without dragging in the kings. The thought of the division of their father's land then draws Hesiod on to comment on Perses' subsequent use, illegitimate to his way of thinking, of resources *(alla te polla . . .)* remaining in their common possession or of ambiguous status.

A passage from *Iliad* Book 1 provides a parallel to this interpretation. When Agamemnon insists that, if he must return Chryseis, he alone should not go without a prize, Achilles retorts that all that the Achaeans have won has already been divided *(ta dedastai: 125)* and it is not right for the army to collect the booty back up again (λαοὺς δ' οὐκ ἐπέοικε παλίλλογα ταῦτ' ἐπαγείρειν: 126; i.e., for a redistribution). Hesiod's *ouketi . . . estai* (34) corresponds to Achilles' *ouk epeoike.* Now that the land has been divided, it would contradict propriety and the norms of the community for it to be recollected and divided once again—apparently, the thing that Perses intends to ask the kings to do.

As I reconstruct the opening scenario, then, no dispute between the brothers has yet gone before the kings of Thespiae (so Verdenius 1985 ad *W&D* 35 [*neikos*]), the kings have rendered no judgment, and Hesiod has not lost his land. Following, presumably, their father's death, Hesiod and Perses divided his land between themselves (*W&D* 37). Whether the division provided equal shares to each son or not, we cannot say, but it was no doubt carried out within the limits of community norms. Although Perses did not prove a successful farmer (*W&D* 27–34), he began to cultivate the nobles of Thespiae with honorific gifts (*W&D* 37–39) and to frequent their

8. For this use of *alla* see LSJ s.v. II.2, Cunliffe 1963, s.v. 3, and Denniston 1959, s.v. II.4. For *gar* see Denniston 1959, s.v. II.3, roughly the equivalent of LSJ s.v. I.1.b, and Cunliffe 1963, s.v. 1. Denniston 1959, s.v. III.4, lists instances where *gar* refers back to something earlier than what immediately preceded it. This is how Hofinger s.v. I understands *gar* at *W&D* 37. I also think that *gar* at *W&D* 37 bears some of the nuance of abrupt objection, in response to the implicit demand of Perses that the *klēros* be redivided, evident in the examples found at LSJ s.v. I.4 and Cunliffe 1963, s.v. 3.

transactions in the *agorē* (*W&D* 27–34).[9] Meanwhile Perses began to rely upon his more successful brother for handouts to keep his own household afloat. As time wore on Hesiod became exasperated with what he considered Perses' indolence and threatened to cut him off (*W&D* 20–29, cf. 392– 400), likely a drastic measure. Perses then countered with his own threat to go before the kings of Thespiae, outside Ascra and the boundaries of Hesiod's influence, seeking a reconsideration of the original division of their father's farm (*W&D* 34–37). *Works and Days* is presented as an attempt to dissuade Perses from so doing. There is no evidence in these lines that the elite of Thespiae exercises regular authority over Ascra or that individual households within the village are under a strong obligation to one another. As I have already acknowledged, we cannot know with certainty whether the scenario of *Works and Days* is based upon factual events or whether it is fictional but achieves a degree of verisimilitude. In either case, I believe that Hesiod's audience took for granted approximately what I have outlined here.

TRADE

The link between Ascra and the world beyond with which Hesiod is most concerned is that of the judicial authority of the "kings." A second form of relationship, for which Hesiod shows less interest and no real hostility, is that of trade. Participation in trade stands as an important issue in our evaluation of the status of Hesiod's community since peasant communities have frequently been coerced by an elite into participating in trade in regional or international markets. Trade as a mechanism of extracting a surplus, as a means of exploitation, characteristically entails unequal terms of exchange for the peasant and the cultivation of cash crops rather than what is needed to feed the community and its households. In order to maintain the conditions required for regularized trade of this sort, an external elite

---

9. Lines 37–39 suggest that Perses made frequent gifts of items whose ownership was at least disputable. I speculate that Hesiod refers to produce from livestock or a garden plot that remained under the brothers' joint management. Exemplary of the sort of gift at issue might be the bit of meat used by Trygaeus in Aristophanes' *Peace* to win over Hermes at the gates of Olympus (*Peace* 192, 378–79) or the cup offered by Priam to the same god at *Iliad* 24.429–39. Cf. Walcot 1970, 102–7, esp. 104. Perhaps comparable is the gift of some cheeses Jesse entrusts to David for the generals at the same time as he sends him with provisions for his other sons in the army (1 Samuel 17: 17–18).

must, of course, be in a position to exercise considerable discipline over a rural community. Trade itself, however, is not diagnostic of a peasant community nor does it necessarily serve as a means of exploitation when peasants participate in it.[10] So, we must consider whether trade appears to operate as a means of exploitation in Hesiod's community, reflecting the power of an external elite.

Trade and the Political Economy

To put the question another way, should the sort of trade described by Hesiod in *Works and Days* be regarded as a part of the subsistence economy, something conducted at the level of the individual household in pursuit of domestic goals, or should it be understood in terms of a larger political economy? Johnson and Earle discuss trade as part of the political economy, where it relies upon the leadership of a head trader, a person with connections beyond the village, and serves to bring in needed resources that are in shorter supply locally as the population grows. This sort of trade appears in the company of stratification and political integration and reflects the collective needs of a community (Johnson and Earle 1987, 190–91, 210–11, 222–24, 247). In my view, Hesiod is in fact describing a form of trade that is more sporadic and opportunistic than that and that can function as another mode of storage for the domestic unit (Johnson and Earle 1987, 15–18, 116–17, 147, 186).

Mele (1979) and Tandy (1997 and 2001) provide the most extensive and detailed accounts of trade in *Works and Days*, where Hesiod's evidence is discussed in the context of general treatments of trade in the early Archaic period. Mele, in a characterization that Tandy adopts and extends, designates the type of trade described in *Works and Days* as *ergon* trade (Mele 1979, 40–46, 53–57, and Tandy 1997, 75, 212–14). Mele's *ergon* trade is subordinated both to the necessities of farming and to the interests of the household economy. It is, additionally, autarkic, practiced independently in the interest of the household's autonomy: it is just one *ergon*, one economic activity, among the many pursued by the small farmer as he works to secure his livelihood. This conception of *ergon* trade corresponds quite closely to the notion of trade carried on at the level of the domestic economy.

10. Regarding trade as a mechanism of exploitation see: Redfield 1956, 45–50; Scott 1976, 7–11, 56–90; Thorner 1987, 64–66; Ellis 1988, 51–59. Thorner points out that trade may operate in various ways in a peasant economy; see also Magagna 1991, 36–39 and Wolf 1966, 40–47. Sahlins (1972, 277–314) discusses trade among societies less complex than peasant societies.

Yet both Mele and Tandy locate this *ergon* trade as practiced by Hesiod within a broader context of stratification, strife, and long-distance trade. Mele constructs a sweeping account drawing Ascra into developments shaping Euboea, Aeolis, Ionia, Attica, and even Italy. He has recourse, moreover, to evidence from Homer down through Solon. Tandy, too, contextualizes Hesiod and Ascra within a picture based on data from Lefkandi, Al Mina, Pithecousae, and Attica.[11] For Mele the Ascran *ergon* trader is drawn into a contrast not only with aristocratic, long-distance traders in luxury goods, the *prēxis* trader, but also with an emergent class of professional merchants who possess neither land, like the *ergon* trader, nor ship like the long-distance trader (Mele 1979, 58–78, 92–94, 106–8). According to Mele's analysis, while Hesiod as a small holder and an *ergon* trader may be at odds with the aristocratic long-distance traders, he reserves his hostility for the *emporos*, the professional merchant, who has abandoned agriculture to live exclusively from commerce. Within this picture Hesiod and the aristocratic trader represent a social and political world that will be forcefully challenged by the demos of the rising polis, whose interests the *emporos* serves. For his part, Tandy sees long-distance trade in luxury goods as the instigator of the economic and social transformation that is reducing Ascrans to peasant status. Trade is one of the mechanisms by which the inhabitants of Ascra are held in dependency upon Thespiae and its kings. Specifically, Tandy argues that the nascent polis, in order to finance its continued development, must rely upon the regular exchange of the farmers' produce in its market on terms favoring the city (Tandy 1997, 125–27, 212–14, and Tandy 2001, 167–68, 172–73). As a means of resistance, Hesiod recommends to his fellow farmers that they export their surplus by sea in order to avoid this unequal system and so to undermine the power of Thespiae's *basilēes* (Tandy 1997, 231–34, and Tandy 2001, 165–73).

While I agree with the characterization of Hesiod as a farmer engaged in *ergon* trade, I question the relevance of the broader context into which Mele and Tandy insert Ascra and Hesiod. One can, of course, hardly fault treatments of trade for emphasizing evidence for trade in their discussions of *Works and Days*—Hesiod does after all provide important testimony on the subject. When viewed from the perspective of Ascra, its institutions and organization, however, the accounts of Mele and Tandy risk attribut-

---

11. See Tandy 1997, 159–66, passim and Mele 1979, 18–39, 95–107, passim. Note also Mele 1979, 46, where he asserts the legitimacy of exploiting Homer to supply the "quadro istituzionale" for the forms of trade referred to by Hesiod.

ing to trade too high a profile.[12] In particular, it is my position that the type of trade Hesiod describes corresponds to Mele's concept of *ergon* trade and nothing more. That is, it does not mark a point of contact between Ascrans and an outside elite or of incorporation of Ascra within a regularized system of long-distance trade routes.

In view of the geographic and chronological breadth of the arguments of Tandy and Mele, it seems fair to ask in the first place whether conditions in Boeotia at the time we assume Hesiod to be composing are so similar to what will occur in Attica a century later or to more contemporary circumstances in what are regarded as the most developed regions of Greece in terms of trade and communication with the broader Mediterranean world. A comparison of Coldstream's (1977) discussions of Boeotia with what he has to say about Attica, the Argolid, or Euboea clearly indicates that Boeotian material culture lags behind that of her neighbors.[13] Whitley (1991, 341–46), supported by Morris (1997, 557–59), stresses the obvious conclusion to be drawn from Coldstream's data, that regional variations in the archaeological record imply that various forms and levels of social organization coexisted during the Dark Age. Burford (1993, 17–20) similarly underlines the variety of models of organization and of sizes and densities represented by Greek communities in the Archaic and Classical periods. As I have already discussed, moreover, Boeotia lagged behind the rest of Greece during the Dark Age and the Archaic period in the rate at which its population grew (see pp. 32–33). To focus upon Boeotia's southern neighbor, Attica, we can note as differences, then, not only Attica's more rapid population growth, but also the early advance of synoecism in Attica, producing a region in which one polis dominated all other settlements while Boeotia remained a region of numerous poleis that organized themselves into a confederacy only at a later time.[14] Such fundamental differences suggest that events in Attica and elsewhere during the Dark Age and the Archaic period may not shed much light on contemporary Boeotia, especially considering that Ascra is a village, not a polis at all.

12. See Cartledge 1983, esp. 10–12 regarding Mele's arguments.

13. Coldstream 1977, 50–52, 73–86, 132–37, 152–56, 186–88, 199–201, 201–6. Coldstream (1977, 206), commenting on the epithets of "[b]ackward, clumsy, rustic, derivative" often applied to Boeotian art, explains that "Boeotians were not much concerned . . . with marketing their wares overseas" and that they exhibited an "indifference to commerce." Morris (1997, 548) notes in his regional survey of Iron Age Greece Boeotia's atypicality in this regard for central Greece.

14. Cf. Bintliff's (1994, 225–33) contrast of the development of Attica and Boeotia.

Hesiod devotes only one substantial passage to trade (*W&D* 618–94), with two other indirect references (*W&D* 45, 236–37), and he presents it as an option rather than as an obligatory element of the farm economy (*W&D* 618, 646–47). Hesiod, moreover, provides little indication in *Works and Days* of suspicion or resentment of the *agorē* as a market. He never refers to the marketplace as the site of unjust economic transactions or to trading in the polis at all. Nor does Hesiod suggest anywhere in the poem, implicitly or explicitly, that farmers ought to export by sea in order to avoid the *agorē*. If this had been Hesiod's intent, it seems likely that he would have been as explicit here as he is in denouncing the kings' judicial activities. I also differ with Mele's argument from *Works and Days* 678–91, especially 686 and 689, that Hesiod condemns forms of trade that permit the trader to make a living independently of the farm economy (Mele 1979, 16–17, 21, 40–46, 53–55). Lines 678–87 caution against the dangers of spring sailing, the risk of losing one's life to the sea. Lines 689–93 weigh concern for one's life and one's cargo against the implicit desire to ship as much cargo as possible. Hesiod advises against committing all of one's *bios* to trade since, as he explains, the risk of losing it at sea is too great. Mele's claim that this advice is motivated by a prejudice against professional traders and fear that the farm will be neglected during trading voyages finds no support in these lines, which caution rather against the dangers of seafaring.[15] The specific conflicts within which Tandy and Mele inscribe Hesiod's *ergon* trade based upon the larger geographic and political contexts they construct cannot be substantiated from the direct testimony of *Works and Days*.

If, moreover, the *basilēes* must insure that the tradable surplus from Ascra reaches their own market in Thespiae in order to finance the continued expansion of the polis, why would they permit peasants from a village within their territory to move produce overland across the countryside in order to export it by sea? Again, if Hesiod and other Ascrans are seeking markets outside their territory to escape the unequal terms of their local

15. The philological evidence for Mele's distinction among the *ergon, prēxis,* and *emporiē* forms of trade in *Works and Days* at any rate is weak. Hesiod does not use *ergon* to refer to trade, and the only usage of the word *emporiē* refers to the type of exchange designated by Mele as *ergon* trade. *Prēxis* does not occur in *Works and Days.* Mele's use of that word is based primarily on Homeric evidence, which he believes can be legitimately conflated with Hesiod's testimony. The two occurrences of *emporos* in Homer, however, merely refer to a passenger on a ship, not to a trader.

market, then it is a reasonable extension of the argument to infer that farmers from other areas bring their produce into Thespiae for the same reason (cf. Tandy 1997, 233, and Tandy 2001, 172–73). Either cities engaged in such a competition would have to lower the margin of "incremental centripetal gains" made through exchange rates in their markets in order to attract farmers from other regions, or else farmers would find all markets the same and would as a consequence select them solely on the basis of proximity and familiarity. Such inter-polis competition would in any case quickly lead cities to attempt to control the movement of farmers and goods within their discrete territories. It can be noted, finally, that Hesiod's testimony does not suggest that Ascrans were in any degree dependent upon access to a market. Hesiod makes scant reference to items manufactured outside the household and only to a single service provided by a specialist, a carpenter to fit the plow stock to its tree (*W&D* 430–31), and there is no reason to think that he, the blacksmith of *Works and Days* 493, or the carpenter and potter of line 25, is from the polis or even a full-time craftsman. The simpler assumption is that the *basilées* exercise no extensive power over Ascra and that Hesiod recommends export by sea simply as the most efficient means to find a favorable exchange.

While long-distance trade in metals and other luxury goods is well known from the archaeological record from at least the latter stage of the Dark Age and is attested to by Homer as well, *Works and Days* makes no reference to it. At the same time, Hesiod's trade in subsistence goods cannot be documented from archaeological evidence and was likely a limited phenomenon.[16] Hesiod's Ascra is in my view relatively untouched by the large trade networks in luxury goods and enters into trade in subsistence goods only opportunistically and in modes subordinated to the priorities of the subsistence agricultural economy. That is, it has nothing to do with exploitative relations between village cultivators and an elite of the polis and everything to do with the perceived self-interest of the individual *oikos*.

16. See Tandy's discussion of Homer's testimony on trade (1997, 72–75). Halstead and Jones (1989) generalize about trade "most records of a 'grain trade' in both recent and ancient times in the Mediterranean probably reflect *short term* conditions of surfeit and shortage" (54). See also Garnsey and Morris 1989, 100; Gallant 1991, 98–101; Tandy 1997, 65–66, 118, 120; and Tsetskhladze 1998, 54–63. Mele's (1979, 41) inference from *Od.* 15.446, 456, and 17.250 that Homer testifies to significant trade in subsistence goods does not take into account that Homer uses *biotos* to refer not only to foodstuffs but also to a household's wealth in general (*Il.* 5.544, 6.14, 14.122; *Od.* 3.301, 4.90; *W&D* 167).

Poverty and Kerdos

It is the topic of the best season for sailing that brings up the subject of trade (*W&D* 618–94). Hesiod gives no hint of participation in trade by an elite, of unfavorable exchanges with middlemen or aristocrats, or of traffic in special crops. Rather the farmer owns his own ship (*W&D* 45, 624–29, 670–72), ships his own produce (*W&D* 689–90, cf. 622–23), and decides whether or not to export (*W&D* 646–48), how much to export (*W&D* 643–45, 689–91), and when to sail (*W&D* 618–23, 663–72, 678–83). On the basis of this evidence one cannot argue for trade organized by middlemen, for a pattern of export able to sustain reliably a non-cultivating town population, or for the directing role of an elite. For Hesiod the sole inducement to engage in trade is the expectation of gain, *kerdos* (*W&D* 630–32, 644–47), for the benefit of the individual household. This orientation would serve to inscribe trade within the same logic of autarky, of production for use, that governs the agricultural and craft activities of the household.[17] But what is the profit Hesiod expects, what goal does he pursue through trade? Simply to attribute a generalized profit motive to Hesiod begs the question by posing participation in trade as a matter of human nature.

As a practical matter trade cannot have been undertaken lightly by Ascrans. Fossey notes Boeotia's poor access to the sea generally and characterizes access to Creusis, the most likely port for Hesiod, as a "narrow gorge" carved out by a torrent running into the gulf (Fossey 1988, 4, 157). Overland transport was extremely time-consuming even in later antiquity (de Ste. Croix 1981, 11–12). The problems presented by overland transport in Hesiod's time and place can be inferred from Burford's (1960) discussion of Classical Attica. Snodgrass (1983) in fact rejects the idea that there could have been a regular, long-distance, large-scale trade in grain in the Archaic period.[18]

In *Works and Days* Hesiod expresses an attitude towards trade that is at

---

17. These passages refute Bravo's (1977, 5–10) argument that the trade described in *W&D* is bankrolled and directed by land-wealthy aristocrats. See West 1978, ad *W&D* 618–94; Mele 1979, 14–17; Millett 1984, 93–99; Spahn 1980, 538–41; and Tandy 1997, 216 and 226–27 regarding Hesiod's orientation towards the independence and survival of the *oikos*. Cf. Sahlins' (1972, 74–99) discussion of the domestic mode of production and household production for use. On *kerdos* and trade see Tandy 1997, 224–27.

18. Cf. Boserup 1981, 64–70 regarding the complexities of population density, transportation, and infrastructure for moving food. Tandy (1997, 213), however, argues in detail that communication between Ascra and the sea was relatively easy.

best ambivalent. The expectation of profit from trade is more than offset in Hesiod's mind by the risks of seafaring to which he alludes throughout his discussion of trade. Hesiod opens his discussion of sailing by referring to it as "stormy" (*duspemphelou: W&D* 618) and by describing precisely the worst weather of the year, when one ought to leave one's boat on the shore and stick to the farm (*W&D* 618–23). This same pattern of a qualified recommendation continues throughout his treatment of the topic. At 644–45 Hesiod gushes that a greater cargo will pile greater gain *(kerdos)* upon gain as long as, he adds, the winds restrain their destructive gusts. Later, when he specifies the season of fair sailing, Hesiod reassures Perses that the sea will not at this time of the year break up his boat or drown him—unless, of course, Poseidon or Zeus decides to do so. Immediately thereafter he balances three lines of smooth sailing with five urging a hasty voyage home in order to avoid the coming storms of fall (*W&D* 670–77). Hesiod next considers the time of the earlier, spring sailing season (*W&D* 678–82) but then continues with six lines of grave warnings against this hazardous period (*W&D* 682–91): "possessions," Hesiod generalizes, "become as valuable as life for wretched men" (*W&D* 686). These conflicting concerns of profit and risk, expressed so clearly at line 686, emerge as well in the contradictory advice he offers on how much to commit to trade. Against the lines promising greater gain for a larger cargo (*phortos: W&D* 644) stands Hesiod's closing admonition not to put all of your produce (*bios:* 689, literally, "livelihood") in a ship but keep most of it back; for it's terrible to meet disaster on the high seas (*W&D* 689–94). Hesiod hardly provides a ringing endorsement of trade. Even as he acknowledges the possibilities for profiting from trade—strictly a maritime enterprise in his view—Hesiod insistently warns of the equally significant risks that go along with it. The only alternatives Hesiod mentions for produce are trade and storage. In practical terms, the farmer had to decide how much of his precious reserve, his only protection against destitution and starvation, to keep in storage and how much to risk on export. What circumstances would have persuaded a farmer to pursue the gains available from the riskier option of trade?

The setting for Hesiod's excursus on trade is of course his catalogue of the farmer's calendar. His use of the personal expression *bios* (*W&D* 689) to refer to the produce entrusted to trade makes it clear that he imagines a farmer exporting the produce of his own farm. Hesiod, moreover, assumes in his account that trade is undertaken by farmers on their own behalf; professional traders do not enter into the picture. Hesiod recommends that Perses load his cargo after awaiting sailing weather in order to bring home a profit (*kerdos: W&D* 630–32). "Just as," Hesiod continues, "your father and mine, Perses, you big fool, / used to sail in ships for want of a decent livelihood *(bios)*" (*W&D* 633–34). The conjunction *hōs per*, "just as," entails a close parallel between Hesiod's preceding recommendation to Perses that he load his cargo and bring home a profit and the earlier activities of his father. What is the equivalency established between father and son by this conjunction? The father "for want of a livelihood" (*biou kechrēmenos esthlou: W&D* 634) sought *kerdos* at sea; Perses, because he is failing as a farmer, is advised likewise to go to sea in search of *kerdos*, exporting the produce he will have if he agrees to return to his farm. The easiest and most obvious sense to make of the parallelism required by *hōs per* is that their father was a farmer in Cyme who was driven by poverty to transport his produce by sea and exchange it elsewhere for *kerdos*.

The phrase expressing his motivation, moreover, "for want of a decent livelihood" (*biou kechrēmenos esthlou: W&D* 634), clearly subordinates trade as an activity to the needs of the household, the subsistence economy.[19] Since Hesiod's family immigrated to Ascra in order to flee poverty (*W&D* 637–38), Boeotia, in spite of Hesiod's grim description (*W&D* 639–40), must have provided a higher level of living than Aeolis and presumably less need for going to sea as a consequence. His father's continuing poverty and immigration to Boeotia do not suggest that he was a middleman, a professional trader profiting by the produce of peasants and so a member of the non-cultivating elite of his city. I see nothing in this passage to support the assumption of both Tandy (1997, 121) and Mele (1979, 21–22, 36–38) that Hesiod's father is a professional, full-time trader—certainly Hesiod does not appear to be advising Perses to abandon agriculture for a life as a merchant as the *hōs per* of line 633 would require if we assume that the father was a merchant and not a farmer. Rather, Hesiod appears to regard the risks of trade as something undertaken as the exigency of poverty. This impression is corroborated by his treatment of sailing in his description of the golden-age settings of the city of justice (*W&D* 225–37) and the pre-Pandoran world (*W&D* 42–46). The marvelous plenty of these settings does not result in increased trade but in its disappearance (*W&D* 236–37, 45). This same complex of poverty, trade, and risk occurs in Solon's catalogue of professions (Solon 13.41–46 [W]) where he describes the man whose poverty (*peniē*: 41) compels him to wander the seas

---

19. Mele (1979, 22) notes Cyme's reputation for its agriculture.

with no regard for his life in order to bring home a profit *(kerdos)*.[20] The relationship between want of livelihood—*bios*, the same term used to name the produce of the farm—and risking one's life at sea for gain demonstrates the subordinate position to which Hesiod assigns trade in comparison to farming, the foundation of the household economy.

Hesiod in fact mentions only two items that are likely to have been acquired by Ascrans through exchange: olive oil (*W&D* 522) and *biblinos oinos* (*W&D* 589). The olive was not cultivated in Ascra (see pp. 145–46) and the single reference to it presents it as a luxury item, used as a skin lotion by a maiden in a passage emphasizing comfort and ease. This item could be supplied from as nearby as Thespiae and certainly would need to come from no further than Attica. The Biblos of the Bibline wine is most likely a region in Thrace (Mele 1979, 56, 65), and its place amid the other delicacies of the midsummer feast clearly designates it as a luxury item. The origin of this product does not, however, necessarily link Ascra directly to long-distance trade routes, since any number of short journeys and intermediary exchanges could have brought this wine to Hesiod (Mele 1979, 66–67). It is also important to keep in mind that luxury goods, precisely because of their scarcity and consequent value, comprise an effective means of storage. They can be readily exchanged for food when a subsistence crisis strikes a household. In any case, neither item is essential for the survival of the household.

Hesiod's discussion of trade supplies no evidence for the personal and regularized trading relations common in primitive and traditional economies in which exchange is conducted according to established rates and there exists some obligation to enter into exchange at the discretion of either trading partner.[21] Nor does Hesiod bear witness to a degree of labor specialization that would indicate a high level of production for exchange rather than for consumption in the household. He mentions potter and carpenter—along with poet and beggar—as craftsmen (*W&D* 25–26) and notes a single operation in making a plow that requires a carpenter (*W&D* 427–31) among others that the farmer performs without a craftsman (*W&D* 423–36, 455–56, 502–3). There is, finally, no indication that trade is organized and guided at the village level by a head trader, a man of influence with valuable connections beyond the community. Hesiod does not

20. Cf. Theognis 179–80. See Bravo (1977, 8–9) and Mele (1979, 17) regarding this link between poverty and trade.
21. See Wolf 1966, 38–41 and Sahlins 1972, 185–230.

describe a domestic economy implicated within a restrictive trading network or one driven by extensive needs for products from outside the household.

Calculating Kerdos

Hesiod holds out *kerdos* as the motive for undertaking trade. Since he is not proposing to act as a specialized merchant, a middleman, but is trading his own produce, he cannot designate by *kerdos* the differential profit from buying cheap and selling dear. If, moreover, the farmer already has in hand the produce that he will trade, *kerdos* must represent something above and beyond the value of those goods were he rather simply to store them. In his only use of *kerdos* outside *Works and Days* Hesiod generalizes that "if you sow evil, you will reap evil profits *(kerdea)*" (fr. 286.1 [M-W]). In this agricultural metaphor the favorable ratio of seed sown to seed harvested is designated *kerdos*—the farmer takes away from his field at harvest more than he left there at sowing. The sense of ratio or proportion expressed through the concept of *kerdos* in fr. 286 is reinforced at *Works and Days* 644–45 where Hesiod claims that a larger cargo will bring greater *kerdos* on top of *kerdos* (cf. 631–32). This *kerdos* of trade, however, contrasts with a simpler conceptualization at *Works and Days* 320–24, where it refers to what can be stolen by force or by lying (cf. 349–52). At a minimum *kerdos* signifies for Hesiod an amount of something exceeding what one had before. In the context of theft it is clear enough what *kerdos* means, but what specifically can comprise "gain" in the context of trade such as Hesiod urges Perses to engage in, where goods of one type are exchanged for goods of another?

Hesiod describes in *Works and Days* a farmer exporting subsistence goods by boat in order to realize a *kerdos*. These are the constraints within which a reconstruction of Hesiod's trading system must be undertaken. He does not tell us whether goods are taken to some sort of regular regional market or simply around to neighboring villages and towns. We are not told what trade goods the farmer exchanges his produce for or what he does with his trade goods upon his return home. It must be kept in mind, moreover, that this trade is being conducted through barter, not through money, making the determination of *kerdos* all the more uncertain.[22] The best that we can hope for in filling out this picture is to reach what appear to be prob-

22. There was no money involved in such transactions at this time. *Pace* Mele (1979, 61–63), whose evidence is not specific to Hesiod, cattle and tripods won't do. See Tandy's (1997, 160–63) discussion.

able answers. As a starting point I think it can be assumed that this trade served to move subsistence goods from localities of relative abundance to localities of relative shortage.[23] Such a movement is the precondition of realizing *kerdos* through trade but also limits a farmer's opportunities for successful trade to years and products of relative abundance. Given the primary dependence of food supply upon weather, such trade will become more attractive as the area comprehended within the trading network becomes more extensive so as to include a broader range of climatic variations. This principle offers a likely explanation of why Hesiod does not speak about trading in Thespiae: Ascra and Thespiae would generally experience the same climatic variations because of their proximity. I suspect that any Thespians trading in subsistence goods were likewise trading by sea for the same reason, in order to reach more distant trading partners.

What I have already stated about the organization of trade and the farmer's direct role in it rules out true long-distance trade, which is generally considered unlikely for subsistence goods at this time. What I consider more likely, however, is a sailing trip to villages of at most a few days distance, following rumors or hunches based on past experience, in search of areas experiencing shortages corresponding to Ascran surpluses.[24] In such a setting our farmer could trade wheat, for example, for wine, or wine for barley, or, as seems more likely to me, he might exchange his subsistence goods for non-subsistence, non-perishable, luxury items—metals and metal objects, for example—or even for perishable luxury goods such as olive oil (*W&D* 522) or Bibline wine (*W&D* 589). But how can Hesiod's *kerdos* be accounted for as the result of all this swapping?

Since we can take for granted that Hesiod does not exchange one product for the same product, wheat for wheat, for example, but for something else, it becomes very difficult to gauge his *kerdos* from what he has traded unless we fill in additional stages of the process. He begins with product A, produced on his farm, which he exchanges for product B. If our farmer has realized any *kerdos*, however, this will not be evident until he returns home and is able, whether he actually does so or not, to exchange product B for

---

23. Contra, see the fascinating article of Foxhall (1998).

24. On trade in grain see above, p. 49, n. 16. Osborne (1996b, 42–43) considers this sort of "tramping" to be characteristic of agricultural goods and to operate outside the networks of long-distance trade. Cf. Donlan (1997, 652) on "calling on" trade. Mele (1979, 53–57) jumps to conclusions, I believe, in construing Hesiod's limitation of the sailing season as a whole to fifty days to imply that trade expeditions normally last that entire season.

more of product A than he initially took to market. That is, *kerdos* must be measured on the basis of the rough equivalencies among different goods within the farmer's own locality. There is, after all, no money involved and no universal medium of exchange to serve as a basis for establishing relative values. Such a sequence of exchanges requires that product A be more expensive measured against product B at the point of exchange than it is when measured against product B in the farmer's own locality. To take an example, a good harvest in Ascra lowers the value of grain there measured against iron. This Ascran grain, however, (product A) could be traded outside Ascra's immediate region for iron (product B) at a favorable rate with individuals from a locale where a relative shortage of grain raises its value in comparison to other goods. The Ascran farmer, now back in Ascra, could then reconvert his "cheap" iron into more grain than he initially traded to acquire the iron. This gain in value represents the farmer's *kerdos* whether he exchanges the iron (or olive oil, or what have you) for subsistence goods for immediate use or hangs on to it against future need. Of course, the scarcer a product is locally, and so relatively more expensive, or the more abundant it is regionally, and so less valuable in comparison to other goods, the less likely it is that a farmer will have realized *kerdos* at the end of a sequence of exchanges. What I propose here is speculative, but it can account for the sparse details of Hesiod's account: trade, subsistence goods, and *kerdos*.

In his references to trade, Hesiod emphasizes its risks and presents it as a gamble undertaken in response to poverty. The poor farmer, such as Hesiod's father back in Cyme or Perses now, might trade whatever he had for products perennially scarce in his home village—perhaps olive oil in Ascra, for example—willing to bear the risks of trade in hopes of coming out enough ahead to make do for the year to come. It may be, then, that trade was only a sweepstakes strategy adopted by villagers as a last resort and not an activity in which a farmer otherwise got involved if he could avoid it. It is also possible, however, that even though Hesiod recommends it especially to Perses as one way out of his troubles, trade was an activity in which any Ascran might participate when conditions were favorable. If we can assume farmers to be putting into trade what they consider surplus, especially if it exceeds storage capacity, then this will generally be produce that is plentiful locally, and so cheap in terms of its local exchange value.

The early sailing season (*W&D* 678–88), which Hesiod considers too dangerous to risk, may shed some further light on this question of *kerdos*. This period occurs just before and almost simultaneously with the cereal harvest in early May (see West 1978, p. 253). If the value of farm produce measured against other goods fluctuated with supply, then this point in the year, when supplies from the previous harvest were running low and when it might also be evident that a cereal crop was going to fail, would offer the greatest *kerdos* to a farmer either with stored grain to sell or produce from an early harvest. If there were no special advantage to be had from trading at this season, such as premium *kerdos,* why would anyone risk its hazards, as if, Hesiod claims, possessions were as valuable as life (*W&D* 686)?

Tandy has argued for fixed rates of exchange between different goods within his model of the limited market. This model, however, is based upon trade in luxury goods, primarily metals. The trade in subsistence goods presents some relevant differences from trade in this other type of products. In the first place, since the specific areas experiencing surplus or shortage would have varied from year to year, the direction in which subsistence goods flowed would not have followed fixed patterns as would have been the case with metals and most luxury goods. This variability may have acted against regularized trading relations and fixed rates of exchange. Indeed, which farmers participated in trading subsistence goods may have varied from one year to the next, again discouraging regularized relations. Additionally, trade in subsistence goods may not have taken place in organized markets at all but informally, virtually on the beach near seaside settlements. The chief difference, however, between subsistence goods and luxury goods is the broad annual fluctuations in the local supply of farm products. This variability in their annual, not to mention seasonal, supply produces a consequent variability in their relative value that would seem to work against the possibility of regularly achieving *kerdos* in a market organized around fixed equivalencies between products. If we do assume a fixed rate of exchange, a farmer would be able to achieve *kerdos* only in those years or times of year when the fixed equivalency of the regional market was more favorable than the going rate in the farmer's own locality. Such circumstances would naturally result in at best only sporadic participation in the regional market since farmers would stay away when they could not realize a gain in terms of local rates of exchange.[25]

Hesiod's insistence upon *kerdos* draws us into the area of what Sahlins has termed "negative reciprocity." That is, the farmer's goal of acquiring as

---

25. Tandy (1997) discusses fixed rates of exchange in markets at 119–22 and 212–13. Sahlins (1972, 280–301) examines the uncertainties of profit and loss under a system of fixed exchange and the sense of social obligation required to hold such systems together. Osborne (1996b, 39, 42–43) clearly distinguishes between long-distance trade in luxury commodities and trade in subsistence goods.

much as possible through his exchange, of leaving his exchange partner with less than he himself gets, is primary in the relationship. Economic motives and goals are not mediated by a larger social relationship strong enough to subordinate them to other priorities. To the degree, then, that *kerdos* dominates exchange, the relationship between traders is "disembedded" from other social relationships. Exchanges conducted according to negative reciprocity differ starkly from those made under balanced or generalized reciprocity (see pp. 82–83, 92–102) in which the degree of social connection between traders precludes *kerdos* as a motive and even imposes upon the more prosperous party the obligation to take a loss. The preeminent role assigned to *kerdos* by Hesiod in such exchanges, however, does not necessarily imply that economic relations overall are no longer embedded in social relations or that the embedded economy is in any way threatened. What is acceptable in dealing with strangers at the periphery of a community's contacts with the outside world is not necessarily permitted in dealing with fellow villagers or family members.[26] The boundaries gauging propriety in exchanges expand outward from the family only with the extension of the political economy.

Ascra and Long-Distance Trade

I offer here a rather simple model of trade: a farmer transports some of his produce to the sea, embarks with it upon his small boat, and follows his hunches about where he will find an advantageous exchange for it. He might be motivated to take the risks inherent in trade either out of a desire to enhance an inadequate livelihood or as a means of converting surplus produce into a storable form. Needless to say, Hesiod supplies only the sketchiest of evidence in *Works and Days,* so it has seemed best to me to proceed cautiously in trying to reconstruct how his trading system might have operated. My account remains within the parameters of Hesiod's picture of a farmer bartering his produce by sea in order to realize *kerdos* and corresponds with the values of autarky and the *oikos* so prominent in the poem. If I have characterized Ascra's trade in a primitivist mode, that should not be taken as a general interpretation of the economy of either the Archaic period or antiquity as a whole but as a reflection of the specific circumstances attested to by *Works and Days,* in particular that trade is organized at the level of the individual subsistence economy.[27] It is, of course,

26. See Sahlins 1972, 193–204; cf. Mele 1979, 12–14.
27. For recent reflections on the continued viability of the primitivist model, see Parkins (1998) and Davies (1998).

possible to imagine a more complex system. For example, it could easily be the case that Hesiod's farmer sought out specific settlements where he knew his produce could reliably be exchanged for trade goods in steady demand in Ascra, a certain type of pottery or metal good, for example. This would move Hesiod in the direction of the "targeted" trading networks described by Osborne (1996b), with their interdependent markets. Yet, as Osborne points out, the variability of harvests from one year to the next leaves agricultural products on the margin of such interdependent networks, which grow up around and rely upon trade in manufactured goods.

Even if it is the case that Hesiod describes a mode of trade functioning outside the long-distance networks that we know to have experienced rapid development towards the end of the Dark Age, still farmers like Hesiod could nonetheless have attempted to benefit opportunistically from the operation of long-distance trade where possible. To speculate along these lines, interaction between the sort of domestically guided trade in subsistence goods described by Hesiod and long-distance trade in luxury commodities might have occurred in regional centers established by long-distance traders. That is, a farmer wishing to trade some of his crop might have transported it to the nearest regional center for trade in luxury goods in the knowledge that at certain times of the year he would be able to meet there householders or traders from areas where subsistence goods were in demand. In this way trade which was too irregular and too multidirectional to support an infrastructure of its own could operate more efficiently by taking advantage of exchange centers established for other forms of trade. For Hesiod, this might have meant a voyage to Attica, the Megarid, or Corinth.

The gap separating the sort of domestically oriented trade described by Hesiod from contemporary long-distance networks is opened by Hesiod's boat. The best understanding of *Works and Days* 622–32 and 684–88 (see p. 50) leads to the conclusion that Hesiod envisions the farmer putting to sea in his own boat. If, however, one abides by the assumption that in *Works and Days* Hesiod consistently describes local circumstances in the village of Ascra, then one has to wonder about the boat. At *Works and Days* 807–9 Hesiod does recommend the best day for gathering wood to build a boat and at 817–18 the best day for launching it. Yet boat ownership for an inhabitant of an inland mountain village seems prima facie improbable—do we imagine that the Ascran farmer just left his boat idle on the shore in Creusis for most of the year? Or did he haul it back and forth between Ascra and the sea? It is Perses who is advised to go to sea, yet how likely is it that even a man facing ruin would still own a boat? Hesiod's admission that he has never traveled more than a few hundred yards by sea (*W&D* 648–53) may not surprise in the case of someone farming the slopes of Helicon, but they add to the puzzle of Hesiod's boat.

Hesiod's advice (*W&D* 643) to praise a small boat *(nē' oligēn)* but place one's cargo in a large one *(megalēi)*, suggests that the farmer has a choice between shipping on a large or a small vessel. This line need not pose a choice between a fisherman's dinghy and a twenty- or fifty-oared ship. Given the indications provided elsewhere about the small scale of trade and about boat ownership by the individual farmer, it is most natural to understand the line as referring to a contrast between two boats, not between a boat and a ship.[28] I suspect that the preference expressed for the large boat stems from the theme in *Works and Days* of the risks of seafaring: larger boats are more seaworthy. The following couplet (*W&D* 644–45), assuring Perses that a larger cargo will bring a larger *kerdos*, does not hinder this interpretation unless we imagine a very large exportable surplus indeed— what Hesiod can commit to maritime trade is, of course, limited to what he can transport overland to the coast.

Yet, by offering the farmer a choice between vessels, this line can reasonably be seen as contradicting the testimony of *Works and Days* 622–32 and 684–88 and suggesting an alternative model of trade. If we do imagine that Hesiod is thinking at *Works and Days* 643 of a ship, a merchant vessel, then it is possible that he refers, as Bravo (1977, 8–9, 33–34) maintains, to taking passage along with other traders on a large ship owned by an aristocrat. On this assumption, our farmer would embark at the most convenient port of call, for Hesiod probably Creusis, and travel in the company of other traders to the settlements on the shipowner's itinerary.[29] Since it is likely that most of the passengers would be trading luxury items, such an arrangement would again draw trade in subsistence goods as practiced by Hesiod within the orbit of long-distance networks devoted to luxury trade. While this reconstruction deprives Hesiod of control of his own vessel, it leaves up to him whether to trade or not, when to trade, what to trade, and how much to trade. This model seems plausible enough, it is compatible with other accounts of trade for the period, and it even disposes

28. See Bravo 1977, 25. Mele's (1979, 46) inference, apparently from the reference at *W&D* 627–28 to "gear" *(hopla)* and oars *(nēos ptera)*, that Hesiod's boat requires a crew strikes me as unconvincing. Not every rowboat is a galley.

29. Mele (1979, 40–46) and Bravo (1977, 25–42) argue that Greeks relied upon the use of larger vessels for trade at this time, but see Snodgrass's (1983) criticisms of this view.

of some improbabilities within Hesiod's own testimony, but it doesn't really square with what Hesiod says elsewhere in the poem about seafaring.

Such an arrangement would not alter the character of the farmer's economic relation to the respective regional and local conditions. That is, the decision to trade would still depend upon the immediate needs of the farmer's household, and the destination of subsistence goods committed to trade would have varied from year to year with local supplies. As Osborne states of the relationship between trade in subsistence goods and long-distance networks, "the established network effected the movement of agricultural goods at times of local crisis, but the network itself must have been created to move goods whose supply and demand were very much more consistent" (Osborne 1996b, 43).

In Sum

Hesiod expresses an ambivalent attitude towards trade. The possibility of *kerdos* is offset by the risks presented by sea-voyaging to life and goods. Under the circumstances why would a farmer commit his valuable subsistence goods to trade? In the first place, Hesiod suggests, he would do so out of desperation. Through the examples of his father and of Perses' precarious circumstances Hesiod characterizes the quest for *kerdos* through trade as an exigency of poverty. The emergence of trade in metals and luxury goods may reflect increasing wealth across the Greek world, and the appearance of trade in subsistence goods may rely opportunistically upon that prosperity-based market, but the actual trade in subsistence goods, both committing goods to trade and buying such goods, does not reflect prosperity so much as its opposite. It represents a risk for the trader as well as an expense for the buyer undertaken by both in response to scarcity.

Hesiod illustrates this continuity between trading and farming and the subordination of both to the self-sufficiency of the *oikos* by offering the same reason to turn to seafaring, avoidance of debt and hunger (646–48), as he offers for getting to work on the farm (*W&D* 403–4 ff.; cf. 299, 302, 363). While Hesiod's advice about trade is addressed to Perses, within this frame of reference we can imagine that successful farmers, too, might have chosen to commit to trade that produce exceeding anticipated need or exceeding storage capacity or technology—note Hesiod's advice not to commit all of one's *bios* to trade but to keep most of it at home (*W&D* 689–94). Items acquired by trade might be consumed immediately by the household, as we might expect in Perses' case, or they might be reserved to be exchanged in turn at a later time for food. In the latter instance, trade could serve as simply another means of storage by converting surplus produce into a non-perishable form able to be reconverted into food later when the need arises.[30] In either case trade is subordinated to a farming economy of self-sufficiency that it is intended to support. So, Hesiod describes cultivation of crops for storage and consumption, not for export. Hesiod's account implies, furthermore, that his father abandoned trade when he was able to acquire a self-supporting farm in Ascra.

Viewed in this way, as a secondary strategy employed by an autonomous farmer to insure the security of his household, trade hardly signals the sort of unequal relations that arise between peasants and an elite. The very failure of any expression of hostility for Thespiae over the issue of trade, even though the *basilées* of Thespiae provoke such tremendous animosity in connection with Perses' threatened litigation, suggests that the farmers of Ascra are free of the influence of Thespiae in disposing of their crops. Indeed, one can assume that an urban elite with any real authority over Ascra would itself soak up the sort of stored surplus that Hesiod prizes so highly while at the same time making such household reserves less necessary by providing a mechanism for social storage. Trade for Hesiod's Ascra was probably a side activity at best, entered into sporadically and opportunistically.

SOCIAL STORAGE AND HIERARCHY

By social storage I refer to mechanisms of risk management organized at the level of the political economy. Through social storage a household is able to convert a present surplus of food into a claim against future food supplies of the community. Loans, banquets, favors, services, gifts can all serve as means of social storage. Since control of food offers a source of power, once social storage evolves beyond the circulation of food among rough equals within a network of reciprocity and into a system of redistri-

---

30. See the discussion of this use of trade by Halstead and O'Shea 1982, 93–94, as well as those by Halstead and Jones 1989, 54 and by Johnson and Earle 1987, 196–99. Interestingly, Forbes and Foxhall (1995, 75–76) note that in contemporary Methana farmers periodically commit stored food to trade before its quality declines to the point that it is unusable. Other forms of such "indirect storage" are discussed at pp. 86–89 and 92–102. Gallant 1991, 98–101, argues that the ancient cultivator overwhelmingly preferred to devote surplus to livestock, creation of social obligations through sharing, or simply to storage before turning to trade; see also 121–29 regarding livestock as a form of storage.

bution orchestrated by a Big Man, or a chief, it becomes implicated within hierarchy.[31] Social storage is not only implicated within the internal organization of a community but for peasant communities it functions as a link between the village and the world outside. Thorner (1987, 65–66) notes as a general characteristic of peasant societies that agricultural surplus moves from the hands of the cultivators into those of the elite only to be returned to the peasants, at a cost, during annual periods of shortage. Within such an economy this movement of food is not only the effect of hierarchy but the mechanism of maintaining it since contributions by the elite of the necessities of life during times of dearth give rise both to concrete debt as well as to less tangible social obligations. "Surplus" is, moreover, a somewhat slippery concept. From the perspective of an elite it comprises as much of a peasant household's production as it can get its hands on. From the perspective of the farmer it is as much of his crop as he is willing to dedicate to purposes other than the subsistence of his household. Within an ideology of reciprocity, the peasant views the surplus that must be rendered to the elite to some extent as a form of subsistence insurance.[32] This, of course, is not to diminish the fundamental inequality of the relationship or the reluctance of farmers to hand over a portion of their crop.

As noted, Hesiod nowhere mentions any of the mechanisms by which elites customarily extract surplus from peasants—rents, dues, fines, debts, corvée, and so forth. In view of the outrage he expresses towards Perses' gifts to the kings (*W&D* 37–41), it is hard to imagine that he would not at least mention such obligations. Rather, Hesiod protests bitterly against both Perses and the kings that gifts have changed hands at all. He does not complain in *Works and Days* about generalized assessments that he, too, must render; he does not object that the kings demand too much, beyond their customary rights; and he does not speak of the gifts as obligatory. Rather Hesiod protests only Perses' gifts, complaining that he gives them at all, with the clear implication that they are made voluntarily. After all, why should Hesiod complain about "gifts" that are mandatory and that he himself has made, and why would a peasant complain about the reciprocity that guarantees his right to subsistence during times of shortage? As

31. The relationship between social storage and the rise of hierarchy is explored by Halstead 1989, 68–80 and by Halstead and O'Shea (1982). See also Johnson and Earle 1987, 16–21, 162–71, 197–99, 209, 244–45, 265–66; Sahlins 1972, 185–219, esp. 210–19, who refers to "pooling"; Schusky 1989, 79–97; and van Wees 1998, 25–47.
32. See Scott 1976, 167–92, esp. 182; Gallant 1991, 179–96.

Scott (1976, 180–92) points out, peasants seldom rebel against customary levels of rent (in whatever form that takes) except in times of extreme hardship. These gifts, the only indication in *Works and Days* of exchange between Ascra and the elite of Thespiae, cannot represent the mechanism by which the entire village is held in subordination or serve as the basis for a system of social storage organized within relations between peasants and lords. Yet we cannot rule out that Perses has through his gifts begun to build a personal relationship of clientage with the kings, from whom he might hope to receive the help that Hesiod denies him.

THE KINGS (BASILĒES)

The status and role of the kings remain crucial to the question of relations between Ascra and Thespiae since they embody in their persons a political economy, structuring and uniting a group of households. They serve as the agents of the processes of integration, centralization, and stratification. Hesiod's fable of the hawk's ruthlessness towards the nightingale (*W&D* 202–12) or the scene of the goddess Justice victimized and outraged by the injustices of the kings (*W&D* 219–21) suggest that these rulers are unchecked in their power and able to do as they please. Hesiod appears to fear and detest the *basilēes* in equal measure. These figures serve as the linchpin of the arguments both of Édouard Will and of Tandy since they administer the power of the polis over Ascra and exploit debt to take possession of peasant land. Tandy sees the *basilēes* as the officials of a stratified society, able to control public space, the market, and the movement of goods. For Édouard Will these are aristocrats who exploit their greater wealth to bring the peasants under their control. For both Tandy and Édouard Will these figures chiefly fill the role of creditor. Does the evidence supplied in *Works and Days* support this view of the kings? Is Ascra incorporated within a larger political economy through the power of these figures?

Since at present I am examining Ascra's relations with the outside world, I will focus here upon the question of whether *basilēes* from Thespiae exercise authority in Ascra. In the next chapter I will discuss the question of the *basileus* within Ascra's local hierarchy. I wish to begin by surveying what Hesiod has to say about the *basilēes*, with particular attention to where he places them geographically and to the specific set of activities he assigns to them.

1. At *Theogony* 80–93 Hesiod offers an encomiastic picture of the *basileus* settling disputes in the *agorē* before the assembled people.

The passage's exclusive focus upon the king's role as judge is likely the effect of the overarching theme of the power of the Muses, though the king is again associated with justice at *Theogony* 434. This function, however, is hardly paralleled in Homer, who assigns his kings primarily a military role along with a redistributive economic function at least among the elite. In any case this passage makes it clear, as do others in *Works and Days*, that Hesiod is familiar with a more positive vision of the king.

2. At *Works and Days* 28–30 Hesiod again identifies the *agorē* with the quarrelsome litigation that occurs there and opposes it to the *ergon*, the site of productive labor. The appearance of the gift-eating kings (*basilēas* / *dōrophagous:* 38–39) and their justice at the culmination of this passage makes it clear that they officiate over the quarrels in the *agorē* (cf. *Th.* 434–30).[33] Hesiod contrasts their judgments, moreover, with the "straight judgments" (*itheiēisi dikēis:* 36) that can be had "here" (*authi:* 35), suggesting that the site of the kings' *agorē* lies outside the village (see number 5 below).

3. The fable of the hawk and the nightingale (*W&D* 202–12), addressed to the kings, has been subject to contradictory explanations. In spite of problems it raises for the treatment of justice and violence elsewhere in *Works and Days*, I think that the most direct interpretation equates the hawk with the kings and the nightingale with Hesiod.[34] The hawk's ruthless assertion that the strong can dispose of the weak as they choose provides the poem's strongest expression of the power wielded by the kings. The judicial setting in which we are to situate this allegorical struggle is made explicit in the following address to Perses (*W&D* 213–24), in which the *andres . . .* / *dōrophagoi* (*W&D* 220–21), clearly the *basilēes* (cf. *W&D* 38–39, 263–64), are condemned for their crimes against Oath (*Horkos:* 219) and Justice (*Dikē:* 220) through their crooked judgments.

4. Both the men offering straight judgments (*W&D* 225–26) for the city of justice and those who love *hubris* and *schetlia erga* (*W&D*

---

33. West ad *W&D* 38 makes the plausible suggestion that Hesiod's *basilēas* may refer to the seven *dēmouchoi* said to rule in Thespiae. See also Drews' (1983, 10–97) regarding the *basileus* as member of an aristocratic elite rather than a monarch.

34. See, however, Nelson's (1998, 77–81) recent argument that the hawk represents Zeus and the nightingale the kings, along with bibliography.

238) are certainly *basilēes*. So much is suggested by the use of the same topos at 240–41 and 260–61 (cf. the parallels cited by West ad 240). Likewise, the single man whose wickedness results in the destruction of the entire city (*xumpasa polis: W&D* 240–41) is, I think, correctly identified as a *basileus* by both West and Verdenius. That the specific reference of *hubris* and *schetlia erga* at 238 is ju-ridical is evident from the contrasting terms "straight judgments" (*dikas . . . / itheias:* 225–26) and "justice" (*dikaiou:* 226) in the cor-responding lines from the description of the city of justice. The oc-currence of *polis* at line 240 and of *teichos* ("wall") at 246 show that Hesiod is here again imagining the city as the seat of the judgments of the *basilēes* even if in the expanded sense of a walled settlement as well as its surrounding territory (cf. 233–35).

5. The harangue apostrophizing the kings at 248–64, finally, reiter-ates this exclusively judicial role assigned to the *basilēes* in both *Theogony* and *Works and Days*. As this passage reaches its cre-scendo, Hesiod declares that "it does not escape Zeus's notice what sort of justice *(dikēn)* the polis encloses within it (οὐδέ ἑ λήθει / οἵην δὴ καὶ τήνδε δίκην πόλις ἐντὸς ἐέργει: *W&D* 268–69). This explicit identification of the polis, the city, as the locale for the *agorē* and the kings as they dispense their justice is corroborated by the vengeance Justice launches precisely against the polis for the crooked judgments of the kings (*W&D* 220–24). Similarly it is the polis that flourishes when straight judgments are rendered (*W&D* 225–27 ff.).

This survey of references to the kings in *Works and Days* evidences a consistent association of these figures with the *agorē* and the polis. In fact, in the opening harangue (*W&D* 27–41) Hesiod constructs, as I have sug-gested, a powerful opposition between the village of Ascra and the *agorē* located in the city. According to what I consider the simplest and most per-suasive interpretation of this evidence Hesiod is drawing a boundary line between the village of Ascra and the city, where the kings give judgments in the town square. Beyond this, we see that Hesiod identifies the kings ex-clusively with a judicial role: they judge cases. His sole complaint against the kings, accordingly, is for self-interested, unjust decisions. *Works and Days* provides no basis whatsoever for the claim that the kings of the *agorē* wield economic, political, or military authority in Ascra. Certainly Homer's *basilēes* fill such roles in their cities, and I see no reason to doubt that He-siod assumes as much for the *basileus* of *Theogony* 80–93 or even for the kings of *Works and Days* in their own city, Thespiae. The ruthless exercise of power ascribed to the kings in Hesiod's fable of the hawk and the nightingale does not imply that a *basileus* wields power over Ascra any more than does his portrait of the good king in the city of justice. Through the fable Hesiod links the kings to the Age of Iron, just preceding, and to the city of *hubris*, soon to follow. The hawk's speech is intended to exemplify the merciless arrogance of the kings and to illustrate what the people in the polis must put up with. This is what he and Perses have to look forward to themselves if Perses insists on taking their dispute to the kings. If the centralized and stratified institutions of a polis seem like sheer tyranny to a farmer accustomed to the more egalitarian institutions of the village, that should not be surprising.

Does judging necessarily imply a political economy? If Ascrans resort to the kings of Thespiae for judgments, should we conclude that this occurs in the context of regularized authority wielded by these men over Hesiod's village in spite of the evidence leading us to question such a role for the kings? In his opening harangue Hesiod pleads with Perses not to take their dispute to the "gift-eating kings" in the city but rather to solve it on their own here and now (*W&D* 35–39). Apparently at this stage of the dispute the kings do not yet have any say in how Hesiod and Perses settle their affairs nor is there any necessity to bring them into the dispute. Hesiod presupposes here a voluntary legal system, and specifically one that is not organized by formal statute law and does not grant an automatic jurisdiction to a magistrate. The "judge" frequently functions in a voluntary system more as an arbitrator, seeking a solution acceptable to both parties and that the community will endorse as equitable. It can be noted in this connection that the idealized king of *Theogony* 80–92 is not pictured imposing decisive judgments in defense of law, but rather calming disputes and satisfying litigants through his gentle words. The kings of Thespiae have jurisdiction over conflicts in Ascra only if those disputes have been brought to them voluntarily by one of the parties to the dispute.[35] Hesiod's complaint is precisely that Perses will hand over to the kings in the polis an authority over his and Perses' dispute that they do not otherwise possess. Perses' threat to take their dispute to the kings, then, does not provide evidence for the authority of Thespian *basilēes* over Ascra or for a political economy integrating the two settlements, and, in fact, the evidence already considered makes it appear more likely that Perses would approach the kings as an out-

35. Regarding the limited jurisdiction of the "kings" see Millett 1984, 91–92; Gagarin 1973, 82–83, 90–92, 1986, 19–26, 34–35, and 1992, 61–78.

sider. This is precisely the situation envisioned at *Works and Days* 225–27, where Hesiod praises those who "grant straight judgments for both strangers *(xeinoisi)* and locals *(endēmoisi)* and do not stray from the just." The inclusion in the description of strangers along with local residents accommodates exactly the situation that Hesiod anticipates of an outsider seeking a fair judgment in the city, except that Hesiod entertains little hope of an equitable decision.

There is no evidence to be found in *Works and Days* that the kings function as creditors for village farmers let alone that they hold any general leadership role in Ascra. The lack of any real evidence from *Works and Days* that Thespiae's *basilēes* exercise power in some form over Ascra has, in fact, resulted in contradictory arguments for those assuming that to be the case. Austin and Vidal-Naquet (1977, 49) observe that *Works and Days* attests that the unification of countryside and polis had yet to occur in Boeotia, but maintain at the same time that Hesiod's anger with the kings entails Ascra's dependence and that some form of authority has already been established by Thespiae over the village (51). Spahn (1980, 544–45) allows that the polis is altogether absent from the world depicted in *Works and Days* except for the litigation between Hesiod and Perses (ignoring the importance of *W&D* 35–36), but he goes on to conclude that the peasants remained powerless and without recourse in the face of the *hubris* of the kings rather than that the polis in fact had little influence over Hesiod's community. Jajlenko (1988, 95–97, 111) for his part is troubled that the concept of the citizen, *politēs*, does not appear in *Works and Days*, where the individual and household are the dominant social realities, but argues as a consequence that Hesiod's Thespiae must be therefore a "proto-polis" rather than considering that perhaps Hesiod describes an autonomous village neighborhood rather than a city ruled by an aristocracy. Garnsey and Morris (1989, 100–101) acknowledge that Hesiod gives no evidence for the asymmetrical coalition, nobleman—wealthy peasant—serf, without which no peasant society can survive. They attribute this lacuna to Hesiod's idealizing vision of society as if a member of a local elite would idealize his prominence in the community by dissimulating it rather than by presenting it as noble self-sacrifice or part of the natural order. In Tandy's case, too, banishing the kings from the village would resolves a couple of difficulties: there would no longer be any compelling reason to hold that *Works and Days*, alone of early epic texts, was composed and circulated in writing rather than orally (Tandy 1997, 194–203), nor would it be necessary to explain why the *basilēes* of Thespiae permit Hesiod to trade elsewhere in spite of their power and their dependence upon peasant trade in their own market (229–34).

I don't want to go overboard, however, in minimizing contacts and interconnections between Ascra and Thespiae. The very fact that a judgment from the *basilēes* of Thespiae is an option for Perses requires that there exist some sort of established relationship between the two communities. And Hesiod's reluctance to make the trip to Thespiae can leave no doubt that the kings held some sort of authority in such matters. For me the crucial question is whether the compass of kingly authority extended broadly enough to integrate the two communities within a single political economy. I explore the relationship between Ascra and Thespiae in detail below. For the moment it is enough to recognize that as a larger, wealthier, and more highly organized settlement, Thespiae was no doubt regarded with a certain respect and admiration by Ascrans. They likely turned to Thespiae in times of subsistence crisis or natural disaster even if Thespiae's power provoked suspicion and resentment at other times. It is plausible enough that Ascrans might have turned to the leaders of a neighbor such as Thespiae to seek resolutions to disputes that seemed intractable once local mechanisms for resolving conflicts had been exhausted. Even if such a last resort is sanctioned by tradition, this is not a matter of Thespian jurisdiction in Ascra but of individual Ascrans seeking out a prestigious outsider in a last bid for a peaceful settlement.

Hesiod's opposition to a judgment from the kings indicates that their rulings are enforceable. Since the kings come from outside the village and appear to possess no economic, political, or military authority, enforcement backed up by coercion, a unilateral use of force, can be ruled out. Within a voluntary legal system it is often public opinion that serves as the final guarantor that a judgment is carried out. So, the authority to render a judgment does not entail the power to enforce it. That belongs to the community. I suggest in this line that the leverage enabling only one party to bring a dispute before a *basileus*, compelling the other to participate as well, is community pressure. Unwillingness to present one's case to the judge would be interpreted as a lack of confidence in its merit.[36] If we envision the *agorē*

---

36. See Gagarin 1986, 19–43, esp. 22 and 35. Gagarin's view that Perses cannot compel Hesiod to submit the case to the kings and that the kings would not formulate a ruling entirely unacceptable to Hesiod is acceptable to me, but I think my interpretation of these lines coheres better with the evidence. A significant role for public opinion in judicial and political procedures is evidenced at *Il.* 2.270–77, 18.499–503; *Od.* 2.70–74, 80–81, 161–68, 229–44.

of Thespiae as a last resort for settling quarrels, then sanctions within the village against open strife might exert considerable pressure upon parties to a conflict to agree to submit a dispute for a decision there, and then to abide by the judgment. Referring intractable quarrels to outsiders, moreover, relieves neighbors of the risk of incurring hostility or even retaliation for a judgment against a fellow neighbor, while an outsider to the community is more able to maintain a stance of impartiality. While this is admittedly speculative, I think it explains the authority Hesiod attributes to the kings within the limits of the evidence in *Works and Days,* which does not otherwise support a strong role for the kings of Thespiae within Ascra.

In order to understand the setting of *Works and Days,* it is essential to recognize that all of Hesiod's rancor against kings and city is provoked by Perses' threat to take his complaint to the *agorē* in Thespiae. The fact that Hesiod's discussion of trade provokes no such outbursts, his glowing description of the good king and the city of justice (*W&D* 255–37), and his recollection of the great victory he received from the sons of Amphidamas in Chalcis (*W&D* 654–59) all serve to highlight the restricted nature of Hesiod's hostility towards city and kings. Hesiod does not despise the kings of the city per se but only as recipients of Perses' gifts and as interlopers into the affairs of the village and into Hesiod's own affairs. It is this that provokes his apocalyptic visions of justice for sale.

I discern a specific social and political dynamic underlying the situation that Hesiod describes in *Works and Days.* The larger-scale context I assume is that of two neighboring communities of different sizes and organized at different levels of complexity. Thespiae, as a larger, more hierarchized community, is perhaps interested in expanding its resource base by incorporating settlements such as Ascra within its territory, or perhaps, as I shall discuss later, is interested in Ascra for strategic reasons. Ascra, we can imagine, is interested in benefiting opportunistically from contacts with a wealthier, more powerful neighbor but at the same time wishes to preserve its autonomy and especially its freedom from the costs of full participation in the political economy of Thespiae. This is the delicate geopolitical equilibrium within which I surmise that the individual conflict of Hesiod and Perses is played out.[37]

The particular configuration of opposing interests in Hesiod's Ascra offers openings for distinct personal strategies to each party concerned

---

37. See the fuller discussion of these issues at pp. 166–73.

within the drama of *Works and Days*—Perses, the kings, and Hesiod. There is Hesiod, a member of the local elite and anxious to preserve his position, locked in conflict with a weaker member of the community, who, in order to strengthen his own hand, threatens to appeal to an external elite that may be interested in injecting its influence into new areas. Perses appears to be reduced to depending on others, particularly Hesiod, for some share of his livelihood. The village offers very limited recourse to a Perses in any case, and Hesiod holds all the trump cards in their relationship. The option of taking an intractable dispute before the kings of Thespiae, however, provides Perses with a source of leverage over Hesiod that has been prepared in advance through his gift-giving. Perses' actual objective, however, may be less to get a judgment against Hesiod from the kings than to maneuver Hesiod into acknowledging Perses' continuing claim on his generosity. The kings for their part must see in their role as judges an opportunity to cultivate a network of patronage within a community to which they are strictly external. Indeed, as I have suggested, status as outsiders could have been an important qualification for their role as mediators since they approach disputes without vested interests in the affairs of the community. Yet the same role places them in the position of potential beneficiaries from the gifts of those cultivating their favor in advance and of actual patrons to those whose interests have been defended by their judgments. Any fissures existing within a community can be exploited by the kings in their role as arbitrators so as to enhance their own authority. The less successful members of a community like Ascra would offer a natural constituency for such an attempt to build a base of influence. Gagarin (1986, 121–41), in fact, argues that the development of law and legal procedure after Hesiod's time, in the Archaic period, served in the first place to enhance the power of the polis as an institution. This observation is in keeping with the use to which the kings appear to be putting their judicial role. Note in this connection Herodotus's account of the rise of Deioces, the first king of the Medes, through his reputation as a judge (Hdt. 1.96–98). For Hesiod, however, the kings' willingness to settle a land dispute between himself and his brother is nothing other than the thin end of the wedge, and he urges Perses to resolve the matter locally.

Hesiod's anxiety about the intrusion of outsiders into village and family matters, moreover, can only be heightened by the fact that his dispute with Perses concerns land, the very basis of subsistence. His only recourse is either a defense of village institutions and values and of the legitimacy of the existing settlement or else to accede to Perses' request for further support.

Hesiod's strategy, as I shall argue, is an attempt to mobilize against Perses the full force of the community's moral sanctions in order to constrain him within the limits of that community and that morality.

My analysis of actions and motives operates at the level of individuals pursuing their own self-interest. We do, after all, confront in *Works and Days* a situation formulated in terms of individuals. In fact, Hesiod's failure to tell us more about his community and its organization provides perhaps the chief hindrance to our understanding of the behavior of those individuals. My orientation, however, does not reflect an assumption that rationality and self-interest are free of historical contexts and so available as analytic tools with universal applicability. Rather I take for granted that while rationality itself may be a universal human attribute, what may appear a rational act in one historical context may not appear so in another. For example, as I shall discuss later, the fact that sharing between neighbors in Ascra is conducted on the basis of balanced reciprocity tells us something about the larger social formation within which rationality and rational choices take specific, determinate forms. My focus on motives and goals at the level of the individual in part comprises a concession to the nature of the evidence and in part stems from the stage to which my argument has progressed.[38]

Within this setting of communities organized at differing levels of complexity and agents with conflicting interests, Hesiod, in my reconstruction, argues that the costs of entering the Thespian political economy outweigh the benefits it offers. The two brothers' respective positions within the Ascran political economy—just how undeveloped it is I will detail later—condition opposite views of the Thespian political economy. Perses would appear to be demanding a greater degree of integration and mutual obligation in the community, a stronger political economy, or, to put it concretely, a formal claim upon the resources of other households (Hesiod's in particular) in the community as subsistence insurance. Hesiod, at the point in the dispute represented by *Works and Days*, is trying to buy Perses off with an encomium of hard work and a diatribe on the dangers of the polis. If I am correct about the context within which this dispute is playing out, Perses' initiative in Thespiae has been provoked by a breakdown of relations between a prosperous member and a needy member of the village of Ascra. So, the dominant opposition organizing *Works and Days* would be

38. See Tandy 1997, 84–88 and Wilk 1996, 3–13 and passim.

that between the prosperous and the poor within the village of Ascra while the contrast between village and city would be secondary to this.

I assume, then, both familiarity and regular contact between Ascra and Thespiae. But I do not find that the evidence supplied by *Works and Days* supports the view that Ascra has been absorbed within the Thespian political economy, especially through the agency of the kings. As for Hesiod's vitriol towards the kings, it would admittedly be easier to explain if the power attributed to the kings by Will, Tandy, and others could be substantiated by the evidence. The specificity of Hesiod's complaints to judging and the limits upon the kings' judicial authority, however, are essential to a clear understanding of the context of those complaints. Hesiod, I believe, reacts in the first place to his brother's attempt to prejudice the kings' judgment, but primarily he resents the entry into village affairs of outsiders who threaten to disrupt the local hierarchy by undermining his own authority in the community. In my view Hesiod is not ill-disposed towards the city per se nor is he feuding with *basilēes* generally. His anger has been provoked by a specific dispute in which he fears his immediate interests will unfairly be put at risk.

ASCRA AND THESPIAE

The sites of both Ascra and Thespiae exhibit artifacts from the Geometric period, among the earliest found by the survey conducted by Bintliff and Snodgrass.[39] Significant activity appears only at one end of Ascra's site during this early period while Thespiae's shows several small clusters of habitations. The two settlements lie at about seven kilometers distance from each other. It would certainly be contrary to expectation if two communities in such proximity were not in contact from the earliest times, especially in view of Thespiae's status as the principal settlement of the district. I think that we can assume interaction not only during moments of crisis but on a regular basis because of their nearness alone.

The one piece of explicit evidence found in *Works and Days* for relations between inhabitants of the two settlements is of course Hesiod's complaint

---

39. On the relative sizes and dates of Ascra and Thespiae see Bintliff and Snodgrass 1985, 139–40; Bintliff 1989, 17; and Bintliff and Snodgrass 1989, 287. A settlement existed on the site of Ascra from a time when Thespiae's own size and development precludes its control of Ascra. Regarding the survival of autonomous villages even into the Classical period, see pp. 166–70.

Map 1. Southwest Boeotia, showing the site of Ascra on Helicon and some of the surrounding settlements.

about Perses' cooperation with the *basilēes*. Both Perses' gift-giving and the kings' offices as judges of Ascran disputes testify that established, reciprocal relationships were by Hesiod's time customary between Ascrans and Thespians and they suggest additionally that Thespiae took the dominant role in such associations. As I have argued, however, these relations remain personal and voluntary, operating at the level of the household, not that of the political economy.

Other forms of relationship we might expect to find in this context, though less well attested in *Works and Days,* are those of marriage and *xeniē*. Lines 344–45 of *Works and Days* assume that in-laws live close enough to be expected to answer a distress call quickly, though they are made strangely distinct from neighbors. In the midst of his discussion of marriage at lines 695–705 Hesiod recommends in particular marrying someone who lives close by (*hētis sethen egguthi naiei:* 700), making careful inquiry to insure that one's new wife not become a source of laughter (or worse—*charmata* [701]) for the neighbors. Hesiod's rationale for endogamy here shows little appreciation for marriage even as an alliance able to secure aid from outside the immediate locale in times of need let alone as a means of building the prestige and influence of the family. He seems more interested in a wife as a source of offspring (*W&D* 235, 244) and labor (*W&D* 779) than anything else. Yet the fact that he must advise marriage to a local girl would seem to suggest that marriage outside the community does occur.

While Hesiod's three references to *xeinoi* in *Works and Days* are all quite general, still a *xeinos*—a "guest-friend," someone with whom one shares reciprocal obligations of hospitality—is by definition a relationship with someone from outside the community. At line 183 the *xeinos* is included alongside the *hetairos* ("companion," "comrade") and the *kasignētos* ("brother," "kinsman") as someone who ought to be *philos* ("dear," "beloved"). At 327–34 the one who does a *xeinos* ill is condemned equally with the person who harms a suppliant, cuckolds a brother, injures orphan children, or berates his aged parents. Both passages acknowledge the solemnity of this formal bond between members of different communities. Though Hesiod does not illustrate the utility of the relationship, it imposes obligations comparable to, if not equivalent to, those owed a *hetairos* or a *kasignētos*.[40] For Hesiod's community it seems likely that *xeinoi* might especially be called upon to provide hospitality, food and shelter, in times of shortage or disaster. In this role *xeinia* serves as a mechanism of risk management. It might also comprise an exchange relationship, providing Ascran families with, for example, a source of olive oil. In any case, however, it remains a personal, voluntary relationship, operating at the level of the household.

40. Hesiod does not consider the bond with a *hetairos* equal to that with a *kasignētos* (*W&D* 707), and I think it is safe to assume that the obligation to a *xeinos* would rank below that to a *hetairos*. See pp. 92–94 regarding this hierarchy of intimacy. The occurrence of *xeinoi* at *Works and Days* 225 refers not to an outsider with whom a special relationship exists but simply to strangers generally. Nevertheless, in this opening verse of the description of the city of justice Hesiod praises those offering straight judgments to strangers and to locals alike.

Hesiod says almost nothing of warfare in *Works and Days*. Certainly he gives no indication of its form or frequency for Ascrans or of how they organized themselves to respond to it. It would at least seem probable, however, that Ascra might turn to Thespiae for aid when threatened by another settlement (provided that Thespiae was not itself author of the threat). If that were the case, the Thespian leadership might come to regard Ascra as within their polis's sphere of influence. At the same time, Ascra, poised as it is between the territories of Thespiae and Haliartos, might have tried to play its larger neighbors off one against the other. At the least, considering the likely higher level of conflict among the nascent poleis of the lowlands and the reluctance a smaller community might feel to be pulled into the conflicts of an ambitious neighbor, one can speculate that an Ascra might be discriminating about when to support Thespiae in its disputes (see pp. 169–73).

Works and Days again provides little in the way of information about cult practice or the institutional dimension of the worship of the gods. Hesiod does tell us, however, that he dedicated the tripod he won at the funeral games for Amphidamas to the Muses in the place where they taught him to sing (*W&D* 651–62). This would be on Mount Helicon, as Hesiod tells us at *Theogony* 23, where this tripod is reputed to have resided in the sanctuary to the Muses. The Mouseion of Helicon shows unbroken cult activity from late in the eighth century B.C. till into the fourth century A.D., occupying a site approximately six kilometers from Thespiae and two from Ascra (Schachter 1986, 147–79). While Hesiod claims a close personal connection with the Muses of Helicon and his is the first known votive offering to them, the sanctuary is associated with Thespiae, whose possession it was from the fourth century B.C. at the latest. De Polignac (1995, 11–88) has argued that the territorial consolidation of the nascent poleis over the course of the ninth and eighth centuries was signaled, among other things, by the appearance of sanctuaries on the border of the settlement's claimed territory. Such sanctuaries, moreover, often at least began as sites shared with neighboring communities occupying land on the other side of the boundary. These extra-urban shrines, finally, were generally complemented by a corresponding temple within the walls of the polis in a bipolar structure linking the heart of the settlement to its boundary. Such a temple to the Muses stood within the walls of Thespiae.[41] Allowing for the

---

41. Schachter 1986, 150–53. Schachter 1996, 103, 111, however, states that the cult of Apollo Archagetas functioned as Thespiae's central civic cult.

chronological discontinuities between the development of such cities as Argos, Athens, or Sparta and the cities of Boeotia, it is at least tempting to see in the sanctuary of the Muses on Helicon such a point of contact between Thespiae and Ascra, a place where the representatives and institutions of the Thespian political economy met the inhabitants of a smaller and less complex community.

The extent to which I have had to speculate about relations between Ascra and Thespiae is indicative not only of Hesiod's lack of interest in the issue but perhaps of the informality of such relations as well. It is a further difficulty that, as Schachter (1996, 99 n. 1) observes, not much is known about Thespiae's early history. It seems inherently improbable that there was no contact between inhabitants of two neighboring settlements, and even the limited role of the *basilēes* attested to in *Works and Days* falsifies such a claim. I am of the opinion, moreover, that the difference in size and complexity between Ascra and Thespiae would have exercised a fundamental influence over relations between the two communities. Ascrans would have been more often in need of aid from Thespiae than offering it, somewhat in awe of their neighbor yet suspicious of its intentions, and perhaps a bit grudging in reciprocating favors received. I will examine the organization of Ascra as a community, especially the level of complexity achieved by its political economy, in the next chapter. The evidence considered here, at any rate, suggests that Ascrans interacted with Thespians individually, at the level of the household, and on a voluntary footing. Perhaps the influence of Thespiae's *basilēes* within Ascra represents an unintended, cumulative effect of such atomized, individual contacts.

CONCLUSIONS

The personal nature of external contacts—both through trade and with the kings as judges—shows that we encounter here interactions occurring not at the level of the political economy but at the level of the subsistence economy. The only role allowed the "kings" in the community is that of arbitrators in cases brought to them voluntarily. The trade described by Hesiod does not draw farmers into an exploitative relationship with an elite. Neither form of external relationship, moreover, binds Ascra as a corporate entity to the outside world, but both operate at the individual level on an ad hoc basis. Hesiod does not view his own and Perses' actions in the context of regularized and formal relations between the village of Ascra and the polis of Thespiae, something that must be accepted as a given because it cannot be changed. He does not look to a village leadership to represent the interests of individual village members in trade or before the judges of the polis. Nor, finally, does he present Perses as the victim of powerful outsiders. Hesiod attributes Perses' failure not to a political economy organized to protect an elite but to Perses' mismanagement of his domestic economy, to his indolence; and, as I have suggested, to view the case otherwise undermines the ethical foundation of *Works and Days* that labor alone is the path of justice and prosperity.

Ascra was never in antiquity considered in its own right a polis. Bintliff and Snodgrass (1989, 286; see also Snodgrass 1987–89, 62–64) describe the site as a "satellite" of Thespiae, within whose territory Ascra ultimately comes to be included. Yet Hesiod's testimony does not support the view that any polis or outside elite exerted its authority over his village. Hesiod does not characterize Ascra as a community that is a "part society" economically or politically, nor in cultural terms either. In spite of Hesiod's spleen, moreover, the intervention of the kings in the dispute between him and Perses yet remains a threat within the setting of the opening harangue. It is beginning to look, therefore, as if Hesiod describes a village that is autonomous, outside the territory of any polis, but that may nonetheless be encountering exploratory confrontations and opportunistic encroachments from a powerful neighbor hoping to extend its influence. Autonomy for a village must be a possibility at this early date in the history of the Greek polis, and what is known of Ascra and Thespiae specifically suggests that the two settlements were coexistent from a date making it unlikely that Ascra was within the territory of Thespiae from the outset.

Hesiod expresses unequivocal resistance to hierarchy and outside authority through his denunciation of the kings' intervention into his affairs. Hanson (1995, 16–45, 91–126) argues that Hesiod as an independent small farmer is engaged in actively opposing the power of an entrenched elite whose wealth and power is based upon herding. The heart of this conflict is competition for the use of land for pasture or for arable. Hesiod's Ascrans represent a group of "middling" farmers contesting the attempt of "bribe-swallowing barons" to cheat them out of their property. Tandy (1997, 141–65, 194–227) likewise situates *Works and Days* in a context of ongoing struggle. The kings in the city advance their newly emergent power through lending, judicial authority, and relations of exchange in the market. Hesiod resists them through *Works and Days* itself, especially in the advice to trade by sea, so avoiding the market of the kings, and in his emphasis upon autarky and *oikos. Works and Days* in fact belongs to a tradition of anti-aristocratic poetry (Tandy 1997, 194–201, cf. Donlan 1973, 149–50).

As I shall analyze in detail in my final chapter, Hesiod builds up over the course of *Works and Days* a powerful appeal for the independence of Ascra as he strives to persuade Perses not to turn to the kings. Because Ascra lies outside the boundaries of Thespiae, Hesiod's resistance cannot be directed solely at the power of the kings. Rather, Hesiod repudiates in *Works and Days* the emergent polis system as a whole upon which the kings rely for any prestige they might project into Ascra. The autarky that Hesiod values and seeks to preserve thrives outside the polis, with its elite, its formal institutions and offices, and its fixed territory. For, although Hesiod may not envision incorporation within the political economy of a neighboring polis as an immediate threat, he clearly rejects that eventuality in his hostility towards Perses' overtures to the kings. *Works and Days* does not represent the popular, anti-aristocratic side of a debate being waged citizen-against-citizen within the confines of the city. It is better seen, rather, as the precursor to this tradition, a point of origin for that discourse, which nonetheless stands outside the specific political dialectic within which it is best known.

Morris (1991, 44–50) has argued that Greek history from the Dark Age through the Classical period is distinguished by the highly organized resistance mounted to the emergence of state-level institutions. Hesiod's poem is a clear landmark within this broader struggle that characterizes the peculiar historical dynamic of ancient Greece. But the topoi and sentiments that served Hesiod in his polemic against the incipient processes of stratification and centralization marking the rise of the polis were later adapted to a new context, the narrower battle fought out between citizens within the walls of the polis. The appearance of these sentiments in *Works and Days* suggests, then, that the philosophy of political egalitarianism associated with the democratic regimes of Classical Greece has its roots in village attitudes predating the polis system and perhaps extending back into the Dark Age.

3 Internal Relations

Ascra as Community

There is, then, little in *Works and Days* to support the contention that the lords of Thespiae exercised much influence over Ascra at all, let alone held its inhabitants in thrall to debt and rent or dominated them as a subservient peasant class. I wish now to consider the evidence provided by Hesiod for the internal organization of his community. In the first place I will consider the organization and priorities of the individual household and in the second the mode of integration of these individual households into more complex structures.

I do not mean to suggest, however, by the organization of my own argument that I consider the internal structure of a community to be independent of the sorts of relationships linking it to the world outside its own boundaries. In fact, I consider these two aspects of a community's form so highly interdependent that they virtually provide two ways of asking the same question. That is, if Ascra was in fact a peasant community, under the domination of an external elite, then we would expect to find village life ordered by certain institutions and forms of customary behavior complementary to its relationship with the outside world. So, the question that I address at this stage is whether the institutions and modes of behavior described by Hesiod correspond to a peasant village or to the autonomous agricultural village that I have thus far argued Ascra to be.

Victor Magagna's recent treatment of peasant communities, or, as he prefers, communities of grain, dispenses with the usual preoccupation with relations between cultivators and elite—that is, external relations between peasant villages and cities—and focuses rather upon the internal characteristics of such settlements, how they define and organize themselves. Magagna analyzes how households integrate themselves into a more complex, interdependent entity than the individual households themselves.

The particular form exhibited by these communities results directly from the conditions that make of them peasants: namely, their exploitation by an external elite. For as Magagna argues, a peasantry does not exist in some natural state but is rather created by the power that an external elite, the lords of the city, are able to exert upon an agrarian community.[1] The complexity that Magagna outlines—the integration of households through shared village interests and their articulation within the village into levels of hierarchy—is the effect of what Magagna terms the forces of constraint, the pressure exerted on the community of grain by an external elite through demands it imposes on the community's resources. The specific internal characteristics of the community of grain that Magagna brings to light correspond, then, to a determinate set of external relationships.

Magagna argues that the form of the community of grain springs in the first place from an intense territoriality. The village boundary encloses within it the benefits of village membership and a legitimating folklore of place. At the heart of the notion of village membership stands an obligation to obey village rules, minimally by participating in communal labor at crucial stages in the agricultural cycle, and a reciprocal claim on village resources, ultimately the right to subsistence.[2] These twin functions of distributing the means of subsistence and of organizing production are jealously guarded against outside interference behind the spatial borders of the village. This degree of interdependence and cooperation within the village community is enforced through its local hierarchy. Through features such as communal labor, distribution of village resources, and hierarchy, the community of grain evidences the processes of political integration and social stratification within the village itself, both of which presuppose an intensification of the subsistence regime. The specific configuration of institutions, moreover, marks a determinate balance between the subsistence

1. Magagna 1991. Regarding the emphasis upon external relations in research on peasant communities, see pp. 1–24 of Magagna's book. The concept of a "community of grain" in Magagna's argument, drawing attention to the internal characteristics of the community, in fact replaces the concept of "peasant," which he associates with the attempt to define such communities in terms of their relations with external elites and considers as a consequence inadequate. Magagna remains quite aware, however, of the role of what he terms "the forces of constraint," the power of a supra-local elite, in influencing the form of the community of grain: Magagna 1991, 25–47, esp. 45–47; cf. 122–23, 248. Cf. Wolf, 1966, 10–12.

2. Regarding the claim on subsistence see also Wolf 1966, 77–80 and Scott 1976, 33–55, 176–79; cf. Sahlins 1972, 210–19. It is possible, of course, to overemphasize the cooperative nature of peasant societies. See Gallant's (1991, 7–10) brief but illuminating contrast of what he terms the "moral economy" and the "political economy" approaches to peasant societies.

economy of the household and the political economy of the village at large, a political economy that is itself shaped by its place in the broader political economy beyond the boundary of the village.

Subsistence insurance for village members, let alone a right to subsistence, implemented through some form of hierarchy, necessarily requires a mechanism of social storage, some arrangement for circulating goods, primarily food, among households over an extended period of time. I have already argued that Hesiod gives no evidence for such an arrangement between the inhabitants of Ascra and an external elite. Sahlins, discussing less complex social formations than the peasant society, distinguishes between generalized and balanced reciprocity. Assistance offered under generalized reciprocity gives rise to a counterobligation but without a specific time limit or expectation of full repayment. Failure to reciprocate does not immediately or necessarily bring the flow of assistance to an end. At the level of the subsistence economy (i.e., the individual household) generalized reciprocity is the norm: cooperatively produced food is pooled and shared among all members without thought for an exact settling of accounts. At higher structural levels than the household, generalized reciprocity manifests itself as pooling, a scheme of social storage in which goods are redistributed through accumulation in the hands of one individual who in turn puts them back in circulation. Such a system of reciprocity comprises a central function of the political economy. It defines within its spatial extent a social boundary and creates hierarchy in the person of the agent of redistribution.

Balanced reciprocity, in contrast, is a movement of goods between two individuals. Reciprocation without delay in equivalent value is the norm, and failure to reciprocate brings an end to exchange. These two forms of reciprocity define at the level of the community contrasting relationships between the subsistence and the domestic economies. The extension of generalized reciprocity beyond the limits of the household necessarily alters the balance between the subsistence and political economies: in order to gain access to village resources, the household must surrender some amount of its sovereignty over its own products. As the political economy is extended, the autonomy of the domestic economy is weakened.

If Hesiod's Ascra is a peasant village, a community of grain, subject to the exactions of the kings of Thespiae, then Sahlins' analysis suggests a series of tell-tale features that we can reasonably expect it to exhibit.[3] Are

3. See Sahlins 1972, 188–96 and 210–19. Donlan 1982 offers a careful and systematic examination of the society described by Homer in terms of Sahlins' types

Ascra's villagers interconnected by relations of generalized reciprocity? Can the political economy exert substantial influence over the operation of the subsistence economy? Does Ascra exhibit political integration and social stratification commensurate with the community of grain and does its subsistence regime show the corresponding level of intensification?

THE *OIKOS*

The Household

Although Hesiod mentions the village of Ascra, it is almost completely eclipsed as a social unit by the *oikos,* the house and household. In the verses of *Works and Days* Hesiod views the household almost exclusively in its productive aspect, as individuals organized to carry out labor. So, in a famous passage (405–409) Hesiod advises Perses to first get a house, a woman, and a plow ox and to pack his equipment away in the house so that he won't need to rely on borrowing from others, putting his success at risk.[4] The basic necessities of life for Hesiod are a house, a wife, an ox, and farm equipment.

---

of reciprocity and on that basis draws broader conclusions about the social formation presented in the *Iliad* and *Odyssey*. See also Donlan 1998 and van Wees 1998. I think that it is safe to claim that the modes of cooperation detailed by Sahlins for less complex social forms are retained within peasant communities independent of the relationships between those communities and external elites. The continuity in such practices and institutions between more and less complex societies is acknowledged by Sahlins (1972, 146–48) in his discussion of the failure of chiefdoms to develop, in effect, into states, as it is as well by Wolf (1966, 9–11) when he points out that peasant communities differ from other less complex forms primarily through their incorporation within a state. So Scott argues that the principle of reciprocity upon which peasant attitudes towards an elite are founded is merely an extension to this vertical relationship with an elite of the principle of reciprocity already organizing horizontal relationships within the community (Scott 1976, 184, in general 176–92, and 40–44 on intra-village cooperation in relation to expectations about external elites). See again Wolf 1966, 77–95; and cf. Gallant 1991, 143–58. In their account of peasant societies Johnson and Earle (1987, 271–301) devote far more attention to what they term "free" peasants, whose relations to the market for land, jobs, and manufactured goods is no longer mediated through a local class of elite patrons. Such direct subjection to market forces is precisely the condition that Scott and Magagna portray peasants as struggling to fend off by asserting the obligations of the local elite to their communities. This focus upon a peculiarly modern form of peasant community makes the account of Johnson and Earle less helpful for analyzing a peasant society in the ancient world.

4. If line 406 is retained as genuine, making the wife into a slave woman with the job of plowing, then Hesiod's outlook is made to appear all the more practical; but I remain very skeptical of this line. See West 1978, ad loc. and Sallares 1991, 218.

Hesiod says little about the wife except for scattered bits of innuendo. Women appear to have no role in agricultural labor (except for line 406; see note 4), though he notes their craft of weaving (*W&D* 63–64, 779, cf. 536–38). Hesiod's statements about children reveal a thoroughly utilitarian perspective. He advises (376–78) only one son in order to preserve the family's accumulated wealth (thinking either of the expense of raising more children or of the division of a family plot between two sons). He quickly adds, though, that with more sons it is possible to do more work, so enhancing the family's prosperity (379–80). Here he views sons as a labor force. In his depiction of the Age of Iron it is a symptom of its depravity that children do not pay back their aged parents the cost of their rearing (187–88). Here too children are viewed in terms of economic advantage.

Slaves are mentioned often enough that there can be no doubt about their place in the household. These men—Hesiod mentions no female slaves[5]—are pictured as engaged in agricultural labor. Hesiod also makes brief mention of hired labor. At 602–603 he advises about hiring a thete as well as a female laborer (*erithos:* 602), presumably for the term of a year, one of the only references to the work carried on within the house. One can speculate that once the household possessed a certain number of slaves, a thete was more attractive than an additional slave since he provided the farmer with labor that could more easily be shed from one year to the next. Certain tasks that were more hazardous and those requiring less skill, moreover, might be reserved for hired labor.

Hesiod recommends both a man to sow and a plowman of forty years, mature enough to keep their minds on their work when the attention of a younger man has begun to wander (441–47). His insistent specificity about age suggests that the farmer is able to make a choice among available candidates. The frame of reference may be the farmer's two or three slaves, but Hesiod's firmness in this recommendation, suggesting that the farmer has a choice in the matter, makes it more likely that he is thinking of hired labor.[6] If so, these would be workers engaged only short-term, to alleviate the time stress of the planting season. Hesiod's warning that younger men are too easily distracted from the task at hand by the temptation to look

5. Homer, in contrast, mentions few male slaves. This difference may merely reflect Homer's lack of interest in what goes on in the fields and Hesiod's complementary lack of interest in what goes on inside the house. See A. Edwards 1993b, 46 n. 49.

6. So West ad 441 though Tandy (1997, 210–11) assumes this plowman to be a slave, as might be suggested by *W&D* 459–61.

over at their fellows presupposes a scene of numerous plowmen working near enough to see each other. If we imagine that this represents the communal working of a single man's plot, then Hesiod's counsel to find a plowman over forty makes no sense at all—the farmer could hardly impose such a requirement in a setting of cooperative labor carried on by fellow villagers. It is more likely that the poet imagines several small, adjacent plots each belonging to a different farmer. The passage gives no indication that at a time when farmers find themselves short-handed, neighbors work cooperatively in each other's fields. Rather they turn to temporary, hired workers who are strictly outside the bounds of the *oikos* and its internal obligations.[7]

The core of the household's agricultural labor supply is comprised of the farmer himself, any sons of working age, and his slaves. Then there is longer-term hired labor, the thete and *erithos,* and short-term labor if I am correct that the plowman is a hired hand. The degree to which households depended upon the products of specialized craftsmen remains unclear. Hesiod mentions only a single task that requires the services of a skilled craftsman: joining the plow's tree to its stock—the farmer can handle the rest of the job of making a plow for himself (*W&D* 427–31; cf. West ad loc.). The degree to which an Ascran such as Hesiod would have relied upon the services of the carpenter or the potter mentioned in the poem's introduction (*W&D* 25–26) is difficult to assess. Did these craftsmen live in Ascra, in the polis, or were they itinerant? If Ascrans, did they practice their craft full-time or alongside of farming? Reference to sickles (*W&D* 573) and cutting tools of iron (*W&D* 420) presupposes the skills of the blacksmith whose forge is mentioned at *W&D* 493–95 as a refuge from winter weather. Again, however, it remains uncertain whether Hesiod has in mind a full-time craftsman supported by the village or a part-time specialist who makes and repairs during the winter slack season the few iron tools used in the village. If it is safe to generalize from the example of the craftsman needed for making a plow, Hesiod and his fellow villagers relied upon their own labor as much as possible and only turned to craftsmen for highly specialized tasks.

7. The hired man presumably lacks enough land to support his household and so has time on his hands during planting and a need for additional subsistence, but see pp. 106–9. It seems odd that there is no mention of hired reapers during harvest, a period of even greater time stress I should think (see Halstead and Jones 1989, 47, and Petropoulos 1994, 27–39 regarding labor needs during harvest in the modern period).

Storage

The *oikos* as a physical structure, a building, is most closely associated in Hesiod's mind with the hoarding of grain. As he warns Perses, there is scant concern to devote to other pursuits for a man who does not have a year's supply of grain (*epēetanos bios:* 31) stored within his house (30–32). It is not clear whether Hesiod refers here simply to enough grain to last the year, till the next harvest, or to a true surplus, beyond what it will take to get to the next harvest, that can therefore serve as a hedge against future shortfalls in production.[8] Halstead and Jones (1989, 50–52) observe in their study of traditional agriculture on two Greek islands that farmers always aim at having a year's worth of surplus grain on hand (that is, above and beyond what is needed for the coming year, until the next harvest) as a buffer against a bad year. Gallant (1991, 94–97) argues that ancient peasants aimed at accumulating a ten-to-sixteen month reserve of food. He contends, though, that ancient storage techniques risked high losses of stored food to insects, animals, and mold. Forbes and Foxhall (1995, 73–75), however, argue that traditional storage methods, devised over many generations, were more effective than Gallant gives them credit for and point out that the hulled grains commonly cultivated in antiquity better withstand insects than the naked grains generally used now. In their study of modern Methana they found that farmers aim for a year's worth of food in storage over and above needs for the coming year and generally maintain storage capacity in excess of that.

Hesiod repeatedly urges and celebrates the accumulation of one's harvest within the house. For example, at 475–76 Hesiod congratulates Perses on the good harvest resulting from his advice: "And I expect that you will rejoice when you draw on your livelihood stored inside" *(biotou aireumenon endon eontos),* and in a later passage he moves from the harvest to his next topic with the words: "But after you have stored all your livelihood packed inside your house . . ." *(eparmenon endothi oikou:* 600–601).[9] This

---

8. In fact, though the etymological meaning of *epēetanos* is "lasting a year" (see P. Chantraine 1970, s.v.), the meaning "abundant" is common generally and adequate here. It is the implicit context of the annual agricultural cycle that makes the literal meaning attractive at *W&D* 31. West compares *W&D* 44 in this connection; see Jones 1984, 310. Cf. *W&D* 607 again of a crop and note that the sheep's wool at 517 is likewise "harvested" annually.

9. See also 363–67, 575–77, 611, 632. Equipment is also stored in the house: 407, 422–36, 452–54, 606–7, 627. The *kaliē*, or "granary," is the focus of the link made between house and harvest (300–301, 306–7, 411–12). The use of the word to refer to a shed or hut (503), perhaps equivalent to the Homeric *klisiē*, suggests

grain, harvested, processed, and now stored securely within the house represents for Hesiod security in its most fundamental form, a guarantee that there will be enough food for the months until the next harvest (so 299–307, 477–78, 576–77; cf. 361–64). In fact he recommends that after the winnowing one keep the watch dog well fed to protect against thieves (614–15).

The hoarding of one's harvest serves as the focus of a more generalized theme in *Works and Days* that accumulation and thrift provide a hedge against future need. So, Hesiod advises that one have a spare plow in reserve in case one should break (432–34, cf. 427–29), to have timber for a wagon on hand in advance (455–57), and to advise one's slaves to build living quarters while it is yet summer (502–503). Lines 455–57 and 502–503 also draw upon the related theme of not procrastinating. This topic receives its clearest statement, however, at 410–13, where Hesiod warns that a procrastinator will not fill up his grain bin. Time itself is something that must be used wisely and not wasted in order to avoid ruin (409, 479–92). Hesiod similarly treats fallowing as a sort of saving: reserving the land from cultivation ensures a reliable and bounteous harvest later on (462–64). At the beginning of a passage celebrating the advantages of having all the necessities of life on hand (361–69) Hesiod sets forth the principle that even if one accumulates only little by little, eventually one will possess a great deal. This opening exhortation to save is balanced by a closing couplet (368–69) advising thrift: at the top and bottom of a *pithos* drink freely but in the middle consume sparingly since economy at the bottom of the barrel is an act of desperation. I assume that Hesiod has in mind here a storage jar whose neck and bottom are narrower than its middle section and that he thus recommends in these lines extravagance with small amounts only but parsimony with the bulk of one's livelihood in order to avoid skimping after it is already too late to conserve.

Not only does Hesiod urge assiduous agricultural labor in order to survive, but the produce of that labor must be carefully stored away, little by little, and reserved against future need. This preoccupation with storage and with accumulation pervades Hesiod's worldview and is especially applicable to the most uncertain and perishable necessity of life, food. Indeed,

---

that the *kaliē* was a structure resembling a storage room rather than a bin or ceramic vessel. The phrase [Δημήτηρ] βιότου δὲ τεὴν πιμπλῆσι καλιήν· (300–301) suggests in connection with the association between the house itself and *biotos* that the *kaliē* is part of the house, a storeroom. The *aggos*, a storage vessel for both grain and wine (613), is also associated with the interior of the house (473–76, 600–601).

I have suggested that trade, too, ought to be viewed as a strategy of indirect storage as can livestock rearing and even hosting feasts.[10] All three are means of converting agricultural produce that exceeds storage capacity or household needs into alternative forms—craft items, animals, social obligations—that are reconvertible back into food later. The fundamental challenge confronted by the farming household was that of securing its subsistence. Under the regime of Mediterranean agriculture, with its interannual variability in rainfall, storing a surplus was an absolute necessity.[11] The lower the level of complexity and interdependence achieved by a community, the greater would be each household's reliance upon its own surpluses and storage capacity.

Hesiod practices a rigorous self-reliance adapted to a community in which each household must be prepared to take responsibility for its own survival. He views the household explicitly as an economic enterprise, in effect as agricultural labor. The *oikos* is prepared to procure all of its own labor needs and it processes and stores all the food that labor can produce. Hesiod's condemnation of children who refuse to repay to aged parents the cost of their upbringing (*W&D* 187–88) suggests what can in any case be assumed, that the household practices a generalized reciprocity within its own boundaries. The survival of the household is Hesiod's overwhelming preoccupation and it is what the subsistence economy is geared towards. Hesiod's *oikos* appears, then, to be organized to achieve as high a degree of independence and self-sufficiency as is possible. The priority attributed by Hesiod to the *oikos* is completely consonant not only with peasant societies but with the less complex social formations described by Johnson and Earle.[12] We must consider whether Hesiod provides any evidence for regular, obligatory cooperation or interdependence at any higher level of social organization than the individual *oikos*. Where does Hesiod's description establish a balance between the subsistence economy and the political econ-

10. Gallant (1991, 170–79) discusses the power of feasts to create social debts.
11. See Halstead 1989, 73–75; Garnsey 1988, 8–16; and Garnsey and Morris 1989, 98.
12. Johnson and Earle (1987) discuss the household throughout their account; see especially, however, 11–15, 27–31, 62–65, 91–97, 101–2, 113–17, 144–52, 165–67, 194–203 The role of the household in primitive and peasant economies is discussed by Sahlins 1972, 41–148, esp. 74–78; Wolf 1966, 12–17, 61–65; Gallant 1991, 11–33, 143–53. See Millett 1984, 93–99 and Spahn 1980, 538–41 regarding the primacy of the *oikos* in *Works and Days*. Tandy (1997, 214–27) offers a valuable discussion of the theme of self-sufficiency in *Works and Days*, though I do not agree with the conclusions he draws.

omy? How far beyond the individual household is the boundary between generalized reciprocity and balanced reciprocity drawn? What is the basis for hierarchy in Ascra and how much authority can village leaders exert over individual households? Addressing these questions of political integration and of stratification raises as well the issue of the intensity of the agricultural regime that Hesiod describes.

THE NEIGHBORHOOD

Neighbors

Hesiod's sole reference to his village of Ascra (633–40) assures us that the world he depicts in *Works and Days* is that of a community, a collection of households with some sense of sharing a common location. Yet Hesiod nowhere else refers to Ascra or even to a village *(kōmē)*. Rather he speaks of neighbors. It is not clear whether the "neighborhood" is identical with the village or constitutes a subdivision of it. If the latter, then the neighborhood would appear to be the more significant social unit, and we can imagine Ascra as a cluster of smaller groups of residences, each constituting a neighborhood. I suspect, however, that neighbors and Ascrans are one and the same.[13]

Most of what Hesiod has to say about neighbors appears in a single passage that shades off quite naturally into a discussion of reciprocity (*W&D* 342–60). He recommends inviting a friend to a banquet, especially one living nearby (342–43). If there is some trouble in your village (or the fields), a neighbor will come to your aid before a kinsman will (344–45). A bad neighbor is a bane as much as a good one is a benefit; he profits who has chanced on a good neighbor (346–47). An ox would not be lost unless a neighbor were negligent (348). Hesiod's series of examples presents a picture of occasional help between neighbors—with some calamity in the village or with an animal who has escaped or otherwise gotten into trouble. These are misfortunes that cannot be foreseen but require unhesitating action. Yet Hesiod does not testify here to regularized cooperation among neighbors on routine chores but only to occasional and extraordinary help.

13. This assumption is strengthened if we read *egkōmion* rather than *egchōrion* at *W&D* 344, where Hesiod claims that a neighbor comes to your aid in case of some problem "in the village" more quickly than an in-law. West 1978 reads *egchōrion* at 344 as does Mazon 1914 though *egkōmion* is preferred by Solmsen 1970, Verdenius 1985, Sinclair 1966, and Wilamowitz 1962.

Geometric/Archaic   Classical/Early Hellenistic

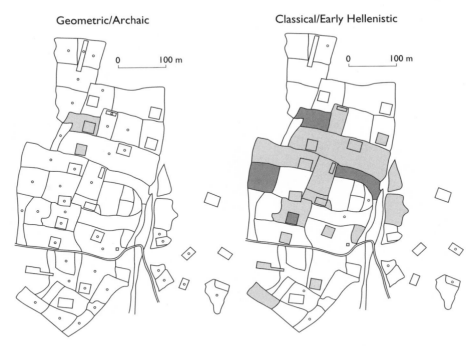

Map 2.   Site maps of Ascra for the Geometric/Archaic period and the Classical/Hellenistic period. Transects with light shading indicate low density of finds, those with darker shading moderate density. Transects marked with a zero are known to have produced no finds. The contrast between these two plans provides a sense of the scale of early Ascra. J. Bintliff and A. Snodgrass, Mediterranean Survey and the City, *Antiquity* 62 (1988) figures 2a and 2b, 62.

The sense in these lines that the neighborhood constitutes an autonomous social world is reinforced at 700–701, where Hesiod recommends selecting a wife from those living nearby (cf. 343–45) and designates the neighbors as the amused audience for the disgrace of a cuckold. Friendship between neighbors is expressed through a shared meal, but one cannot take for granted cooperative relations with a neighbor: he can cause a lot of damage if he is so inclined (346–47). While neighbors clearly have much to gain from cooperation, such behavior depends upon individual goodwill more than explicit social obligation.

While the relationship between neighbors is, as I will continue to argue, limited, it remains the main form of association outside of household and familial connection. Hesiod uses *philos/phileō* to describe a relationship that is changeable, selective, and dependent upon unique circumstances.

Terms familiar from Homer such as *phrētrē* or *politēs* do not occur in *Works and Days,* nor is there any equivalent to Homer's formula of parents, *dēmos,* and *polis* for identifying oneself. The word *dēmos* does occur twice in *Works and Days* (261, 527), but linked in the one instance to a *basileus* and in the other to a *polis.* Ascra is not described by the term *dēmos,* which would designate it as a distinct, spatially defined entity able to serve as the setting for exclusive access to habitation and use of resources. The "neighborhood" does unite a limited space with a set of cooperative relationships, but obligations here are limited and organized as contingent, personal relations. Hesiod's neighborhood, as the geographical locus of a collection of domestic or subsistence economies, does not appear to have progressed far in the direction of political economy.

Eris

The limited cooperation that links neighbors is balanced against a powerful, if constructive, "competition," *eris,* which Hesiod regards as endemic to communities in which farmers live and work near to each other. This rivalry is played out in terms of success at farming, but its prize, beyond prosperity, is social standing.[14] The theme of social standing is announced in the opening lines of the poem when in the course of his praise of Zeus Hesiod claims that the god can make men "both unknown and famous, celebrated and obscure" (*aphatoi te phatoi te / rhētoi te arrhētoi te:* 3–4). Hesiod focuses this general contrast between the illustrious and the obscure into its salient form for *Works and Days* in the following elaboration of the good *eris* (17–26), which provokes even the shiftless to labor out of envy of a neighbor's wealth: "one neighbor vies with another who is striving for prosperity" (*zēloi de te geitona geitōn / eis aphenos speudont'* [23–24]).[15]

The difference in prosperity existing between the industrious man and his lazy neighbor gives rise to the circumstances in which the good strife operates. Hesiod repeats the idea that the indolent man envies the prosperity of the diligent at 312–13, though without explicit reference to neighbors. This relationship of rivalry is triggered by the gaze of the shiftless and impoverished man at his industrious and wealthy neighbor ("for,

---

14. See Walcot 1970, 87–92; Millett 1984, 93–99; Hanson 1995, 99–102.

15. See West's note on lines 3–4. In support of the connection between 3–4 and the relationship expressed through *zēloi* at 23–24, note the use of the contrast of *arizēlon* with *adēlon* at line 6 to reformulate the oppositions *aphatoi te phatoi te / rhētoi te arrhētoi te.*

somebody lacking work himself, gazing at another who is wealthy . . .": *eis heteron gar tis te idōn ergoio chatizōn / plousion . . .* [21–22]). Those who prosper through their industry serve as the objects of admiring envy for the indolent. This gaze shows up again at 477–78, where Hesiod tells Perses that in the wake of a bumper harvest he will not need to gaze admiringly at others (*augaseai*: 478) and a few lines later at 482 Hesiod warns that in the wake of a failed harvest no one will look at him (*thēēsontai*: 482).[16] The phrase *geitona geitōn* (23), moreover, explicitly establishes the neighborhood, the village, as the arena for this sentiment of admiring envy in *Works and Days*.

Hesiod's sense that this rivalry is an elemental force in relations among neighbors hardly rules out the possibility of cooperation within the boundary of neighborhood or village. But I think that it is safe to say that he endows *Eris*, "Strife" or "Competition," with a centrality and speaks of it with an intensity that far exceeds anything he has to say about cooperation. The power attributed by Hesiod to *eris* reinforces the sense of autonomy and isolation of the individual *oikos*. From this perspective each household stands against all other households. Even if we do not ascribe to *Works and Days* the zero-sum logic of a "limited good" theory of wealth, *eris* must certainly operate to mask the shared interests that induce neighbors to cooperate.[17]

Sharing

For a small agricultural community such as that described in *Works and Days*, saving, the ability of one household to accumulate and store a surplus, raises immediately the issue of sharing that surplus with other households that find themselves short of food. As noted, Magagna considers subsistence a fundamental right within the community of grain. The extent of such obligations among households can provide a gauge of the level of integration, of the strength of the political economy, in the community. For Hesiod, however, claims against the reserves of others in the name of sub-

16. Cf. regarding the gaze *Il.* 3.342, 12.312, *Od.* 7.71, 8.169–73, 20.166. This same gaze is thematized for *Works and Days* at 6 in the contrast between the *arizēlon* and the *adēlon*, literally, the "very visible" and the "invisible." Cf. West 1978, and Verdenius 1985, ad loc.

17. Millett (1984, 95) argues that Hesiod takes the "negative view of wealth and prosperity as being feasible only at the expense of other people." According to this notion of "limited good," since land and wealth generally are limited for a peasant community, if one family's fortunes rise, then those of another must fall in equal degree. Gallant (1991, 146–48) considers the limited good mentality consistent with the values of Dark Age and Archaic Greece as well.

sistence are at best contingent. Sharing as a practice for traditional communities such as that described by Hesiod is governed by its specific conventions of reciprocity. That is, sharing is always really a form of exchange even when the giver receives nothing in return except the recipient's sense of obligation and indebtedness. In a setting in which some have more and others less, sharing functions as a mechanism of redistribution that easily evolves into pooling or social storage, and serves as the basis for hierarchy. What Hesiod has to say about sharing, then, is central to the questions we are raising about the community he depicts in *Works and Days*.

Sharing and the terms of sharing vary with the degree of social obligation, and Hesiod supplies enough evidence to construct a rough hierarchy of obligation extending from kin outward. His condemnation of the depraved men of iron for failing either to respect their parents or to repay them in their old age for the cost of their own rearing (*W&D* 185–88) indicates that a relationship of generalized reciprocity is normative, as one would expect, between parents and children. Hesiod recommends that a brother *(kasignētos)* should be superior in one's esteem to a *hetairos* (*W&D* 707), a non-kin associate, and that he should be *philos*. The advice to smile when insisting that a brother swear an oath (*W&D* 371) implies that while brothers were related closely enough that a contract seemed an affront to their intimacy, still the relationship between sibling households was bounded enough that the terms of mutual cooperation and obligations could require explicit spelling out. Such preciseness and control, however, would risk undermining the amity of generalized reciprocity. Hesiod's statement that a neighbor will come to one's aid before an affinal kin, *pēoi* (345), should, I believe, be taken as an ironic affirmation that the obligation between in-laws is expected, at any rate, to be stronger than that between neighbors.

The distinction between *hetairos,* "companion," and *philos,* "friend," would appear to be slight at best in view of Hesiod's use of *philos* as a synonym for *hetairos* (707–14). Hesiod's bracketing of his discussion of neighbors (*W&D* 342–55) with advice about dealing with *philoi,* moreover, assumes a high degree of congruence between these two categories, as between *philos* and *hetairos.* Though Hesiod counsels not to make a *hetairos* the equal of a brother in this passage, if one should nevertheless do so, he goes on to recommend a high degree of loyalty and formality to ensure that the relationship endures. Status as *hetairos* appears to be a rather formal matter and one that can approach the intimacy and commitment expected of kin (cf. 183, 716). Hesiod's admonition that the wage *(misthos)* promised to a *philos* must be adequate (*W&D* 370) asserts a standard of equity in dealing with "friends" while acknowledging at the same time that friend-ship can join unequals, employer and employed. The relationship entailed by a *misthos* would appear to contradict the ideology of generosity and equality ingrained in generalized reciprocity. As I shall argue below in con-nection with *W&D* 342–55, Hesiod rather describes a regime of balanced reciprocity organizing relations with friends and neighbors. The degree of obligation lessens among community members as distance from the inti-mate kinship of the household grows. What, however, is the concrete obli-gation among various classes of individual in Hesiod's Ascra, especially where relations of close kinship leave off and those defined by mutual membership in the community begin?[18]

Hesiod discusses sharing and reciprocity in the same passage in which he discusses neighbors (*W&D* 342–55). The principle of reciprocity opens the passage as a whole with the injunction to invite one's friends to din-ner (*epi daita*: *W&D* 342), especially neighbors, but to pass over enemies (*W&D* 342–43).[19] As West and Verdenius both note, the topic of the ban-quet emerges from that of sacrifice in lines 335–40. It is thus the same sort of setting that Hesiod has in mind later in references to the "banquets of the gods" (*W&D* 736 with West's note, 742). As 342 makes clear, at-tendance at such events is by invitation *(kalein)* of the sacrificer (cf. 722, again with West's note). Feasts can serve as a limited mechanism of shar-ing within a community, but as the topic of neighbors and reciprocity un-folds in these lines, it becomes apparent from Hesiod's insistence on strict balance that such an invitation imposes a very concrete obligation for re-payment. The banquet as ceremony, a religious and social event, moreover, appears to be organized at the level of the *oikos* rather than that of the broader community, and consequently participation is a matter of one-to-

18. Sahlins (1972, 196–204) discusses the attenuation of generalized reciproc-ity into balanced as the degree of relationship declines from household member to-wards stranger. Also see his analysis of how domestic units will produce above and beyond their own needs in order to be able to meet needs of the community as a whole (102–15). Gallant (1991, 153–58) offers an illuminating discussion of the relative advantages of kin and neighbors in a support network constructed by a household.

19. The *dais*, though probably, I think, a generic for "banquet," is associated by Homer and Hesiod with the *eilapinē*, the type of banquet for which the host sup-plies the food *(Od.* 1.225–26, Hes. fr. 274), as distinct from the *eranos*, to which each guest brings a contribution. I follow West's interpretation of 722–23, accord-ing to which *dais* in 722 would be an *eilapinē*. In general, see Tandy's (1997, 94–101) discussion of reciprocity in connection with lines 342–55.

one personal relationships between host and guests—the host's *philoi* alone are invited—rather than of status as a citizen or "village member." The banquet does not function as a mechanism of generalized reciprocity in the community but appears to be governed more by the values of balanced reciprocity and serves as ceremony to promote the bond among a group of *philoi* rather than across the village as a whole. *Works and Days* 722–23, presenting a contrast in its advice (to the host, presumably) not to be a grouch at a *dais* and its observation that a pot-luck style banquet *(ek koinou)* is cheaper and more fun, rates saving expense and preserving household resources above the sort of sharing that can create long-term obligations among households.[20]

Following his praise of neighbors Hesiod advises paying back what one borrows from a neighbor exactly and in full measure and even more, if possible, in order to ensure further aid when in need again in the future (349–51). Hesiod appears to refer to food here and speaks explicitly of the need compelling the recipient to borrow.[21] Such assistance is organized as a one-to-one exchange between neighbors with a concrete expectation of repayment. Hesiod says nothing about a time limit for repayment, but from the context of food we can safely infer a loan intended to help get a household to the next harvest. This assumption entails a period of a year at most while the firmness of the injunction to repay suggests a period not much longer. Hesiod reinforces the precision and formality of this obligation in the next line with the admonition not to profit unfairly (*mē kaka kerdainein:* 352), forbidding evasion of repaying one's debt to a neighbor in full. The care Hesiod advises, moreover, in order to prepare the way for future loans makes it clear that such assistance is contingent, the product of a voluntary relationship that could lapse. Hesiod does not describe here a generalized reciprocity in which all members of the community simply share and share alike or redistribute goods through the agency of a local Big Man or

20. Again, I am in agreement with West's interpretation of these lines; contra, see Sinclair ad loc. See Mazarakis Ainian's (1997, 290–93) discussion of archaeological evidence for the importance of ceremonial dining to chiefly authority in Dark Age Greece.

21. I take *metreisthai* (349) and *metrōi* (350) to indicate that Hesiod has foodstuffs in mind. Cf. *W&D* 392–97, 600, Hes. fr. 278.7–12. Sahlins (1972, 215–19) discusses the special status of food as an item of generalized reciprocity. Millett (1984, 99–103) points out that the excess repayment recommended by Hesiod has the very specific purpose of creating a counterobligation so as to prevent the relationship itself from lapsing when nothing is any longer owed by either party; cf. Sahlins 1972, 222–23.

chief. This resembles more closely the conventions of Sahlins' balanced reciprocity.[22]

Hesiod concludes this topic with three verses asserting explicitly the principle of balanced reciprocity in social relations (353–55): love the one who loves and be in front of the one approaching,[23] give to the one who gives and don't to the one who doesn't, one gives to a giver but one does not give to a non-giver. Essential to grasping the importance of this passage is the recognition that rather than expressing a general obligation to share with all members of the community, Hesiod discriminates among individuals on the basis of specific personal relationships. In these lines conclud-

---

22. Gallant (1982, 112) categorizes the transaction described at *W&D* 349–51 as an example of Sahlin's generalized reciprocity, arguing "the exchange need not be simultaneous or of equal value. There is no time limit on return." Hesiod, of course, specifies repayment in the exact amount plus a little extra. Although he does not specify a time frame (would his audience have simply assumed a customary period?), a very concrete expectation of repayment is unmistakable from the implication that there will be no more loans if there is no repayment (*W&D* 350–51). Sahlins states that balanced reciprocity "may be more loosely applied to transactions that stipulate returns of commensurate worth or utility within a finite and narrow period" (1972, 194–95). This seems like a pretty close fit to me. The correspondence of a loan of food to a neighbor, however, to the contexts specified by Sahlins for balanced reciprocity—trade, buying-selling, ceremonial gift-exchange, peace treaties—is pretty poor. This inconsistency may be what led Gallant to what I consider a mistaken identification. The implication, as I shall discuss below, is that Ascra has reached only a very low level of complexity indeed.

23. I am not sure what to make of 353b (τῷ προσιόντι προσεῖναι). I would prefer to render it "oppose the one opposing you." Lines 354 and 355 each comprise two antithetical hemistichs composed respectively of "like to like" sentiments. The interpretation offered by LSJ s.v. πρόσειμι (εἶμι) I.2, based upon the discussion of this line in Σ *Od.* 1.406, that προσεῖναι is the equivalent here of προσίεναι and that both verbs carry a hostile connotation is attractive since the hemistich *kai tōi prosionti proseinai* would then balance the opening phrase *ton phileonta philein* according to the formal and semantic pattern found in 354 and 355. Cf. the contrast between *phileont'* and *echthron* at 342, the line opening this passage. But it seems quite a stretch to take προσεῖναι as the equivalent of προσίεναι, a possibility uniformly rejected by Sinclair 1966, Hofinger 1978 s.v., West 1978, and Verdenius 1985—though G. P. Edwards (1971, 114–15) defends the position with reasonable arguments. Even at that, a hostile connotation is attested for προσίεναι (Hom. *Il.* 10.339, 11.742; Hes. *Sc.* 425), making an interpretation of "oppose the one attacking you" possible if we can attribute to προσεῖναι a fairly literal meaning here of "oppose" in the sense of "be against," "be in front of" (cf. Lat. *obsum*). West's "and give your company to him that seeks it" (ad loc.) makes sense of the Greek *kai tōi prosionti proseinai*, but disrupts the formal balance so rigidly applied otherwise in the passage and flatly contradicts the required sense that one respond to like with like, not that one bestow favors on whoever asks. Verdenius's suggestion "be at the disposal of the one who comes for help" makes no better sense in the context and the meaning "come for help" for *prosionti* is poorly attested.

ing the section on neighbors Hesiod provides a general principle, dividing the world into those with whom one shares and those with whom one does not. In the lines introducing the topic of reciprocity (349–51) Hesiod explains the principle for maintaining relations of sharing. Sharing for Hesiod is conducted within a relationship of strict reciprocity that is maintained through precise repayment of what has been borrowed. While Hesiod uses words based on the verb "to give" *(didōmi)*, it is clear that this mode of giving requires a countergift by way of repayment.

Since such sharing permits one household to draw directly upon the precious food reserves of another, which may itself not be so far from shortfall, Hesiod's rigidity and exactitude are not surprising. For, as we have seen, the entire process of producing and consuming food is closely identified with the autonomous household. Hesiod mentions no communal mechanism mediating the direct exchange between the household with a surplus and that with a shortage. That is, there is no formal political economy able to structure and organize relations among household-level subsistence economies through some scheme of regularized social storage. Rather, the relationships of reciprocity within which sharing occurs are strictly personal, solely dependent upon the goodwill of neighbors. These relationships of reciprocity among *philoi* could, as lines 707–14 testify, come to an end. Hesiod's norms of reciprocity depart dramatically from those organizing behavior in the chiefdoms described by Homer. In the Homeric poems there is emphasis upon ceremony and display in the act of giving, and asymmetry in exchange or deferral of repayment serve the giver's interest by enhancing his authority and prestige.[24] Reciprocity within Hesiod's community is not organized as a system of obligatory and generalized sharing aiming to maximize the distribution of the community's common resources. We observe rather a network of dyadic relationships that are formed voluntarily, that might be discontinued at any time, and that require a certain effort and maintenance to prevent them from lapsing. In Hesiod's village one cannot expect help from neighbors outside of preexisting, voluntarily established relationships of balanced reciprocity. Such reciprocal relations of mutual aid presumably function in Hesiod's world as a hedge, a stopgap in the face of misfortunes overwhelming the resources of an individual household—that is, as an ad hoc, rudimentary mechanism of social storage.

The contingency of sharing in Hesiod's community is best illustrated by

24. See Qviller 1981, 120–27, Donlan 1982, esp. 169–71, and Donlan 1993, 159–72. This is the regime of Sahlin's generalized reciprocity.

instances where loans are flatly denied. Following his recommendation of a house, a woman, a plow-ox, and all the necessary equipment, Hesiod explains that with this secured, Perses will not need to try to borrow from someone else who might refuse and leave him at a loss while his farm goes to ruin (408–409). A little later Hesiod imagines the helpless distress of a man who has no ox or wagon of his own in plowing season and is refused when he tries to borrow them in order to do his planting (453–54). In the first passage no reason for refusal is hinted at; in the second the adverb *rēidion* (454) suggests that the excuse is disingenuous. These passages indicate that there was only a limited obligation that households share with one another. This is hardly the picture of a community in which members were obliged to labor collectively during periods of seasonal time stress.

While these passages deal with equipment, an earlier and more detailed passage (*W&D* 394–404) pictures Perses begging food first from Hesiod and then from his neighbors. Perses, Hesiod claims, will beg from other households but accomplish nothing just as now he has approached Hesiod, who will give him nothing more. Perses should get to work lest he find himself begging from neighbors, who will help two or three times, but after that he will beg in vain. Hesiod in this passage permits us to infer the gradations of obligation between the generalized reciprocity within the household and the balanced reciprocity between neighbors. Does Perses, as close kin to Hesiod, enjoy a relationship of generalized reciprocity with him, like a member of the household, or as head of his own household does he exchange with Hesiod's on the same footing as a neighbor? Hesiod's prediction that Perses will turn to his neighbors now that he will give him no further aid (note the prefix *epi-* of *epidōsō* and *epimetrēsō*: *W&D* 396–97) implies that a household turned first to kin for help, where there is a stronger obligation, and then to neighbors.[25] Hesiod claims that the reciprocity between neighbors can tolerate two or three advances before sharing ceases because of failure to repay (cf. *W&D* 349–51). Yet Hesiod asserts nonetheless that there is a limit to his obligation too.

Specifically, Hesiod ties his refusal of further assistance to an exhortation that Perses get to work and see to his own needs. Perses is like the shiftless drones who consume the toil of others and whom men and gods

---

25. The hierarchy of relationships implied here is supported explicitly by the injunction not to count a friend the equal of a kinsman (707) as well as by the apparent paradox exploited by Hesiod at 344–45 that neighbors come to one's aid even before kin. See pp. 93–94. Gallant (1991, 153–58) discusses the hierarchy of obligation between kin and neighbors and the relative advantages of each.

blame (*W&D* 302–306). In Hesiod's mind his obligation even to a close kinsman is qualified both by duration and by the behavior of the individual in question. The charge that Perses' troubles are due to sheer laziness precludes, moreover, a context of a general subsistence crisis such as might strain one household's ability to come to the aid of another. Hesiod does not claim that he cannot help Perses for want of resources but simply that he should no longer need to. Hesiod's prediction of what Perses can anticipate from neighbors, moreover, may suggest the limited obligation imposed by the community generally even in matters of food. The same expectations that may have sanctioned sharing with kin to begin with require such assistance only up to a certain point. The realization, then, that Perses, because of his indolence, may become a chronic drain on his resources leads Hesiod to refuse further aid. This reaction presupposes that there is an expectation even among close kin that reciprocity will be balanced. As it appears progressively less likely that this expectation can ever be satisfied, Perses' status moves further from that of household member and closer to that of neighbor. No doubt, Hesiod's estrangement from his brother was only accelerated by Perses' threat to take it before the kings. In sum, when it becomes apparent that the giving could go on indefinitely with no expectation of a return, then even for a kinsman the giving comes to an end.

Sharing pits the interests of the *oikos* quite directly against those of the larger community. It is in the interest of the individual household not to share its resources but instead to reserve them for its own use. But a generalized reciprocity better serves the interests of the community at large. Indeed, even an individual household that guards its own resources jealously would value a claim on assistance from other households in a time of shortage, but a household can acquire such a claim only if it is willing to acknowledge reciprocal claims against itself on the part of other households. Sharing points up the trade-off of advantages against attendant disadvantages that a household deliberating whether or not to participate in a political economy must confront. The values of autarky and intra-village cooperation and solidarity are fundamentally opposed and as a consequence are not easily negotiated.[26]

In peasant societies this tension between the interests of the individual household and the interests of the community animates village relations, but the community's expectation that the well-off will share with the

26. See Gallant 1991, 7–10, 143–58; Johnson and Earle 1987, 11–15; Sahlins 1972, 95–99, 123–39, and 210–19; and Forbes and Foxhall 1995, 84.

needy overcomes the impulse to hoard in all but the most extreme circum-stances.[27] This is the logic of the peasant society and of other relatively complex social formations. Hesiod, however, perceives only a collection of discrete households. His sense of community obligation and interdepend-ence is by comparison highly attenuated. The claim of one household upon the resources of another, even in the case of kin, is dependent in Hesiod's community upon goodwill and is subject to definite limits. Indeed, it can-not be said that Hesiod encourages sharing at all if one considers the rela-tive balance of exhortations to cooperate, share, or further the interests of the neighborhood to those encouraging work on one's own farm and hoard-ing one's own produce in order to see to the interests of one's own *oikos*.

Under the regime of balanced reciprocity described by Hesiod the flip side of sharing is debt *(chreos)*, the obligation assumed by the recipient of assistance to restore its value in an exact amount. In the passage discussed above (*W&D* 394–404) Hesiod continues, after warning Perses that his neighbors will not give more than two or three times, that he should rather find a deliverance from debts *(chreiōn: 404)* and a means of avoiding hun-ger *(limos: 404)*. This complex of neighbors, food, and debt appears as well in the passage at *W&D* 349–51 in which Hesiod gives instruction about paying back neighbors. Both passages warn of the need to repay in order to maintain the relationship of reciprocity. The only other occurrence of "debt" *(chreos)* in *Works and Days* (646–47) is likewise joined to hunger. Debt in these passages is a relationship between neighbors and it is con-tracted over food as an alternative to hunger. The fact that the sharing of food results in formal debts again testifies to the low level of integration and interdependence among households in his community. Debt occupies a relatively small place in the community. Its impact is limited for both borrower and lender since failure to repay results in neither repossession nor expropriation but only in the breakdown of continuing reciprocity. If such a breach of reciprocity could eventually culminate in a reduction of status—the necessity to labor for a *misthos* as a thete or even taking shel-ter as a prosperous man's *dmōs* (whether or not that could happen is, of course, a matter of pure speculation)—still that would not result from a creditor's active pursuit of his debtor but from the passive withdrawal of further aid and the individual's own failure as a householder.

As Millett and others have already observed (p. 36), this debt of which Hesiod speaks has nothing to do with the kings. It is not a matter of ex-

27. See Gallant 1991, 7–10; Scott 1976, 40–44; and Wolf 1966, 77–80.

ternal relations between Ascra and Thespiae but a relationship between prosperous and poor within the village. Why precisely does Hesiod disapprove of this debt between fellow villagers? Of course, for Hesiod debt does not involve such complications as money, interest, or collateral. Even among the simplest, most egalitarian communities, "debt" in the form of sharing food can be viewed in a positive light. The debt incurred by the borrower comprises simultaneously the generosity of the lender and it credits the lender with a claim in the future for reciprocal generosity from the borrower. Regularized and multi-directional debt relations among the households of a settlement not only provide a mechanism of subsistence insurance but they also ensure that food is consumed efficiently within the village and they bind villagers together, easing the tensions and animosities that arise in living at close quarters.[28] Such debt is the fundamental expression of a political economy. Hesiod, however, appears to resist the creation of a claim against the future production of his own household, perhaps fearing that he will not be able to make the timely repayment his neighbor expects. Hesiod prefers to adhere to the monadic logic of the individual household (i.e., the subsistence economy). In Ascra the collective constraints of a political economy over the impulses of the subsistence economy again appear to be only weakly developed. Hesiod's admonitions against debt signal not the unchecked power of an overbearing elite or Ascra's integration within a complex regional system so much as the autonomy of the village and the low level of hierarchy and integration within its boundaries.

In sum, relationships between households in Hesiod's Ascra were based on a form of balanced reciprocity. Good relations among neighbors were highly valued, and the assistance available to Perses from Hesiod himself and from neighbors implies public sanctions to aid families in distress. But any right to subsistence attached to village membership remains highly qualified in the community depicted in *Works and Days*. Giving is a discrete, one-to-one transaction linking individual households and it entails a finite expectation of repayment in at least an amount equal to the original donation. Sharing among households in Hesiod's Ascra is not comprehended within a complex system of reciprocities, within a developed political economy. The movement away from strict balanced reciprocity and towards the regime of generalized reciprocity observable in the extended period between loan and repayment does mark, however, a compromise of the individual household's autarky in the interest of the community. Even

28. See, e.g., Johnson and Earle 1987, 79–80; Sahlins 1972, 123–39.

at that, though, the form of reciprocity described by Hesiod offers a mini-mal mechanism of subsistence insurance. Lacking generalized reciprocity, some form of regularized social storage within the limits of the commu-nity, there is no truly integrative mechanism at work. Not only has the bubble of Thespiae's political economy not expanded to enclose the village of Ascra, but Ascra's local institutions evidence little development beyond the boundaries of the subsistence economy. The political integration asso-ciated with the emergence of a political economy is at any rate absent. What level of social stratification could such a simple system of interobligation support?

Hierarchy

If Ascra lies outside the political economy controlled by the *basilēes* of Thespiae, what is the extent of its own, local social stratification? As I have just pointed out, the self-sufficiency of the Ascran household and the rela-tively weak obligations among neighbors do not offer a strong foundation for hierarchy, but Ascra, as a permanent agricultural village, can hardly be expected to exhibit the sort of egalitarianism we might encounter among a group of foragers. First I will outline the statuses that receive explicit ac-knowledgment from Hesiod. Then, I will examine the material basis for status distinctions in Ascra. Lastly, I will return to the question of the *basi-leus:* Did Ascra have its own, local *basileus?*

Homer presents the men whom he designates as *aristoi, kaloi, esthloi,* among other labels, as a group formally distinct from those he regards as *kakoi* or *deiloi.* The social context for these terms is the distance between *basileus* and *dēmos* familiar from the Homeric polis, where their use be-comes implicated within an ideology of *genos,* of birth, unknown to *Works and Days* (see Edwards 1993, 60–66). In contrast, it is the opposition of prosperity and destitution, themselves direct reflections of how hard a man is willing to work, that provides the reference points for Hesiod's ethical terms. Hesiod does on occasion use terms such as *esthlos, agathos, kakos,* or *deilos* in reference to moral quality alone (*W&D* 191–93, 316, 346–48, e.g.). The social grounding for these terms, however, is provided by the contrast of diligence and shiftlessness. So much is made explicit in the sweat that the gods have placed before the path of *aretē* in contrast to the ease of the path of *kakotēs* (*W&D* 287–90). Similarly, it is just before Hesiod re-peats his counsel to get to work (*W&D* 295–99) that we are told that the *esthlos* listens to good advice. These terms do not refer to class or status group as something formally distinct and homogeneous over the long term. For Hesiod's community they relate in the first place to prosperity, which Hesiod, of course, links directly to how hard one works.[29] For Hesiod these ethical terms do not imply an inherited or permanent status. They do not serve as the independent variable, so to speak, from which other mental, physical, and social traits can with probability be inferred. In *Works and Days* one's status varies with one's success as a farmer.

What Hesiod tells us in *Works and Days* suggests three distinct statuses, although we cannot be certain that an Ascran would have organized his social world in precisely this way. In the first place it is possible to distinguish between the *dmōs*, usually rendered "slave," and the non-*dmōs*. Within the latter category of the free we must again distinguish between the *thēs*, or thete, and the non-thete, the self-sufficient farmer. To consider the first group, "slaves," it can be noted that Hesiod does not use words formed on the stem *doul-*, more closely associated with strict chattel slavery, but only *dmōs* and its variant *dmōios*. Morris proposes that "dependent" might be a better designation for the *dmōs* than "slave." The phrase *Athēnaiēs dmōios* (*W&D* 430) for a craftsman perhaps supports a rendering of "dependent" rather than "slave."[30]

Dmōs/dmōios occurs on eight occasions in *Works and Days*. Leaving aside the *Athēnaiēs dmōios* mentioned above, five of the seven remaining attestations refer to the tasks of planting, harvesting, and winnowing (*W&D* 430, 459, 573, 597, 608). At *Works and Days* 502–503 Hesiod recommends that one's slaves be commanded to build a *kaliē* while it is still summer. *Kaliē* here most likely denotes some sort of shelter for the winter months, but something less than a proper house—a shed or hut. Later, Hesiod specifies the propitious day for giving instructions to slaves (cf. West ad 765), reviewing their work, and passing out rations (*W&D* 765–67). While these last two passages suggest that the *dmōs* might dwell separately from his master, the *kaliē* and dispensation of rations do not support the view that he is a farmer, with house and land, who has been forced into dependency upon a more well-to-do neighbor, having become something like a serf or even a sharecropper. The *dmōs* does not appear to head an *oikos* of his own.

Admittedly it is easier to enumerate questions about status as a *dmōs* than it is to enumerate facts about that status. How does one fall into this state? Is the *dmōs* a war captive, a failed Ascran farmer, or just some un-

29. Contra, see Zanker 1986, 26–27.
30. Morris 1987, 177–79. West ad loc. compares *Mousaōn therapōn* at *Th.* 100 to *Athēnaiēs dmōios*.

fortunate captured and held in bondage? Can the *dmōs* own property or head a household. Is he property himself, a thing to be sold, exchanged, or given? Is this status permanent, is it inherited? Is status as a *dmōs* something that might be assumed voluntarily as an alternative to destitution? Certainly, Hesiod never suggests that Perses is in danger of becoming a *dmōs*. What percentage of Ascra's population did *dmōes* comprise? Can this status be said to embody a true social class? Is the *dmōs* a permanent alien in the community, cut off even from acquiring kinship relations through marriage or parenthood? In the face of these questions and others we can only say that Hesiod's *dmōes* were agricultural laborers constrained by some form of dependency upon the farmer for whom they worked.

The question at hand is less how the institution of slavery was organized in Ascra than what the presence of slave labor there tells us about hierarchy in the community. Yet, to deal with the issue of hierarchy, it will be necessary to consider the general question of organization. Meillassoux (1991, 35–40), whose study focuses upon the institution of slavery on the African continent, makes the point that the presence of slaves in a society does not make of it a slave society in the strict sense. In fact, within Meillassoux's account, Ascra would not appear to qualify as a slave society. That social formation is characterized by the presence of a fundamental boundary drawn between slaves, on the one hand, and, on the other, the free population, including a class of masters whom slaves preserve from the need to work. The slave, moreover, by definition stands outside all forms of kin relation (Meillassoux 1991, 14–15, 23–26, 85–86, 99–100). Meillassoux's slave society, because it depends upon the labor of slaves, must, in order to reproduce itself, secure a steady, reliable supply of captive labor. Meeting this need requires the services of both a martial aristocracy to engage in the warfare through which slaves are acquired as well as a merchant class to transport and trade in these captives. Stratification and centralization, of course, accompany the warfare and trade upon which this social formation depends, and the slave society consequently exhibits a relatively high degree of complexity (Meillassoux 1991, 39–40). The individual master-slave relation, moreover, is embedded within an enduring, institutionalized relationship between two distinct societies, the one plundering the demographic resources of the other in order to secure a supply of human labor (Meillassoux 1991, 43–53, 72, 75–76, 85–86, 95–96).

Meillassoux contrasts the slave society with the simpler social formation of the domestic society. Here again slaves remain completely isolated from kin relations and are not permitted to reproduce themselves socially, but the domestic economy of this society has not been undermined by insertion within a larger market. Under these circumstances the slave is exploited, but the supply of slaves is too unreliable to permit the consolidation of a discrete social class of slaves or for distinctive social institutions to form around them (Meillassoux 1991, 23–26, 33–40).[31] Under the domestic economy the slave labors side by side with other members of the household and what he produces remains in the community, mixed with the production of others, and distributed according to prevailing norms. Under the domestic society the labor of slaves is not employed to produce an exchange value, a commodity (35–40).

Within the framework of Meillassoux's model Ascra corresponds more closely to the domestic society than to the more complex slave society. The strongest evidence is Hesiod's testimony that the farmers of Ascra work in their own fields at the sides of their slaves, and that such labor is not stigmatized in *Works and Days* as something slavish and unfit for a free man. Hesiod, moreover, betrays no ambition to free himself from the need to work by acquiring more slaves. It can also be noted that the mode of trade described by Hesiod is not adequate to providing Ascrans with a sustained supply of slaves, nor do Ascrans appear to be employing slaves to produce commodities, items intended for exchange rather than use. It is certainly the case that the presence of slaves in Ascra creates a status hierarchy, a degree of stratification, but in terms of Meillassoux's model of slavery, this feature of Hesiod's village does not in itself imply a high degree of complexity, such as characterizes the full-blown slave society.

Finley (1980, 67–77) draws the same distinction as Meillassoux between a society that owns slaves and a slave society. In his view the latter social formation emerges in Greece only in the Classical period, preeminently in Athens, where it presupposed (1) a concentration of land holdings, (2) development of trade, markets, and commodity production, and (3) the unavailability of a readily coercible local labor force (Finley 1980, 77–86; cf. Garlan 1988, 37–84). Garlan argues, moreover, that for the society depicted by Homer the status of the *dmōs* is not defined through an opposition to non-slave. Rather, the line between elite and non-elite is a more significant distinction for Homeric society, leaving the position of the *dmōs* somewhat ambiguous in relation to other low-status individuals—thete and *therapōn*, for example (Garlan 1988, 30–31, 35–37). Yet Homer attests to more numerous categories of servile labor than Hesiod by far, a reflection of the role of elite households in Homer's poetry (Thalmann

31. Finley (1980, 77), however, denies that slaves in ancient Greece or Rome ever comprised a *social* class.

1998, 49–67), and the picture of Laertes working side by side with his slaves conveys a far different impression in the *Odyssey* from that of the Ascran farmer walking out to the fields in the company of his slaves (Edwards 1993b, 63–66).

This evidence suggests that the distance separating slave and free in Homer's world is less than what is observed in the slave societies of the Classical era, but greater than in the village of Ascra. I suspect that the supply of slaves to Ascra was irregular, dependent upon taking the occasional wanderer captive, taking in victims of famine, perhaps enslaving prisoners of war, or through barter (cf. Meillassoux 1991, 33–35). I would speculate that the attraction of such unfree labor for farmers in a village like Ascra would have been two-fold. Meillassoux (1991, 86–96) demonstrates that the profits of slavery derive from the savings the slave society realizes when it acquires laborers in whose rearing it needed to make no investment. Gaining a laborer after he has reached the point at which he is able to produce a surplus above his own subsistence needs could offer considerable advantage to a household. Additionally, as I will detail more fully in a moment, an attraction of servile labor may also have been the control it provided the farmer over the fertility of the slave and so over the ratio of producers to consumers within the household (cf. Meillassoux 1991, 86–89).

To be compelled to work in the interest of another rather than for oneself, to be held as the property of another, to exist as a permanent outsider in one's community (cf. Finley 1980, 67–75)—if these characteristics of the chattel slave do indeed all apply to Hesiod's *dmōs*, they establish a status group defined by its inequality with other members of the community. While some are in a position to accumulate wealth over the course of a lifetime, others are not able to do this and may not even have the opportunity to found households at all. But the institution of slavery does not in itself imply a significant degree of stratification or centralization for a community.

Hesiod makes one reference to the *thēs* (*W&D* 602), alongside the *erithos*. In the *Iliad erithoi* show up as laborers on the *temenos* of a *basileus* (*Il.* 18.550, 560, but cf. *Od.* 6.32). The Homeric *thēs* works for the term of a year for a specified *misthos* (*Il.* 21.444–45). The insulting offer made by Eurymachus to Odysseus to become his *thēs* (*Od.* 18.357–61), the pairing of thetes with *dmōes* (*Od.* 4.644), and Achilles' preference to be the thete of a poor man rather than king of the dead all suggest that the *thēs* occupies a low status. The simplest assumption is that Hesiod's *thēs* and the *erithos* represent community members reduced to working in exchange for a *misthos*. It seems most likely that these would be individuals from households possessing inadequate improved land and livestock to support themselves. A household experiencing difficulty with day-to-day subsistence needs would probably be unable to spare the labor necessary to prepare new land for cultivation. A more effective option would be to work for another household experiencing a labor shortage.

A thete, then, is someone who works on someone else's land in exchange for a wage. The Homeric evidence, moreover, attests to social inequality between thete and master. Aside, however, from questions of status, thetage can also be viewed as a mechanism for efficiently distributing labor among households of the village in response to the specific ratio of available land to available labor within individual households. As Gallant has shown, a major problem facing households was achieving a favorable balance between members able to produce more than they consumed and members, such as the very old or very young, who consumed more than they produced.[32] In the course of its typical life cycle a family progresses through periods of a favorable ratio of producers to consumers and periods of an unfavorable ratio—that is, periods of surplus and periods of inadequate labor. As family size fluctuates, moreover, so does the amount of land needed to feed it. The sensitivity of the ratio between workers and consumers in a household may explain Hesiod's advice that the *erithos* have no children of her own and that the thete be without an *oikos*, a household of his own.[33] Not only would such workers find their attentions more focused upon the needs of their employer's house but they would also make smaller demands upon the resources of his household since the labor they supply is balanced against only a single mouth to feed. I have already suggested that a similar logic may be at work in the case of slave labor.

The two household ratios, that between workers and consumers and that between food needs and available land, permit the construction of at least four different scenarios: (1) a favorable ratio of labor (workers to consumers) and enough land (or more) for household needs; (2) a favorable ratio of labor but inadequate land; (3) an unfavorable ratio of labor but enough land (or more) to meet nutritional needs; and (4) an unfavorable ratio of labor and insufficient land. Of course, according to Gallant's model a single household might cycle through several of these scenarios over time. A household of type 1 remains self-sufficient and in a position to pro-

32. Gallant 1991, 11–33, 78–92, 101–12; cf. Sahlins 1972, 69–74, 87–92 on the variations in the amount of labor available to households.

33. This seems to me the most likely way to take *thēta t' aoikon poieisthai* (602). So West 1978, ad loc. and Burford 1993, 187. For a year as the term for which labor is hired, see *Il.* 21.444–45 and Solon 13.47–48 (W); cf. *epēetanos* at *Od.* 18.360. Contra, see Tandy 1997, 210.

duce a surplus. This might represent Hesiod's ideal. Such a household could also send out a member to work as thete though it might not have a strong motive to do so. A household of type 2, controlling adequate labor to meet its needs but not enough land, would be the most likely source of a thete. A household of type 3 would be most likely to take in a thete since its basic problem is a labor shortage. Households of type 4 are in a bind. Their insufficient labor might still be adequate to work the land they possess, but its produce will not meet the family's nutritional needs. Or, it might not even have enough labor to work its already insufficient land. Hiring a thete might be no better than the lesser of two evils in such a case.

Any household with more labor than needed to work its land might wish to benefit from this surplus by hiring out a family member to a household experiencing a labor shortage, but this would be especially true of a household that is short of land. Households of type 2 and type 3, then, would naturally participate in an exchange: the one contributing labor and the other in effect contributing land. Hesiod's advice to bring in extra labor during planting season (*W&D* 441–47) attests to the availability of labor even during periods of seasonal time stress. Such individuals certainly would come from households with more workers than are needed to cultivate their own land. Putting a child at a neighbor's disposal on either a long-term or a short-term basis could have offered a household a means of reducing its own subsistence needs and even of bringing in additional resources in the form of a *misthos*. Thetage would thus represent an attempt by the thete's household to benefit from its labor resources when they exceed the demands of available land and an attempt by the household of the master to expand production beyond the limits imposed by its own labor resources.

Within a given community the gap separating households with enough land (or more) and those with too little can be substantial or slight. In the context of the Homeric polis, for example, it seems unlikely that the son of a *basileus* would labor as a thete for a household from the *dēmos*. But in a village setting, in which the distance between the prosperous and the poor is far less pronounced, such as I believe Hesiod's Ascra to be, it is not inconceivable that a relatively prosperous family might hire out a member as a *thēs* even with a relatively poorer family. Indeed, Hesiod's injunction that adequate compensation (*misthos*: *W&D* 370) must be offered to a *philos* could be taken to indicate that such labor arrangements operate with relative indifference to the status hierarchy. The question I am raising here is whether the *thēs* represents a social status in Ascra or simply a form of labor. While the thete may belong to a landless class constrained to toil for a *misthos* on the land of others, comparable to the Athenian census class of thetes, thetage might equally represent a labor agreement entered into by families differing chiefly in their respective ratios of labor to land. This remains a matter of speculation, but certainly Hesiod provides no evidence in *Works and Days* requiring that thetage represent a fixed and permanent social status for a household.

To return briefly to the topic of slavery, the use of servile labor suggests the presence of households of type 3, possessing more land than they can manage to cultivate on their own. Hesiod at *Works and Days* 376–77 advises that there be only a single son since in that way the household's wealth will increase. According to one interpretation, this passage warns against the division of the family land and possessions between multiple heirs. If Ascrans did seek to avoid the division of patrimony through restraints on production of heirs, then slavery might have complemented such a practice by supplying labor without making further claims against the household's wealth.

It is clear from the preceding discussion that land is related to the issue of social status at least insofar as thetage represents a social status. It is worth noting, however, that Hesiod never explicitly indicates that poverty is due to an insufficient holding or that prosperity is the result of the quantity or quality of a family's land. He attributes poverty and prosperity rather to the energy with which one cultivates the land one does possess. Yet the institution of thetage supplies indirect evidence regarding land tenure since it would seem to be best explained, as I have suggested, in the first place by reference to the relations of a family's holdings to its subsistence needs and in the second by reference to the ratio of a family's holdings to its labor force.

Hesiod claims title to his plot as a private holding, his *klēros*, and it is inheritable (*W&D* 35–39). His reference to farmers cultivating different regions (*W&D* 388–93) reinforces the impression of settled farmers cultivating fixed plots. Land, moreover, is alienable (*W&D* 342). Ascra itself, finally, as a permanent settlement, indicates permanently held fields. Of course, individual households would not bother to lay claim to specific plots unless it were possible for value to accumulate in the land. This certainly took the form of the vineyards to which Hesiod refers. Plow agriculture, moreover, requires that fields be cleared of stones, stumps, and roots and that they be contoured for plowing, proper drainage, and to avoid erosion. Aside from value due to investment, one plot can hold greater value than another because of such features as its proximity to the settlement, the quality of its soil, its slope, exposure, ground water, or the amount of rain-fall it receives.

It is not contrary to expectation that in a sedentary, agricultural com-munity improved land should have a value. That does not entail, however, that unimproved arable is in short supply. Nor should we assume that every family experiencing a shortage of land would immediately devote its energies to preparing new land for cultivation. While bringing new land under the plow adds to the long-term wealth of a family, the effort required to do so subtracts labor from the immediate task of feeding itself. House-holds of type 4, with inadequate land to meet their subsistence needs and with an unfavorable ratio of workers to consumers, would not be in a posi-tion to invest labor in preparing new land for cultivation and might find it difficult to work such land even if they had it. Households of type 2, with a favorable ratio of consumers to producers but possessing insufficient land, might still find thetage preferable to clearing additional land since that in effect gives the family access to another family's resources without the ini-tial time lag and investment required to bring unimproved land under cul-tivation. This would be especially true for a family that did not anticipate a long-term shortage of land. I think that the household most likely to de-vote labor to clearing new fields would be those of type 1 or 2, enjoying a surplus of labor, which are also anticipating in the near future a long-term increase in subsistence needs. For example, a family with several sons who have yet to marry and begin producing children of their own might prefer to invest in preparing new land for cultivation.

While Homer presents thetage as a relationship governed by a status hierarchy, it is clear that it presupposes a specific ratio between a family's supplies of land and labor. Hesiod does not clarify whether for *Works and Days* thetage, as a labor relation between families experiencing different labor and land conditions, is structured within any more comprehensive status distinction than that between the more and less prosperous families of the moment. One might be reasonably inclined to attach a status dis-tinction to the institution, but, as I have indicated, it is at any rate possible that a wealthier family might send a thete to a poorer. Additionally, under certain circumstances a family might find thetage as a solution to a land shortage preferable to bringing new land under cultivation. As for the land itself, we see that land can have value and that a family can experience a shortage of land even in a setting of plentiful unimproved land. It follows, moreover, that the fact that some households might be short of land does not in itself imply that land has been concentrated in the hands of a few large holders or that unimproved land is not available.

The most significant status distinction to which Hesiod attests is that between the *dmōes* and the free population. The difference separating the thete from the non-thete is more slippery. But even if we assume that thetage does not comprise a formal social status, it would nevertheless be more attractive to households whose land does not suffice for their needs and that are by that measure less prosperous. What Hesiod presents in *Works and Days* is not a community lacking in stratification, but one in which the upper stratum appears to be relatively large and undifferentiated. We see subaltern groups in the form of the *dmōes* and possibly the thetes, but Hesiod identifies no distinct elite. On the top of the pile, there are only farmers, a group able to accommodate both Hesiod and his ne'er-do-well brother. The hierarchization within this group cannot be conceptualized in terms of formal social statuses.

A system of hierarchy, distinguishing a primitive elite from the rest, does in fact function within this latter group, but it does not resemble the hierarchy of *basileus* and *dēmos*. Within the relationships of the neighborhood the social phenomena of sharing and of competition for prosperity result in a sort of hierarchy that itself in turn reinforces sharing and competition. That is, the ethical hierarchy of the successful and less successful farmer structured by the good *eris* operating among neighbors finds concrete expression in the hierarchical relationship between lender and borrower. I have already noted in this connection the role of the good *eris* in establishing social standing (pp. 91–92). In the midst of a passage praising the advantages of hard work Hesiod specifies the sources of status and prestige in the community:

εἰ δέ κεν ἐργάζῃ, τάχα σε ζηλώσει ἀεργός
πλουτέοντα· πλούτῳ δ' ἀρετὴ καὶ κῦδος ὀπηδεῖ· (312–13)

If you get to work, soon a shiftless man will envy you
as you grow prosperous; for prestige [aretē] and honor [kudos] accompany prosperity.

Hesiod urges Perses that if he gets down to work, the shiftless man, the equivalent for him of the poor man, will envy/admire *(zēlōsei:* 312) Perses as he becomes wealthy since (δ': 313) prestige/standing (*aretē:* 313), and honor/reputation (*kudos:* 313) accompany wealth. Prosperity won from labor, then, is the foundation for the *aretē* and *kudos* that place a man before the eyes of his neighbors. *Aretē* occurs in only one other passage in *Works and Days* (286–92), that contrasting a road of *kakotēs* (wickedness, evil) with a road of *aretē* (prestige, excellence). The ease and accessibility of the former road (287–88) and the sweat (*hidrōta:* 289, cf. 290–91) placed before the latter repeat the contrast encountered at lines 312–13 of indolent poverty versus industrious wealth spanned by the envy and admiration directed by the impoverished man toward the prosperous. Here again Hesiod asserts that there is an *aretē*—reputation, standing, dignity—for the man who has gained a measure of prosperity from tireless labor expended upon his fields.[34] A similar ensemble of associations appears at line 319, where Hesiod contrasts the shame *(aidōs)* that belongs to poverty *(anolbiē)* with the confidence *(tharsos),* or even "insolence" (so West ad loc.), that accompanies wealth *(olbōi).* Even if *tharsos* is understood as a negative quality, a pitfall of wealth, it refers nevertheless to the standing of the wealthy man in the community much as *aidōs* refers to the self-respect that the poor man cannot afford. Within the bounds of the neighborhood, authority, prestige, and celebrity accompany the prosperity of the successful farmer.[35]

The specific link between the prosperity of the successful farmer on the one hand and his prestige and authority in the community on the other, aside from the inherent attractiveness of wealth itself, stems from the obligations springing up between the well-to-do and their poorer neighbors. While the successful farmer wins *kudos* and *aretē* in the eyes of his neighbors, the failed farmer is pressed by need and is driven to ask his more prosperous neighbor for a loan to keep his household alive. In fact the same gaze that expresses envy and admiration for prosperity simultaneously conveys the need that the poor man has of a wealthier neighbor. This need comprises the concrete foundation for the standing and distinction of the successful farmer. This link between the admiration felt by the poor for the prosperous and the appeal made by the poor to the prosperous is evident in

34. West 1978, ad loc. is right, I think, to insist that *kakotēs* and *aretē* "are not 'vice' and 'virtue' but inferior and superior social standing, determined principally by material prosperity." But I believe that Hesiod did not distinguish sharply between the notions of virtue, hard work, and superior social standing. See also Verdenius's (1985) comment on 289.

35. Hesiod's concern with reputation is further evidenced by *W&D* 760–64. I think that Tandy (1997, 106–11, 135–37, 225–27) and Mele (1979, 50–51) misunderstand the intent of *W&D* 313. Hesiod is not complaining there about a degenerate world in which prestige and reputation follow wealth. He is rather celebrating through both wealth and standing the success that comes from hard work on the farm. The observation that reputation follows wealth means that villagers approve of diligent farmers, not that a mercantile class is corrupting accepted values as it displaces an aristocracy.

an implicit equation drawn between the two at lines 473–78. Hesiod sums up the satisfaction Perses will take in a good harvest with the boast that "you will not look (*augaseai:* 478) towards others, but another man will be in need (*kechrēmenos:* 478) of you." The gaze of admiration, which Perses will not now need to direct at anyone else in view of the status his new success brings him, corresponds to the need others will have of him because of that same prosperity. The gaze of admiration *(augaseai)* and the sense of need *(seo . . . kechrēmenos)* serve as virtual synonyms in *Works and Days*. Perses will not look upon others with admiration since he has no need of their help; the poor man's request for aid from Perses will be expressed in the first place through an envious gaze. So, Hesiod warns Perses only a few lines later, in the event of a bad harvest no one will look at him *(pauroi de se thēēsontai:* 482).[36] In the poor man's gaze, expressing both his request for aid as well as his admiration for someone who has made it, Hesiod merges the role of the prosperous as patrons of the needy with the status they enjoy in the community. The same admiring gaze that rewards prosperity with *kudos* and *aretē* can serve as well to solicit the help that underwrites the local prestige of the successful farmer.

To put it bluntly, then, the prosperous in effect purchase their prestige through their capacity to make loans to less successful neighbors. I suggest that assistance, even if it must be paid back in full, places an obligation upon its recipient which can be balanced out only when the initial aid has been repaid and a reciprocal loan has subsequently been extended to the original creditor. If over the long run assistance between households should always move in the same direction, then there would result a cumulative debt of gratitude in spite of regular repayments. Thus, if Hesiod has already extended support to Perses' household, then Perses' threat now to turn to the kings in order to get another share of the *klēros* would certainly be seen as a betrayal of the gratitude owed by Perses, making Hesiod's outraged indignation all the more understandable. This scenario harmonizes what Hesiod tells us of the nature of reciprocity and exchange in his community with what he tells us of status and authority. This is, of course, a scantier foundation for hierarchy than the obligations fostered by a regime of generalized reciprocity, but the principle is the same.[37]

36. Proclus explains *augaseai* with *hōs epikourias deomenos*. Regarding this gaze of admiration and reverence see pp. 91–92 and Walcot's comments 1970, 82–83 apropos of this passage on the convergence of practical advantage and social prestige in the accumulation of wealth.

37. As Sahlins (1972, 133) puts it: "generosity is a manifest imposition of debt, putting the recipient in a circumspect and responsive relation to the donor during

In the interest of clarity I should offer two qualifications at this point. First, words such as "wealth," "prosperity," or "success" can easily suggest an economic distance between households beyond what I have in mind. As will become clearer by and by, I envision Ascra as a community of subsistence farmers in which distinctions in wealth are inadequate to support anything but the most primitive stratification or elite status. For Hesiod the line between prosperity and shortage is significant, but in practical terms the distinction boils down to how much grain one has locked away in one's corn crib; the sort of treasure amassed by a Homeric *basileus,* and the distance separating such a figure from a common member of the demos, belong to another social universe altogether. Second, it is solely the prosperity won from hard labor on one's farm that Hesiod prizes. The kings, for example, would do better to dine on the impoverished fare of asphodel and mallow (*W&D* 40–41) than consume the gifts of those currying favor with them.

I have already noted (pp. 94–95) that the banquets to which Hesiod refers, probably occasions for sacrifices to the gods, can be understood in terms of ceremonialism. Hesiod recommends inviting one's *philoi (ton phileont')* and one's neighbors (*W&D* 341–42). The ceremony of the meal offered by the host to his *philoi* and common worship of the deity serve to reinforce individual relations between the host and his various guests. Ceremonies can be used in this way to make alliances within the community, to create networks of exchange partners, and to acquire personal prestige. The sort of gathering Hesiod describes here, however, does not function to unify and express the identity of an entire village, let alone link separate villages; rather it binds together informally a collection of households from within the village. It does not express the intention of the village to celebrate its own identity or of a leader to assert his preeminence over the community as a whole, but the desire of an individual household to strengthen its ties with neighboring households and to build its reputation.[38]

The *kudos* and *aretē* available to members of Hesiod's community have little to do with inherited excellence or with heroic deeds on the battlefield. Rather they depend upon the vagaries of farming. Hesiod's confidence that even Perses could readily raise himself to prosperity demonstrates Hesiod's awareness of the mercurial nature of success on the farm and, therefore, of status within the neighborhood. The mutability of human fortune and

all that period the gift is unrequited. The economic relation of giver-receiver is the political relation of leader-follower." Cf. Schusky 1989, 81–83.

38. See Johnson and Earle 1987, 102, 159, 196–97, 202.

fame serves, after all, as the central theme of the poem's proem.[39] Hesiod's cautious, even stingy attitude towards sharing testifies to the narrow margins upon which prosperity depends. All that Hesiod has to say about the hardships of survival on the land would indicate that even the successful farmers of Ascra possessed from one year to the next only a small surplus available for loans to neighbors. By "surplus" here I refer to what is in excess of that devoted to the needs of the household and can therefore be committed to the political economy to finance a career for the farmer as a man of *kudos* and *aretē*. Even a small surplus achieved consistently over the years would lead to a steady place among the local elite of Ascra.

Paul Halstead has in fact proposed that such a regular surplus, in this case produced intentionally, could have served as the mechanism in just this way for the appearance of an elite.[40] Hesiod provides no explicit testimony that a "normal surplus," regular over-production planned as a hedge against routine levels of crop failure, was a strategy employed by the farmers of Ascra, though I have already noted that the phrase *bios . . . epēetanos* (*W&D* 31; see p. 86) may refer to a surplus beyond what is required to see the household to the next harvest. Farmers practicing short fallow plow agriculture in semi-arid regions such as Greece characteristically aim to keep in storage a year's worth of food over and above what is needed to supply the household until the next harvest. Even failing such a surplus, however, the mere tendency of one farmer's plots to produce over the course of the years more than the immediate needs of his household would be enough to enable him to make the loans to less prosperous neighbors that would endow him before the community with *aretē* and *kudos*. If over the years loaner and debtor households tend to remain the same, loaner households could come to constitute a primitive elite.

Perhaps Hesiod's endless exhortations to work and the sure connection he establishes between *aretē* and relentless toil are to be understood in this light. While Hesiod views work in the first place as the best form of subsistence insurance available for his own household, beyond that, production of a surplus exceeding the immediate needs of the family provides the means of occupying a position of prestige and influence in the community.

---

39. *W&D* 280–85 or 320–26 can be taken as a further development of this theme first announced in the proem.

40. See Halstead 1989, 73–80 and Bintliff 1994, 221–22. Not all of Halstead's argument seems applicable to Hesiod (see my further discussion below in the section on Hesiod's agricultural regime: pp. 135–39), but the proposed connection between storage and hierarchy is illuminating. Cf. the discussion by Halstead and Jones 1989, 55; Johnson and Earle 1987, 161–65; and van Wees 1998, 25–47.

Sahlins (1972, 65–68, 135–37, 206–209) describes how in societies where rank is not so firmly established as to be inherited but must be achieved by successive leaders, such "auto-exploitation" of his own household by the aspiring Big Man serves as a starting mechanism to make possible the displays of generosity through which nobility is accumulated. Yet, while Sahlins considers auto-exploitation the weakest basis for leadership, he nonetheless shows it functioning within a regime of generalized reciprocity, which, once it takes hold, can begin to operate to the Big Man's profit, enabling him to consolidate and even extend his authority. Hesiod's Ascra, however, does not appear to operate at the level of even Sahlin's weakest case. The balanced reciprocity described by Hesiod cannot command the sort of obligation created under generalized reciprocity and as a consequence it remains inadequate for creating lasting and well-articulated hierarchy, the sort of self-sustaining authority enjoyed by a *basileus*, for example. The form of balanced reciprocity observed in *Works and Days*, with its limited capacity for redistributing the community's produce or for creating enduring obligations, might produce rather a community characterized by continuous, tight competition among successful households for superior standing, a sustained state of *eris* pitting neighbor against neighbor as each strives to gain greater *kudos* and *aretē*.

In the opening lines of *Works and Days* Hesiod describes how the good *eris* stirs even the shiftless man to work when he sees how his neighbor grows prosperous as he plows, plants, and sets his house in order (*W&D* 20–24). In Hesiod's Ascra a man with ambitions to be respected must discipline himself, work hard, and produce good harvests to be stored away in his *kaliē*. His example sparks *eris* among those in the community who wish to equal or surpass his *kudos* and *aretē*. Such prosperous households can expect to be called upon for assistance by neighbors of lower standing, whose needs exceed what their own households have produced, and who must look up to the families that can help them. This is the political economy of Ascra. No strong political integration or stable social stratification can emerge in a community in which the power of the atomized subsistence economies has yielded so little to the interests of the political economy.

By this reconstruction Hesiod's community risks looking like the society of the *Odyssey*'s Cyclopes or the community of discrete monads composing Sahlins' domestic mode of production.[41] The "commonality" inher-

---

41. As Sahlins characterizes this "ideal type" (1972, 74–75), "The domestic mode anticipates no social or material relations between households except that they are alike. It offers society only a constituted disorganization. . . . The social

ent in the concept of community appears to be to a large degree missing. But such a comparison would go too far since *Works and Days* does reveal the outline of a primitive system of exchange based upon a form of balanced reciprocity. Direct, reciprocal exchange, its transactions of giving and repaying separated by a certain passage of time, permits one household to convert its surplus into a claim against the surplus of another household in the near-term future. This rudimentary mechanism of social storage, moreover, supports an equally rudimentary hierarchy within the village. It may be that we discern in Hesiod's Ascra a community evolving towards a regime of generalized reciprocity, able to induce greater interdependence and a steeper hierarchy. So much is suggested by the delay tolerated between accepting a loan of food from a neighbor and paying it back. That is, Ascra may be moving towards a greater complexity under which its boundaries will be defined and its membership fixed by the limits of a *basileus*'s generosity, the expanding bubble of a political economy. As it is, however, Hesiod presents a picture of a group of householders exploiting their own families in order to compete for status as men of influence within the village. None has succeeded in gaining preeminence over the others and establishing himself as a village headman. This failure may be due not in the least degree to the fact that the majority of Ascra's inhabitants have up to this point, at least, foreseen no compelling advantage from the costs that generalized reciprocity and greater complexity will impose on them. Ascrans have resisted the processes of centralization and stratification, the emergence of a *basileus,* since they do not consider the benefits of such leadership worth the troubles it brings. We confront, then, in Ascra a somewhat unstable group of men of influence—a council of elders perhaps—who are locked in close competition among themselves but who taken together comprise an incipient elite for the village.

We must assume that the level of complexity constitutive of the polity

---

economy is fragmented into a thousand petty existences, each organized to proceed independently of the others and each dedicated to the homebred principle of looking out for itself. . . . Nor is any higher cause entertained by the household's access to productive resources, or again by the economic priorities codified in domestic pooling. . . . Divided thus into so many units of self-concern, functionally uncoordinated, production by the domestic mode has all the organization of the so many potatoes in a certain famous sack of potatoes" (Sahlins 1972, 95). Max Weber (1978, 360–63), in fact, briefly describes a type of community comprised of an autonomous neighborhood in which the regularly occurring exception of interhousehold loans responds to unexpected crises and provides the basis for hierarchy. Cf. the discussion of neighborhood communities by Radermacher 1918, 252–59 and Johnson and Earle 1987, 20–21.

depicted by Hesiod reflects both the needs and the resources of a remote and sparsely populated valley as Greece emerged from the Dark Age. Yet such a social formation was undoubtedly too fragile to withstand the pressures that could be exerted upon it by the nascent polis as the Archaic period gathered momentum. Their *kudos* and *aretē* placed a relatively anemic power in the hands of this fluid village elite. While Hesiod can threaten, cajole, entreat, and preach to Perses, it is clear enough that, once he has cut him off, persuasion is his sole means of turning Perses from the "kings."

THE KINGS (*BASILĒES*)

I have already argued from a survey of the references to the *basilēes* in *Works and Days* that Hesiod locates them outside the village, in the polis of Thespiae, and that from there they are able to exert only limited influence over Ascra, which remains outside Thespiae's political economy. The question remains, however, whether Ascra might not have had its own local leader. There is after all a growing consensus that the *basileus* was already a ubiquitous fixture in Greek settlements of the Dark Age, making it a reasonable expectation to find such a figure in a village of the early Archaic period.[42] Bintliff (1994, 213) observes of Dark Age settlements that "with abundant resources and merely a shortage of manpower to make full use of them, with long-distance trade reduced to a minimum, with the disappearance of kings, bureaucrats and taxes, one would expect Dark Age society to return to a state of social equality, with political authority being reduced to the joint decisions of adult males in autonomous hamlets or farm clusters." He goes on to argue, however, that this established view must now be revised in view of several factors: the continuous occupation of certain important sites from Mycenean times through the Dark Age; the differentiation of Dark Age sites into larger and smaller communities by the eighth century in an increasingly competitive landscape; and the discovery in some of the excavated sites from the Dark Age and early Archaic period of a relatively large building, interpreted as the house of a village leader (Bintliff 1994, 213–20).[43] All of this points to the presence of formal leadership in Dark Age settlements.

42. See, e.g., Bintliff 1982, 107–8; Garnsey and Morris 1989, 99–101; Whitley 1991; Donlan and Thomas 1993, 65–66; Bintliff 1994, 219–21; and Thomas and Conant 1999, 46–59.

43. Cf. Snodgrass's (1993, 35–37) somewhat more skeptical discussion of the same problem.

Of course, the very survival of the word *basileus* itself, the title of a subordinate Mycenean official, attests to the continuance of some sort of apical leadership through the Dark Age. Mazarakis Ainian (1997) provides an exhaustive survey of the occurrence of large structures in Dark Age settlements, which he identifies as either cult buildings or rulers' dwellings. As Mazarakis Ainian (1997, 271–76, 286) acknowledges, the exact uses of these edifices are difficult to specify with certainty. But even if they are not the halls of *basilēes*, their size nevertheless bears unmistakable witness to the existence of some level of political economy in these settlements, since it is hard to imagine how they could have been built without broad participation of the community at large. Out of the total of 183 sites discussed, Mazarakis Ainian identifies 27 possessing a ruler's house.[44] Whether more Dark Age sites might yet reveal such a large structure, and especially whether Ascra might conceal such a ruler's house, remains an open question. Mazarakis Ainian concludes, however, that during the Dark Age there was "no uniform type of government in the Greek world" nor did sociopolitical evolution proceed at the same pace in all regions (1997, 270). The obvious context for the endurance of such an institution would be the larger, continuous settlements indicated by Bintliff. Yet, as Snodgrass (1993, 36) points out, these are the exceptions for the Dark Age, when settlements tend to be sparse, small, and relatively short-lived. While it appears much more certain now than formerly that there existed some sort of hierarchical leadership in the Dark Age, perhaps along the lines of a Big Man as suggested by Whitley (1991, 348–52), it is also becoming clearer that broad generalizations about Dark Age social organization are risky.

Just the same, I think many would be unwilling to concede that a Greek village of the late eighth or early seventh centuries, the conventional time frame for Hesiod's life, could lack a *basileus* or some other form of stratified leadership. It has been an assumption of my argument that a community will not bear the costs associated with hierarchy unless an elite fills a function which is somehow necessary for the community and through that role comes to exercise control over essential resources or activities. Otherwise there is no basis for elite power. Bintliff (1994, 221) acknowledges precisely this problem, pointing out that the availability of unexploited land during the Dark Age would have prevented elites from controlling commoners by monopolizing land and that the same circumstance would have enabled dissatisfied families simply to leave settlements if they fell into conflict with

44. See Mazarakis Ainian 1997, Maps 1 and 2 and Table X. See also Coldstream 1977, 303–12 and Thomas and Conant 1999, 38–39, 52–57, 94–97, 102–7.

a local *basileus*. In order to circumvent these obstacles to the emergence of hierarchy under the conditions of the Dark Age, Bintliff, following Halstead (above, p. 115), proposes that the most successful farming families invested in the acquisition of large herds. These supported in turn "extravagant feasting with meat and a status symbolism emphasizing large flocks" as a basis for status as a Big Man or *basileus*. I have already declared my agreement with this line of argumentation, though the general reciprocity that Bintliff appears to assume and the emphasis upon meat would correspond more closely to the polis of Homer than the village of Hesiod. The question remaining to be pondered, however, is how much hierarchy, how much real power would such feasting and ceremony support? Would such a figure be the peer of the Homeric *basileus*?

The Homeric *basileus* presents us with an extensive ensemble of social roles and status markers. He appears to serve in the first place as the community's leader in warfare. The *basileus* keeps a retinue of armed followers, a hall in which to entertain them with feasts, and horses, armor, and treasure. A herald attends the *basileus*, and his household includes a poet as well as numerous specialized slaves. The Homeric *basileus* also maintains relations with men of his rank from other cities, his *xeinoi*, based upon ceremonial gift-exchanges. Additionally, the *basileus* also tends to seek his wife from an elite family of another polis. The *basileus* is also distinct from his fellow citizens in possessing a genealogy, generally leading back to a divine progenitor. The *basileus*, finally, possesses a *temenos*, a grant of choice farmland from the community, and keeps extensive herds. These resources, along with his share of the booty from wars and pirating, permit the *basileus* to serve as the center of a redistributive economy integrating the community within a web of reciprocity and enriching his own household even further. If we evaluate the *basileus* in terms of Johnson and Earle's four categories of warfare, trade, technology, and risk management, he clearly fills multiple roles. I think it is correct to see him as primarily a war leader. But ownership of the large ships used for warfare place him in control of an important technology. The example of Mentes might additionally suggest for the *basileus* a role in long-distance trade that would also presuppose control of a ship. The redistributive economy he orchestrates serves, of course, as a means of risk management.

Ascra certainly cannot support the equal of the Homeric *basileus*. I have already shown that trade and risk management for Ascra are organized at the level of the individual household. Similarly, Hesiod does not refer to any technology—irrigation, terraced plots, ships, roads—that would require the organized effort of the community at large. If we wish to hypothesize some sort of apical leadership for Ascra, all that remains is some form of war leader. This is a likely choice in view of what I have argued about Ascra so far since such leadership is not based upon an extensive political economy, it is sporadic, and its authority is limited. Although Hesiod's complete silence about such a figure in Ascra hardly argues in favor of a war chief's presence, it equally precludes our ruling out his presence in the village. It may well be that in a poem devoted to the good *eris*, references to war, a form of the wicked *eris* (*W&D* 14–15), are blocked. The same simultaneous feelings of dependency and hostility felt by a smaller settlement towards a larger, more highly organized neighbor that could induce Ascrans to rely upon the *basilees* of Thespiae for judgments might also lead them to prefer their own leader in war. Yet if such an institution amounted to much more than an ad hoc willingness to follow a man whose courage and judgment were respected in the village, then we might expect to encounter in Ascra a group of warriors who consider themselves the *aristoi* and who distinguish themselves through the possession of weapons. But the poem makes no reference to displays of hospitality and luxury goods or to the fetishization of arms and horses. The only standard of merit Hesiod articulates in *Works and Days* is that of success in farming.

In the opening of Book 2 of the *Odyssey* Homer narrates a somewhat anomalous scene, an assembly at which there is no presiding *basileus*. This odd circumstance makes this scene of special interest to the question of social hierarchy in *Works and Days*. Aegyptius in fact observes at the outset that no such *agorē* has been summoned since Odysseus left for Troy (*Od.* 2.26–27). Aegyptius's comment suggests that it is an extraordinary event to call such a meeting in the absence of the legitimate *basileus*. Equally interesting, however, is the fact that in the absence of the *basileus* it is Aegyptius who rises to call the meeting to order, not Telemachus, the son of the absent *basileus*, nor one of the suitors, Antinous or Eurymachus, for example, who are all themselves *basilees* or the sons of *basilees*. Present at the assembly are the *laoi*, the commoners, to whom Telemachus appeals, his mother's suitors, and Telemachus himself. Just before Aegyptius arises to speak, we are told that Telemachus took his father's seat and the old men *(gerontes)* made way for him (*Od.* 2.13–14). This detail argues that within the assembly, the old men, the *gerontes*, comprised a distinct group, standing together around the seat of the *basileus*. Aegyptius, we are told, was bent with old age but knew countless things (*Od.* 2.16). Later, in the wake of Antinous's speech and at another crucial moment in the scene, it is Halitherses, also a *gerōn*, who rises to interpret Zeus's omen. Homer tells us that Halitherses surpasses his generation at the interpretation of birds

(*Od.* 2.157–59). Finally, following Telemachus's response to Eurymachus, Mentor, the *gerōn* to whom Odysseus entrusted the care of his household (*Od.* 2.225–27), initiates the final sequence in the scene by delivering a rebuke both to the suitors for their violence as well as to the *dēmos* for their indifference to the house of Odysseus.

The problem confronting the Ithacan polis is the absence of legitimate political authority because of the absence of Odysseus, its *basileus*. While Telemachus and the suitors speak as adversaries, accusing and defending before the assembly, it is old men, *gerontes*, presumably men of prestige and standing, who in Odysseus's absence quite naturally assume a role of authority in the community, officiating over the meeting in Odysseus's absence and attempting to guide the community towards a settlement. Such legitimate political authority as there remains in Ithaca is embodied in these elders of the polis, an informal Ithacan *gerousia*.[45] This scene implies that there is another tier of authority in the community, weaker than the *basileus*, but upon which the *basileus* relies, and ready to assert itself when a crisis occurs at the top. If the institution of the *basileus* represents a level of hierarchy and complexity beyond what exists in Hesiod's village, then this picture of a polity directed by the advice and influence of its old men may not be so far from what I have proposed for Ascra. If anything, the Odyssean version of this institution might be weaker than what would be found in Ascra since Ithaca's old men seek to defend the interest of their beloved *basileus* and, to do so, must face the intimidation of *basilēes* from other communities. In effect, I am suggesting that the temporary elimination of the head of the Ithacan body politic reveals beneath it its institutional predecessor. For Ascra, this form of hierarchy was all that there was, the leadership of Hesiod's men of *aretē*, a system not so far removed from Bintliff's characterization of now obsolete assumptions about the organization of Dark Age communities.

I gladly concede that the *basilēes* of *Works and Days* present uncertainties for my argument, and I will seem to some to have gotten myself out on a limb. While I remain confident that I have made the strongest case that the evidence allows, I cannot claim that the results are absolutely conclusive. I consider it highly unlikely that the *basilēes* sat in judgment in Ascra rather than Thespiae, but it is certainly not impossible. Yet even if that were granted, the only activity Hesiod permits them is judging cases on

---

45. Cf. *Il.* 18.497–508, where a group of *gerontes* sit in judgment of a dispute with no reference to a *basileus*.

a voluntary basis. He gives no hint of the mechanisms by which elites normally maintain themselves nor of the functions they perform. Likewise, my conclusions regarding hierarchy in Hesiod's Ascra are at odds with what I consider the emerging consensus that the *basileus,* a leader on the order of a Big Man or a chief, was a ubiquitous fixture in Greek settlements of this period. Even if we must rule out the influence of the *basilēes* of Thespiae over Ascra, could there not have been a local *basileus* in Ascra? Of course, the argument from silence, that Hesiod nowhere mentions such a figure, can never in itself be conclusive. The presence of such a figure in Ascra would not undermine my central thesis that the models of Solonian Athens and the peasant society are not compatible with the picture Hesiod provides of Ascra, and in some ways an Ascran *basileus* would actually strengthen my case. A local *basileus* in Ascra would serve to sharpen the boundary between Ascra and Thespiae that I claim Perses threatens to violate. Additionally, such a local leader would be more in line with what comparative data lead us to expect (see pp. 161–63). Yet I hesitate to propose such leadership for Ascra because Hesiod attests to no basis for its power. There is no evidence in *Works and Days* for an elite's control of land or a system of social storage or for regularized leadership in war. Clearly I do not deny that hierarchy and different levels of wealth existed in Ascra but only that Hesiod gives any indication that they reached such a degree as to be able to support a *basileus.* In larger settlements or in more densely populated regions a higher degree of stratification probably was the rule, but it does not appear to have been the case in Ascra.

CONCLUSIONS

I have already argued that Hesiod gives no evidence for the external relations between village and supra-local elite that are distinctive of peasant societies. It is this hierarchy of peasant and elite, with its exploitative relations, that is to a large extent responsible for the interdependence and the internal hierarchy of the peasant village. In terms of this internal organization I believe that Ascra again falls far below the level of complexity characteristic of the peasant village. I would hazard a guess that all traditional cultivators, not just peasants, seek to minimize risks and to maximize sources of potential assistance during crisis. Peasant societies are distinguished, rather, by the additional strain placed upon their means of subsistence through obligation to a non-farming elite. This burden reduces surpluses in good times and pushes households closer to the brink in bad times. The characteristic forms of cooperation within peasant villages are the product of this circumstance. Autonomous cultivators, such as those depicted in *Works and Days,* however, might well find the cost of such strategies in terms of hierarchy and preservation of household resources to outweigh their benefits.

The neighborhood as Hesiod characterizes it is too weak a structure to support a strong sense of boundary, a folklore of place, or a sense of village membership. Indeed, the absence of a well-developed generalized reciprocity among households (i.e., a system of social storage) leaves village membership bare of any large advantage and the village boundary with nothing much to enclose. Within the peasant village, hierarchy, the guarantee of subsistence, and intra-village cooperation each reinforces the others, and both the ideological integrity and the practical utility of the system they comprise are enhanced by the pressure exerted upon the community by an external elite. It is my contention that *Works and Days* displays no trace of this arrangement of institutions, customs, and forces.

Rather than a "community of grain," Hesiod portrays an independent farming village in which there are only minimal distinctions in wealth or social standing. Authority in Ascra is informal and based upon individual prestige, not on age, office, or some form of inherited status. Members of this community are not bound together by formal obligations of law, by accountability to a higher civic authority, or by relations of long-term economic dependence. Rather the looser ties of proximity and the mutual advantage of occasional cooperation are what make of Ascra a community. Hesiod gives us a glimpse of a community that is less complex, less stratified, and less integrated than what we observe even in Homer.

The absence of any evidence for cooperative labor during periods of seasonal time stress and the apparent weakness of the obligation to share could taken together indicate either a community surviving under conditions of terminal shortage or else circumstances of general security and availability of resources that obviate any need for regularized cooperation or sharing.[46] Hesiod's complacent optimism about the efficacy of hard work argues for the latter scenario. In my view the loose-knit character of Hesiod's community, its lack of hierarchy or centralization, and the low level of cooper-

---

46. Sahlins (1972, 127–33) describes such a breakdown of sharing within the community, leaving households reliant solely on their own resources, on the island of Tikopia during a severe famine. See also 101–23 where Sahlins contrasts two communities in terms of sharing and hierarchy.

ation among households result from its autonomy from outside control and its access to relatively plentiful resources.

Ian Morris (2000, 109–54) has argued that the democracy of the fifth century was based upon a "strong principle of equality," that is, a prevailing judgment that all members of a community are equally qualified to make decisions about the conduct of public affairs. Morris ties this political philosophy specifically to the class of citizens he terms the *mesoi* or "middling" men, who began to take form as the core of Greek communities in the eighth century. These middling citizens occupied the social zone between the elite, men of wealth, and the poor, those unable to support themselves from their own land. By the time of the democratic polis, however, middling status was more a matter of attitude and manner. The *mesos* exercised restraint, exemplified propriety, and did not permit his appetites to exceed moderation. The assertion of personal distinction and achievement was deferred by the middling citizen in favor of a celebration of the superiority and fame of the city, the collective identity of all *mesoi*. The values of the *mesoi* and the privileging of the city over the individual served as the foundation for consensus within the polis. Hanson (1995, 16–126) focuses upon this same group of middling citizens, located between the wealthy and the poor, especially in their capacities as hoplites and independent yeomen. The circumstances of the lives of these middling men fostered an ethos of quietism, stubbornness, self-reliance, and a respect for hard work. The dynamic of Archaic society is supplied in Hanson's view by the struggle of this group to win formal political power commensurate with their economic and military importance.

Morris has characterized Hesiod, as we see him through the lens of *Works and Days*, as "the middling man incarnate," asserting that "*Works and Days* is the oldest example of a peculiarly central Greek conception of the good society as a community of middling farmers" (Morris 2000, 164, 166). In Hanson's (1995, 91–126) view as well *Works and Days* exemplifies the values and outlook of the middling man. Hesiod's preoccupation with work, self-reliance, and autarky, as well as the scale of his farm, place him within this middling tradition. Both Morris and Hanson demonstrate the close connection existing between *Works and Days* and the ideology of the Classical *mesos*, illuminating the genealogy of later democratic ideology. But Hesiod's own status as a true "middling man" seems to me questionable.

I have argued that Ascra is a community without a formal and distinct elite, and to the extent that there exists a status hierarchy there, Hesiod speaks as a high status member of the community, a man of *kudos* and *aretē*. The values which *Works and Days* promotes, then, are not those of a "citizen" who lies sociologically between a landed elite and the landless poor. They are the values of a villager living outside the stratification of the polis system, and their egalitarianism simply reflects the conditions of village life. Ascra lacks the cooperative institutions of the city, a political economy, within which the values discussed by Morris and Hanson operated. As a consequence, the *oikos* and the individual claim a primacy in *Works and Days* that is antithetical to the middling ideology of the polis. In fact, Hesiod's defense of daily toil, the autarky of the household, and the nobility of the small man arose in reaction against the polis. Yet Hesiod's perspective as the successful farmer who expects to wield influence in his community, who values hard work, who demands equal justice, and who shuns laziness and luxury holds special appeal for the *mesoi* of the Classical period even if the cooperative, hierarchized institutions of citizenship, hoplite phalanx, and *politeia* are lacking in his world. The testimony of *Works and Days* suggests that the ideology of the *mesos* preserves the values and egalitarianism of the villages, reaching back to the Dark Age, which preceded the rise of the polis. The *mesoi* themselves, moreover, no doubt are the heirs of those former villagers who over the generations somehow succeeded in defending their position against the pressure that the elite of the polis were able to bring to bear on them. Here again *Works and Days* provides a piece not of the history of the polis but of its prehistory.

4 The Agricultural Regime of *Works and Days*

FARMING SYSTEM, POPULATION DENSITY, AND COMPLEXITY

In my view the evidence from *Works and Days* leads to the conclusion that Hesiod's Ascra was neither very centralized nor very hierarchized as a community. It is generally agreed that social complexity is intimately connected with the factors of agricultural regime and population density. Johnson and Earle argue that integration and stratification in a community are preceded by subsistence intensification that is itself the result of population growth.[1] A growing population after all must be fed. Initially, then, new land is taken under cultivation at the existing level of intensity in order to meet a growing demand for food. Once this option is exhausted, however, the only alternative other than emigration is to produce more food on the fixed amount of land available to the community. This is achieved through intensifying the utilization of available land.

Such intensification, however, comes at a cost, as Ester Boserup has shown. Boserup's research has revealed that while intensification succeeds

---

1. See Johnson and Earle 1987, 3–5, 11–14, 70–72; Boserup 1965, 11–14; Boserup 1981, 15–28, 35–42; Schusky 1989, 8–12. Earle (1997, 41–46, 75–89), however, has shown how under certain circumstances chiefs are able to spur intensification independently of population growth through their control of the means of subsistence production. Tandy (1997, 30–34) offers a valuable analysis of the positions of the Malthusians, insisting that technical advances in food production lead to population increase, and the "anti-Malthusians," who argue that the reverse is the case. I believe that there is a case to be made for population as the first cause (cf. Johnson and Earle 1987, 4–5, 15), but Livi-Bacci remains skeptical of making a judgment one way or the other (1997, 80–111). The papers collected by Aston and Philpin (1985) supply an illuminating exploration of the complicated relationship between population density and social complexity. The dynamics of population growth are discussed by Sallares (1991, 42–46, 65–73) and Livi-Bacci (1997, 1–34).

in increasing the net produce from available land, the amount of labor required to produce a given amount of food also increases. That is, even as the *total* output per unit of land increases, the output per unit of labor, per-hour productivity, declines.[2] Intensification of cultivation brings larger harvests, but farmers must work disproportionately longer to produce them. It is for this reason that farmers do not willingly hasten to intensify their farming regime at the earliest opportunity. After all, who would want to work harder just to maintain an existing, acceptable level of prosperity?[3] Such common companions to growing population and agricultural intensification as permanent settlements, land ownership, disparities in wealth due to disparities in size and quality of holdings, need for communal capital investments, dependence upon trade, and especially reliance upon social storage, taken together result in the emergence of hierarchy, of greater social complexity.[4]

Boserup gauges the level of intensity at which land is utilized for agriculture in terms of fallow, the length of time during which land is allowed to lie dormant between cultivations.[5] The longer the fallow period, the more land that is required to support a given population since a smaller fraction of it is under cultivation at any particular time. As population rises, a fixed amount of land must be farmed at shorter fallow intervals in order for food production to keep pace with population. A sparse population cultivating at extended fallow periods normally exhibits a habitation pattern of scattered, low-density, impermanent settlements, often no more than homesteads. Conversely, nucleated settlements tend to accompany a denser population employing shorter fallow periods.[6] Fallow becomes shorter as cultivators become tied to a specific holding, population becomes denser, and centralized settlements begin to be formed on a more permanent basis.

---

2. See Boserup 1965, 28–42, 53–55, 65–69, 75–76; Boserup 1981, 46–50; Wood 1998; Schusky 1989, 25–26; Cohen 1977, 27–40; Sahlins 1972, 41–74, 87–92. See also Tainter (1988, 91–127), who argues that this tendency towards "diminishing marginal returns" affects not only agriculture and resource production as a society becomes more complex but also other aspects of social organization.

3. See Sahlins 1972, 87–92 on "Chayanov's rule."

4. See Boserup 1965, 70–87, esp. 72–75; Johnson and Earle 1987, 11–22; and Schusky 1989, 79–97.

5. Boserup 1965, 11–14; Boserup defends this principle at Boserup 1981, 15–16.

6. See the discussions of Boserup 1965, 72–75; Sahlins 1972, 95–99; and Johnson and Earle 1987, 18–22, 62–83. Schusky (1989, 17–21) claims that permanent villages can be supported by long fallow cultivation, but still I believe that the principle relating habitation patterns to fallowing regimes remains fairly obvious.

Boserup (1965, 15–22) categorizes the various forms fallowing can take within five basic regimes. Forest fallow and bush fallow are forms of shifting agriculture, also known as swidden or slash-and-burn agriculture. Such regimes use fire to clear the land and specialize in root crops.[7] Under forest fallow plots are planted for one or two years and then left fallow for twenty to twenty-five years, long enough to permit the forest to regenerate. Bush fallow allows for one to two years of cultivation followed by a shorter fallow of six to eight years, long enough for bush to grow on the plot. The preferred tool for cultivating under these regimes is the hoe. Scattered sites of habitation are characteristic of both of these regimes as the land supports only a low population density and farmers must frequently move in order to find new plots.

Under the short fallow regime fields are allowed to lie uncultivated for from one to two years, allowing only grasses to grow upon the plot. Since neither fire nor the hoe can adequately destroy the roots of grasses, the plow is the preferred tool for cultivation under short fallow. The appearance of grasses as the dominant wild vegetation on fallow plots, moreover, simultaneously provides fodder for draft animals. This system can be used without irrigation even in dry regions. Boserup (1965, 35–36) specifies that in order for short fallow and draft animals to be a viable agricultural system one of three conditions must be met: (1) a considerable percentage of available land must be devoted to permanent grazing; or (2) the period of cultivation must be shorter than the fallow period, permitting draft animals to graze for a good part of the year on fallow; or (3) part of the harvest must be devoted to feeding draft animals (i.e., a special fodder crop must be cultivated). Boserup generalizes that if animals are to be fed with non-cultivated fodder (options 1 or 2), one third of available land is the maximum that can be devoted to cultivation at one time. Option 3 represents the most intensive of the three since additional land must be cropped in order to feed the draft animals. This results in a substantial increase in the amount of land under cultivation. Short fallow is a relatively extensive exploitation of the land, though it is far more intensive than long fallow. Boserup (1965, 48–51) also notes that the short fallow regime is characterized by two seasons of peak activity: the plowing/sowing season and the harvest. Labor demand follows this rhythm, resulting in underemployment during the slack seasons.

7. See the discussions of Johnson and Earle 1987, 62–83, 104–17, and 138–52 and of Schusky 1989, 45–63. Boserup's scheme of fallowing regimes is discussed in connection with Greek agriculture by Gallant 1982, 113–15 and 1991, 52–56.

The last two fallowing regimes can be characterized as intensive. Under annual cropping fields lie fallow for several months between annual crops. This regime can accommodate a rotation of cereal and fodder (pulse) crops. Under multi-cropping two or more successive crops are grown per year with only a minimal fallow period intervening. Multi-cropping in general depends upon irrigation as does annual cropping in drier regions. Both require the use of fertilizer.

Needless to say, I hope to use Boserup's sequence of fallowing regimes to contextualize the farming practices described by Hesiod. But can we assume that this entire range of fallowing schemes was available to Ascrans? As population levels sank into their nadir in the Dark Age, might the inhabitants of Greece have reverted to shifting agriculture?[8] Boserup and Schusky both maintain that agriculture entered Greece in the form of shifting cultivation by 6000 B.C. Certainly if shifting agriculture were a viable option for Greece, it would most likely be so during the initial phase of the neolithic. Yet Barker (1985, 17–18, 63–65, 141–43, 167–70, 197–98, 234–35, 248–49) now rejects the role formerly attributed to shifting cultivation in Europe north of the Mediterranean zone and does not discuss it at all in connection with Greece. Sallares has recently argued that Boserup's long fallow regimes are less the first stages on a developmental continuum than systems uniquely adapted to tropical ecosystems and poorly adapted to temperate zones.[9] Long fallow as an agricultural system relies upon the use of fire—to efficiently clear land, to leave behind a residue of fertilizing ash, to destroy weed seeds and insect eggs—but, as Boserup points out, fire is ineffective against grasses since burning leaves

8. Tandy (1997, 35–38) suggests that Messenians abandoned grain cultivation altogether during the Dark Age. Contra, see Coldstream 1977, 313–14; Garnsey and Morris 1989, 99; and Cherry 1988, 26–30. See Palmer's (2001, 45–50) review of the question. Her argument (2001, 66–77) for the continuity of cultivation through the Dark Age strikes me as certainly correct.

9. See Boserup 1965, 56–57; Boserup 1981, 56–58; Schusky 1989, 16–21; Jarman 1982, 133–46; Barker 1985, 17–18, 63–65, 141–43, 167–70, 197–98, 234–35, 248–49; and Sallares 1991, 81–84. Sallares' argument that the plow was adopted because it makes cultivation easier, of course, agrees with Boserup's principle that farmers seek the easiest means of meeting their needs (see Boserup 1981, 46–50). See Sherratt 1981, 263–72 regarding the date of the plow's introduction into Europe. Halstead (1981, 319) likewise argues that shifting agriculture is less attractive outside a tropical setting. The soils of tropical and temperate zones are quite distinct as are the processes by which they are replenished. Whittle's (1996, 34–71, esp. 66–69) summary of the arrival of the neolithic in southeastern Europe does not consider shifting agriculture. See Lele and Stone 1989 and Stone and Downum 1999 on the need to qualify Boserup's scheme in line with ecological constraints.

their root systems intact. Halstead and Cherry have argued that through both herding and clearing neolithic farmers in Greece rapidly converted woodlands into grasslands, and Boserup herself argues that the plow was introduced into Europe by the second millennium in response to spreading grasslands. I conclude, then, that even if long fallow cultivation could have been employed in Greece at the outset of the neolithic, it would not have been an option for Greek farmers in a post-neolithic landscape.[10]

I believe that by Hesiod's time the least intensive agricultural regime that could be practically employed was plow cultivation. Since fields are not cleared and graded for the long fallow regimes, the hoe and digging stick are the primary cultivating tools. For the more intensive regimes, introduced when the shortage of land makes draft animals too expensive, the hoe again appears as the chief tool.[11] The use of the plow, then, implies short fallow, and short fallow arguably is the most extensive regime possible in Greece. Even if for the present purposes we must truncate Boserup's developmental sequence in this way, still short fallow cultivation permits of various levels of intensity and these bear a direct connection to the density of population. That is, there is a substantial difference in the intensity of land use between a regime allowing, on the one hand, for both two years of fallow and enough dedicated pasture to feed draft animals without the need to grow a special fodder crop and a regime, on the other, utilizing a three-field system in order to raise a special pulse crop as fodder.[12] The latter system would reflect a less favorable ratio of people to land and would require the farmer to work harder in order to produce a given amount of food.

Remaining within the logic of Boserup's argument, if we can assume, as I think is likely, that an extensive form of short fallow cultivation is the

---

10. See Boserup 1965, 24–25 and 1981, 46–50, 56–59; Halstead 1981, 310–12, 320–37; Cherry 1988, 12–17. Boserup (1981, 18–24) shows in tables 3.3 and 3.5 that short fallow in tropical zones is adopted at higher population densities than in non-tropical zones, indicating that long fallow is more productive under tropical conditions. Rackham's research (1983, 339–47) attests to the long-term stability of the Boeotian landscape, in which grasses figure prominently.

11. Regarding tools and intensity of cultivation see Boserup 1965, 24–25 and 1981, 46–52, 85–86; Halstead 1987, 83–86; and Gallant 1991, 50–52.

12. Schusky (1989, 56–58) notes the tremendous cost draft animals impose upon farmers in the form of fodder, doubling their work or more. Halstead (1987, 83–85) estimates that it takes over twice as much land to support a family through farming with draft animals, and Halstead and Jones (1989, 47–50) estimate that the need to harvest fodder crops and to harvest straw for fodder along with cereals more than doubles the amount of work that must be done at harvest.

lowest level of intensity available to Greek farmers of Hesiod's time, then we would expect to see this regime along with permanent settlements and fields functioning at comparatively low densities of population. That is, might we not observe an agricultural regime of short fallow cultivation in a setting of relatively more abundant land and lower levels of social integration and political stratification than one would find in tropical zones for the simple reason that short fallow is the least intensive regime practicable at any population density in Greece at this time? Since plow agriculture requires certain improvements in the fields (clearing, removal of stones, contouring) and fields vary in quality because of soil, water, exposure, and so forth, even in a context of abundant land households would wish to protect their investments and advantages by holding on to plots on a permanent basis. Of course, this attachment to specific fields would be even stronger in the case of perennial crops such as vines.

HESIOD'S AGRICULTURAL REGIME

Boserup (1965, 56–64) notes that in most places several fallowing regimes will be found in use simultaneously depending upon the variation in the soil, the size of the holding, the form of land tenure, and so forth across a locale. I assume that this principle applies not only to the local district but to the larger geographical region as well. That is, the regime described by Hesiod may be localized, dependent upon the ecological, social, and demographic conditions prevailing in Ascra, but not necessarily representative of other regions of Greece. As I have already suggested, I think that it is mistaken simply to assume that *Works and Days* can be taken as representative of conditions across all or most of Greece at the time of its composition. If certain expected elements are missing from the agricultural system presented by Hesiod in *Works and Days*, that does not mean that they were not present or even widespread elsewhere in Greece, but only that they were not characteristic of agriculture in Hesiod's Ascra. More intensive regimes of farming may have been practiced in the Dark Age or in the Classical period or elsewhere in Greece contemporaneously with Hesiod. My present purpose is to understand the testimony of *Works and Days* in isolation, on its own terms, and without regard for its role as evidence for practices elsewhere in Greece.

Hanson and Halstead on Intensive Cultivation

Victor Hanson (1995, 91–126) has made a detailed examination of the agricultural regime practiced by Hesiod, arguing that it exemplifies intensive cultivation. Hanson (1995, 50) provides a list of six characteristics that comprise his definition of intensive cultivation: (1) homestead residence; (2) irrigation; (3) slave labor; (4) diversified crops; (5) reclamation of marginal land; (6) processing and storage of food on the farm.[13] As we have seen, Boserup's definition of intensive cultivation focuses solely upon the frequency with which the land is cropped, ranging from long fallows measured in decades to multi-cropping within a single year. The features of irrigation and reclamation of marginal land, items 2 and 5 in Hanson's list, exhibit this same focus. Irrigation is essential to multi-cropping, the most intensive form of cultivation, which justifies the expensive infrastructure required.[14] Reclamation, however, the bringing of new land under cultivation, generally offers a means of providing additional food for a growing population without cropping existing arable more frequently at the cost of more intensive labor. As far as land use goes, then, one would expect to see reclamation before irrigation. Slave labor and a wide variety of crops, items 3 and 4, express in Hanson's argument the intensity of cultivation in terms of labor. That is, a broad spectrum of orchard, garden, and field crops keep the farmer busy all year round with little slack time, and it is this circumstance that makes slaves, a labor force available continuously throughout the year, efficient. Both of these elements derive from the intensity with which the land is utilized. Homestead residence and processing and storage of produce on site, items 1 and 6, for the most part express the autonomy and independence attributed by Hanson to his new class of yeomen. Hanson's notion of what comprises "intensive agriculture" is much broader and more heterogeneous than Boserup's narrow focus upon fallowing, yet close consideration demonstrates that Boserup's concerns with land use and the intensity of labor are present in Hanson's definition. The question remaining is whether or not Hanson's account of intensive agriculture can actually accommodate the regime that Hesiod describes in *Works and Days*.

To turn to Hanson's list of criteria, about items 3 and 6 there is not much to debate. Hesiod does take for granted slaves who work side by side with the farmer in his fields. He also clearly refers to threshing and storing grain as well as to making wine locally. The claim that Hesiod's dwelling is an isolated farmstead upon a contiguous plot appears, however, to contradict the

13. See Hanson's discussion of Laertes' farm in terms of these criteria at Hanson 1995, 47–86, where each is given detailed consideration.

14. Schusky (1989, 63–78) generalizes that irrigation tends to accompany the rise of cities and social stratification as the effect of a centralized authority. See also Boserup 1965, 25–26, 39–42 and Johnson and Earle 1987, 207–11, 246–48.

clearest indications Hesiod gives us on this matter. Hesiod tells us that his father settled "near Helicon in the wretched village of Ascra" *(W&D* 639–40). The simplest and most obvious meaning of *oizurēi eni kōmēi / Askrēi* is that the dwelling was within the village. It is difficult to guess, moreover, whom Hanson imagines to live in Ascra if not farmers. Hesiod does, of course, refer to neighbors in a number of places in the poem (see pp. 89–91). The statement that a neighbor will come to your aid before an in-law (345) would appear to suggest that neighbors are nearby. Indeed, the field survey of the vicinity of Ascra and Thespiae, *pace* Hanson, indicates that isolated homestead farms become a common phenomenon only much later than Hesiod's time.[15] Finally, it is not at all certain that Hesiod's fields are contiguous, a feature closely associated by Hanson with intensive cultivation and without which homestead residence offers no advantage (Hanson 1995, 51–55, with note "*" on 54, 59). Hesiod refers to taking supplies out to slaves periodically and inspecting their work (765–67, cf. West ad loc.) as well as to slaves building shelters (502–3), both suggestive of dispersed fields, distant from the main residence. At 579–81, moreover, Hesiod indicates pretty clearly that the road lies between a man and his morning work, an impression corroborated by the need for a wagon to take seed out to a field for planting (453–54). Greek inheritance and dowry customs, finally, make contiguous holdings highly improbable over the long run, as Hanson himself (108) notes apropos of *W&D* 376–77.[16]

Of irrigation Hesiod simply makes no mention. The argument that it can be taken for granted in a semi-arid country like Greece would rule out its role as a distinctive feature of intensive cultivation.

The heart of Hanson's definition of intensive agriculture is the cultivation of a wide variety of crops. I discuss the problem of the mix of crops cultivated by Hesiod below (pp. 141–47). Suffice it to say here that the only crops discussed in the agricultural calendar *(W&D* 381–617) are cereals and grapes. This hardly provides convincing evidence that Hesiod's farmers cultivated a broad array of crops.

15. Bintliff and Snodgrass (1985, 139–40) state that sites identifiable as homestead farms only begin to appear in the sixth century, one hundred to seventy-five years after the composition of *Works and Days,* and they do not become common till later still. Cf. Bintliff and Snodgrass 1989, 287–88 with figures 41, 42, and 43, and Snodgrass 1987–89, 54–56. These sites coexist with densely populated villages and cities, and result from the need to bring every last acre of land under cultivation in the face of increasing population density.

16. See the discussion of Snodgrass 1990, 126–27. Farmers tend to prefer scattered, non-contiguous plots since they spread the risks of unfavorable weather, pests, and crop diseases (see, e.g., Gallant 1991, 41–45).

What Hanson leaves out of his discussion of Hesiod's agricultural regime and his argument that it represents intensive exploitation of the land is that the products of intensive cultivation are more expensive than those of extensive cultivation not only in terms of the amount of labor they require of the farmer but also in terms of the overhead to support an elite and institutions of social storage. These are burdens that cultivators do not undertake except out of necessity. In fact, the autonomy, independence, and spatial dispersion of households tend in general to decline precisely as the intensity of cultivation increases.

Paul Halstead's research has also sparked a reevaluation of the received view that ancient Greek farming resembled the traditional agricultural regime of Greece in the modern period, a system based upon short fallow and cultivation with plow and draft animals. Halstead and those following his work argue for a regime of intensive agriculture practiced from neolithic times in interdependence with small-scale stock rearing. I remain interested in evaluating this approach exclusively as an account of the specific regime described by Hesiod. While more intensive regimes may have been in practice elsewhere in Greece during Hesiod's time and likewise before and after, for the moment suffice it to say that the farming regime described by Hesiod does not correspond to the intensive regime attributed by this school to small holders in early Greece. I will demonstrate this below point by point when I examine the evidence supplied by Hesiod himself for this question. Since, however, Halstead's approach has implications for the relationship between population, social complexity, and agricultural regime, I will also discuss it from a theoretical perspective.

Halstead argues that when population densities are low and land is consequently plentiful, then a homestead habitation pattern is adopted enabling farmers to live close to their land. This proximity of spatially contiguous fields permits these farmers to practice an intensive regime of cultivation. Specifically, this is an agricultural system employing hoe and dibble cultivation, a rotation of pulse crops with cereal crops, little or no fallowing, and manuring. This last element entails the interdependence of farming with husbandry in an integrated regime of "mixed farming."[17]

17. Halstead associates extensive cultivation with transhumance in an agricultural system that thus deprives fields of manure for a good part of the year. This overstates the case, however, since short fallow presupposes the presence of draft animals and since the proximity of herds to fields otherwise depends upon the location of pasture—that is, land not under cultivation. The use of fallow for winter grazing provides a natural link between cultivation and husbandry. The term "transhumance" itself is not entirely helpful since it disguises what may only be a dis-

According to this argument it is only with the development of larger, centralized settlements, incorporating individual households within a hierarchized and integrated community, that farmers turn to extensive cultivation. Larger settlements require that farmers walk longer distances to reach their fields, and this increased travel time in turn reduces the amount of time available to be spent working in the fields themselves. As a consequence farmers adopt an extensive regime since it requires a smaller investment of labor in the fields, which are now dispersed and more difficult to reach.[18] According to this argument, if Hesiod describes a fairly extensive agricultural regime, then Ascra ought to be a densely populated, hierarchized settlement since those are the circumstances attendant upon the shift from intensive to extensive cultivation. But does Ascra fit the scenario elaborated by Halstead?

Whether or not intensive agriculture can be successfully practiced at low population densities is itself open to debate.[19] Beyond that, however, lies the question of whether farmers would prefer to cultivate intensively rather than extensively if they were given the choice. Halstead appears to regard the intensive regime as inherently advantageous, but we must consider why farmers might prefer one regime to another. Under what circumstances do the advantages of the one outweigh those of the other? While Halstead focuses his arguments upon the increased travel time resulting from distant and dispersed fields, he acknowledges as well the considerable advantages offered by dispersed fields: that they serve as a hedge against insects and crop diseases as well as variability of rainfall (Halstead and Jones 1989, 50–52, Halstead 1989, 72–75). Garnsey (1988, 93–94) summarizes the advantages of extensive cultivation as follows: fallow allows the soil to rebuild its nutrients, especially if livestock are turned onto it; fallow alone conserves moisture from rainfall, a process enhanced by frequent tilling to reduce weed growth and evaporation; fallow diminishes the occurrence of weeds and other pests. Similarly Boserup (1981, 23–26)

---

tinction between "infield" and "outfield" pasture behind the connotation of movements of nomads over long seasonal migrations. See Skydsgaard 1988, 76 and Hodkinson 1988, 51–58, who notes (53–54) Hesiod on Helicon as exemplary of the infield/outfield conceptualization.

18. The principal statement of this argument is found in Halstead 1981, especially 327–31. The argument is developed in Halstead 1987, Halstead and Jones 1989, and Halstead 1989. See also Osborne 1996, 60–63 and Jones 1987, 120–23.

19. As Halstead observes (Halstead 1981, 317–20 and 1987, 81–83) a shortage of labor is a frequent impediment to the rotation of cereals and pulses, which is the heart of intensive agriculture as he describes it. See also Boserup 1981, 18–23, 46–50.

notes among the benefits of fallowing that it prevents soil exhaustion, reduces weed growth, and limits the spread of plant diseases. As she goes on to point out, these same results can be achieved under an intensive regime of annual or continuous cropping by applying manure, by weeding, and by removing insects by hand, but such measures can be implemented only at the cost of considerable labor (presupposing the availability of a considerable labor force). For, as Boserup demonstrates (above, pp. 127–28), while the intensive regime does provide more food per acre, it does so at the cost of more labor per unit of produce. This observation leads us to the chief problem with Halstead's thesis: namely, why would farmers practice a regime requiring them to work harder if an easier alternative were at hand?

As I have noted above, it is generally accepted that population growth, reducing the amount of land available per capita, is the primary factor forcing farmers to intensify their cultivation of the soil. It is for this reason that the case for intensive agriculture strikes me as far more compelling in the context of the fifth and fourth centuries. Halstead, however, argues the contradictory position that farmers practice a more intensive regime when population density would allow them to cultivate more extensively and that they introduce extensive agriculture when increased population density would more likely require them to intensify cultivation. This inconsistency in Halstead's theory presents itself clearly in his account of the emergence of large nucleated and stratified settlements. In Halstead's view these larger, hierarchized settlements bring considerable disadvantages to the typical householder. He notes longer traveling times to the now more distant fields; cultivation of pulses in the "infield" and of cereals in the "outfield," precluding rotation; less efficiency in weeding and manuring operations; stratification between those with draft animals and land close in to the settlement and those without these advantages; these various hindrances to cultivation in turn force households to rely more heavily upon the emerging elite (Halstead 1981, 327–31, 1989, 76–81). And although Halstead asserts that the chief burden of these circumstances is the loss to small householders of efficiency in cultivation, one must not minimize the added cost to every household in these larger settlements of supporting an elite who both do not work at farming and insist on living better than the norm. What force or attraction sufficed to draw householders into such disadvantageous settlements?

The logic of Halstead's argument requires that these settlements must have been located amidst abundant arable and pasture since, just as these settlements establish themselves, farmers are being compelled to adopt a regime of cultivation that requires at least twice as much arable as well as additional grazing land for draft animals. Without a plentiful supply of arable land, farmers could not have made the transition from annual crop-ping under an intensive regime to the biennial fallowing of a more exten-sive regime that requires that a minimum of half of a farmer's land remain uncultivated in any given year. If large amounts of land are available, as Halstead's argument requires, and large, concentrated settlements are so disadvantageous, then why is it that farmers do not simply move off into new land to establish new villages or homesteads rather than endure the costs of hierarchy and a shift to what Halstead characterizes as a more de-manding farming regime in centralized communities? How can an elite re-quiring control of a substantial surplus to support itself emerge precisely at the moment when per capita production is declining because of a change from intensive to extensive cultivation and time lost to travel? Why do farmers consent to trade a good thing for a bad thing: ease and efficiency of cultivation for dependency upon an elite and shorter rations? As the ratio of land to inhabitants becomes less favorable why would an agricultural re-gime requiring more land to produce a given amount of crop be intro-duced? As Boserup (1981, 64–70) demonstrates, moreover, a precondition to the appearance of such large settlements is the availability of an agricul-tural surplus within a proximity making transport into the central settle-ment economically feasible. On this score again the transition from inten-sive to extensive farming, which entails greater spatial dispersal of cultivated land, would operate to reduce the potential size of the settlement in the very moment that it is forming and consolidating its control over its territory.

Under conditions of the early neolithic when Greece's landscape was still dominated by woodlands and before the arrival of plow and draft animals, intensive cultivation of small plots with dibble and hoe would have pre-vailed. But these were not the environmental or technological circum-stances confronted by Hesiod. As regards the relationship between inten-sive and more extensive regimes, however, I do not see how a transition from an intensive to a more extensive regime alone, leaving aside addi-tional factors such as trade or warfare (see p. 162), can have played the role in the emergence of hierarchy attributed to it by Halstead. As long as land was plentiful, Halstead's farmers would have dispersed themselves across it in villages rather than put up with the disadvantages of more densely pop-ulated settlements.[20] The circumstance that produces large, stable settle-

20. See p. 128, n. 6 and Boserup 1981, 74–75.

ments is a density of population that has filled in available land and so precludes moving into areas of lower concentration. At this point, extensive agriculture is no longer an option since population density requires the more efficient land use offered by intensive cultivation. In my view, then, if Hesiod can be shown to describe a relatively extensive regime, that should be understood as an indication of sparse population and a smaller, more egalitarian settlement rather than of a larger, more hierarchized settlement.

Land Tenure

Hesiod claims title to his plot as a private holding, his *klēros*, which is heritable (*W&D* 35–39; see above, pp. 109–10). His reference to farmers cultivating different regions (*W&D* 388–93) reinforces the impression of settled farmers cultivating fixed plots. There is, finally, Hesiod's reference to the village of Ascra itself. As I have discussed above, permanent settlements indicate permanently held fields. These features together suggest that considerable investment has accumulated in the land. The dispute between Perses and Hesiod over their paternal *klēros* and the alienability of land support this conclusion. Yet I have also argued that the population density of Ascra is low and that unimproved land is available for cultivation. There is a contradiction here only if it is assumed that improved land has no more value than uncleared land, and that, of course, is not the case. Vines add considerable value to land, as do the clearing and contouring required for plowing. Proximity to the settlement as well as soil and climatic characteristics are equally important factors. I assume, in fact, that the effort required to bring new land under cultivation is adequate to account for the dispute between Hesiod and Perses, and possibly thetage and even slavery as well. These tenure and habitation patterns suit the short fallow regime that, it will become clear, Hesiod describes in *Works and Days*.

Fallow

The most important passage for understanding the fallowing regime described by Hesiod occurs at *Works and Days* 462–64, where he praises fallow and recommends plowing it three times per year. The injunction to plow in spring (*W&D* 462) must mean before the cereal harvest has occurred since a plowing after that time would be in summer (see pp. 154–55). A plowing done before the harvest of the cereal crop in the fields requires that there be some fields that were not planted the preceding fall, but were left as bare fallow at least since the last harvest. Presumably this plowing serves to knock down weeds and to protect water stored in the soil from evaporating as the weather becomes hotter and drier. If the fallow has been grazed, plowing would also serve to work in manure lying on the ground. Summer plowing (*W&D* 462) could not occur before the harvest and threshing, so it must fall in late July or August (see p. 155). This plowing's chief purpose is likely to prevent evaporation by destroying capillary passages connecting the dried surface with deeper levels in the soil. The unrestricted form of this recommendation (θέρεος δὲ νεωμένη οὔ σ' ἀπατήσει: *W&D* 462) implies that Hesiod is thinking here of all of a farmer's arable land. If this inference is correct, Hesiod does not assume spring-sown summer crops. The recommendation to sow when the soil is yet light and friable (*W&D* 463) refers to the fall plowing at planting season. Hesiod describes the fields to be sown as *neion,* fallow. This passage guides us to the conclusion that Hesiod describes a system of at least biennial bare fallow, though the fallow period could be even longer than a year.[21]

At lines 379–80 of *Works and Days,* after recommending only one child as heir, Hesiod goes on to qualify his statement with the observation that greater wealth easily comes to a larger family (*pleonessi:* Hesiod seems to have sons in mind) since there is more effort *(meletē)* from more hands *(pleonōn)* and greater increase *(epithēkē).* One way to understand these lines is as a reference to intensification, to a shorter fallow cycle enabling the household to utilize more labor in order to produce more food. Yet short fallow cultivation is characterized, as I mentioned above, by seasonal underemployment. Intensification of the short fallow regime normally results in longer months of agricultural employment over the year for the existing labor force. The additional labor capacity would be valuable only in the instance of cultivation of another crop whose cycle came into competition with the sowing or harvesting period of the cereal crops.[22] It seems

---

21. Tandy (1997, 208) characterizes Hesiod's fallowing regime as either a two- or three-field cycle of bare fallow. Burford (1993, 120–21) and Isager and Skydsgaard (1992, 21–26, 44–50) both understand Hesiod to describe a two-field, short fallow system. Gallant (1991, 52–56, cf. 1982, 114) argues that Hesiod describes either short fallow or multi-cropping. I see no justification for positing a more intensive regime than short fallow (two-field).

22. Hesiod's description of the Isles of the Blessed at *W&D* 172–73 perhaps deserves brief mention in connection with the topic of intensification. Could the amazing fertility he attributes to the place of three crops per year be more than mere utopian fantasy and actually reflect knowledge of a continuous-cropping regime? It is, of course, not only possible but highly likely that Hesiod knew of agricultural practices that were not current in Ascra. If this chances to be so, however,

Figure 1. The site and setting of Hesiod's home village of Ascra. Photograph by Robin Osborne.

more likely to me that Hesiod means here that a larger family controls the labor necessary to improve new land and bring it under cultivation, simply extending the existing fallowing regime into a new area in order to meet an increased demand for food.

Cereal Cultivation

References to cereal crops through generic nouns are common in *Works and Days*. Hesiod uses *sitos* at *W&D* 146 (but cf. 604), the noun *aktē* is used three times (*W&D* 466, 597, 805; the occurrence in line 32 may refer to produce of all types), and grain crops are referred to by *karpos* five times (*W&D* 117, 172, 237, 576, 775; at 563 the word occurs as a generic for produce, cf. *Th.* 216). The only direct references to specific grains exhibit the same generic quality since they occur in noun-epithet phrases: *zeidōros aroura* (*W&D* 117, 173, 237) and *purophorois . . . epi ergois* (*W&D* 549).

---

he has sanitized his picture by omitting reference to the increased burden of labor such an agricultural regime requires.

The first phrase (*zeia*: emmer wheat) is well attested in Homer and *puro-phoros* (*puros*: wheat proper) is also found there.[23] Hesiod provides, however, some indirect evidence that is more helpful. At *Works and Days* 443–44 he mentions *artos*, wheat bread, as an especially nourishing food and at 582–97 he puts *maza*, barley cakes made with milk, on the menu for the midsummer break. Emmer, wheat, and barley are the most likely cereal crops for Hesiod.[24] The various items of equipment mentioned by Hesiod complement cereal cultivation: mortar and pestle for milling cereal grains (*W&D* 423), a mallet for breaking clods of earth (*W&D* 425), a wagon and wagon parts for taking seed and grain to and from one's fields (*W&D* 424, 426, 448–57, 692–93), a plow (*W&D* 427–36), and a sickle (*W&D* 387, 573).

Obviously enough Hesiod describes the cultivation of cereals with a plow and he likewise makes frequent reference to draft animals, primarily oxen, though he does mention mules and even horses in one passage. The frequency with which the ox is mentioned suggests that this was the preferred animal. Hesiod presents it as essential equipment for the house (*W&D* 436–37, 405–7; cf. 795–97, 814–16). The ox is associated with the plow at lines 436–40, 580–81, 795–97, and 814–16, and is identified as the draft animal for wagons at 453–54.[25] Hesiod (*W&D* 441–47) describes the plowman as distinct from the man sowing the seed, though the manner in which he juxtaposes them in the passage implies they are working together, perhaps with the man sowing going ahead of the plow as West suggests. The phrase *spermata dassasthai* (*W&D* 446) clearly describes broadcast sowing. Hesiod warns against *episporiēn*, an uneven distribution of seed on the soil. While broadcast sowing is not the most efficient method of getting the seed into the soil, in Hesiod's account the seed deposited on

23. Isager and Skydsgaard (1992, 21) identify *puros* as *triticum vulgare* or *cereale*. See Sallares' (1991, 313–26) detailed analysis of the identities of ancient wheat varieties.

24. Regarding the identification of these different cereals, see Richter 1968, 107–23. See also Isager and Skydsgaard 1992, 21–26 and Burford 1993, 130–331. Hesiod at *W&D* 414–36 gives far more detail about the different types of wood needed to make a plow than he ever does about the cereals to be cultivated with said instrument. There's not much here for the novice farmer. Regarding the barley cakes of the midsummer break, see the encomium of the barley cake at Braun 1995, 25–33, esp. 29. Braun points out that although the Boeotian lowlands are well-adapted to wheat cultivation, the uplands are better for barley (see 29, 32–33).

25. See Sheratt's (1981, 263–72) fascinating discussion of the intimate historical connection between the use of domestic animals for traction, the plow, and the wagon, and their role in the spread of plow agriculture in the Near East and Europe.

the soil is covered over by another slave using a hoe (*makelē: W&D* 470).[26] Hesiod relies upon his draft animals during the threshing process as well when, presumably, they are called upon to trample the grain or to pull a sled over it (*W&D* 607–8).

The agricultural system described by Hesiod incorporates draft animals at many stages : *erga boōn* (*W&D* 46) are synonymous with agriculture in *Works and Days.* Such reliance upon draft animals characterizes short fallow, plow cultivation. In order to evaluate the intensity with which the short fallow regime is practiced in Ascra, however, we must determine how Hesiod imagines his draft animals to be fed: are they grazed upon permanent pasture, upon fallow fields, are they stall-fed on fodder crops raised specifically for that purpose, or is some combination of these methods employed? The first of these options would signal the least intensive use of the land and would require the least effort of the farmer (see p. 129).

Hesiod claims that if it were not for a bad neighbor, no one would ever lose an ox *(W&D* 348). Hesiod presupposes here a setting in which neighbors would frequently see each other's livestock, either the village, where oxen are kept within family compounds for stall-feeding, or else pasture close in to the village. In another passage Hesiod recommends fattening up one's oxen indoors (*endon eontas: W&D* 452) in anticipation of the fall plowing season. Several features of the passage suggest that this is special treatment. First is the "oxless man" (*andros abouteō: W&D* 451) whose request to borrow oxen at peak season is to be denied. Second is the approach of the most intensive work season of the year for these draft animals. The simultaneous desire to provide them with rest and to build up their strength with special feeding are linked to the explicit reference to keeping them indoors. If oxen were always kept indoors and stall-fed, then why does Hesiod bother to spell out these measures specifically for this season? There is also the implicit assumption that the oxen must be kept under a watchful eye during plowing season in particular so that they are not borrowed without permission by the needy "oxless man." Complementing the extra feeding endorsed for plowing season, Hesiod recommends half rations in the depth of winter (*W&D* 559–60). Such control over consumption of food might imply stall-feeding at least during this part of the year. Yet the epithet of "oxflayer" (*boudora: W&D* 504) given to the month of Lenaion and the inclusion of oxen among the catalogue of domestic animals victim

26. Halstead (1987, 77–79) lists broadcast sowing among features characteristic of extensive farming.

to the north wind's blasts (*W&D* 515–18) suggest that oxen normally winter out of doors along with other livestock even during the coldest months. The epithet applied to the ox in the phrase *boos hulophagoio* (*W&D* 591) offers further evidence for pasturing, though the line's context in a description of a banquet suggests that the reference may not be to a draft animal. If oxen were pastured during the winter months, then the recommendation of half rations at *Works and Days* 599–60 most likely refers to a practice of moving animals less frequently in order to make pasture last longer.[27] Taken together, these passages suggest that draft animals were stall-fed on fodder likely during the fall plowing season and possibly for part of the winter.

The most important passage for our understanding of this question remains to be examined. At *Works and Days* 597–608 Hesiod describes the final stages of the cereal cycle, threshing, winnowing, and storing the harvested grain. In 606–7 he directs Perses to "bring in the fodder *(chorton)* and the sweepings *(surpheton)* so that there will be enough for the oxen and mules." The words *chortos* and *surphetos* are generics, the one indicating merely provender and the other whatever is swept together, with the implication that it is refuse. The words themselves hardly suggest a special fodder crop. To the contrary, their inclusion in the description of final processing of the grain harvest implies that these are by-products of grain cultivated to supply food for the human population. The simplest interpretation of the words is to take *chortos* as "straw" and *surphetos* as "chaff."[28] Understanding *chortos* and *surphetos* as the products of specialized fodder crop entails the abrupt and unprepared-for introduction at this point of another crop whose planting and harvest have not otherwise been mentioned.

My interpretation is in essentials the same as that of Isager and Skydsgaard (1992, 25 n. 13), who reject Gallant's (1982, 114) argument that *surpheton* at *W&D* 606–7 refers to stubble from the grain fields but that *chorton* likely refers to a pulse crop sown in the spring. Halstead (1987, 83–85) notes among other features of the extensive regime the necessity of harvesting the straw along with the grain in order to utilize it as fodder. As Halstead (1987, 81–83) points out, however, the work under the intensive

27. Boserup (1965, 36–39) notes that farmers practicing short fallow in its most extensive form prefer starving their animals on inadequate pasture during off-season to the considerable additional work of cultivating fodder crops. Regarding fodder and winter pasture for oxen in *Works and Days* see Skydsgaard 1988, 76.

28. *Chortos* can accommodate the meaning "hay" but nothing in the present context is required beyond the more generic "fodder."

regime of harvesting both cereals and pulses at the end of spring can create severe time stress—it is more work than bringing in the straw along with a single grain crop. While a pulse-cereal rotation may have been practiced in early Archaic Greece, it seems to me, finally, an insurmountable objection to attributing such a system to Hesiod that he says nothing about pulses or rotations in *Works and Days*.

The most likely scenario appears to be that Ascrans practiced limited stall-feeding by utilizing by-products of the cereal harvest, the straw and the chaff. Certainly there is no discussion in *Works and Days* of the substantial fodder crops that would have to be raised in order to support stall-feeding throughout the year. Hesiod does not clarify for us whether oxen are pastured on dedicated pasture land or on fallow (stubble and weeds). If the former, then he describes the most extensive form of short fallow regime; if the latter is the case, then he describes a more intensive pattern of land use, one that benefits fallow through the direct application of manure.[29] The reliance upon draft animals, plow, broadcast sowing, and limited stall-feeding typify the short fallow regime practiced at a low degree of intensity.

Other Crops

The other major crop discussed by Hesiod is the grape. He briefly mentions the pruning and trenching of the vines (*W&D* 564–72) and later describes the gathering and processing of the grapes (*W&D* 609–17).[30] The vines receive the most detail from Hesiod after the cereal crop and clearly claim an important position in the household economy. Once we leave behind cereals and grapes, matters are no longer so clear, however.

Although the nutritional triad of cereals, grapes, and olives was arguably a thousand years old in Greece by the Archaic period, Hesiod makes no mention of either the cultivation of olive trees or the processing of the fruit. In fact in his only reference to the olive Hesiod places its oil in a setting of luxury where it is used as a lotion (*W&D* 519–24). It is Rackham's (1983, 313) judgment that cultivation of the domestic olive has spread into

29. Regarding this latter option see Hodkinson 1988, 42.
30. The practice of permitting the grapes to lie in the sun for ten days and then in the shade for five more before crushing them (*W&D* 612–13) is defended by both Mazon and West ad loc. Isager and Skydsgaard (1992, 56), however, believe that this must be a reference to making raisins, apparently conflated with a description of processing grapes for wine. Hanson (1995, 96, 150–51) also appears to assume that Hesiod is talking about raisins.

inland Boeotia only in the last 150 years. Hesiod may be referring to oil collected from the wild species or else to a luxury good acquired from another region through trade.[31]

The only other cultivated plant mentioned by Hesiod is the fig (W&D 681). Though the word *kradē* does not necessarily mean "fig," that seems likely here in view of the comparison of the leaf to the imprint left by a bird's foot. *Kradē* does not necessarily refer to the domestic variety of the tree, either (cf. Eur. fr. 679.1 [Nauck]). Hesiod elsewhere mentions the fruit of the wild fig (*olunthos:* fr. 278.1 [M-W]) but refers nowhere to the domestic fig *(sukeē)* or its fruit *(sukon)* though both are named by Homer. In any case, Hesiod mentions the *kradē* not in connection with its cultivation or its fruit but as a weather sign for the spring sailing season. If the fig is cultivated in Ascra, as it may be, Hesiod does not give the impression that it is a significant crop.

References by Hesiod to specific crops are now exhausted, but some generic references remain. Hesiod uses the verb *phuteuein* two times in *Works and Days* and the noun *phuton* three times.[32] The contrast between *sperma* and *phuta* at line 781 distinguishes *phuta* as crops that are planted, not sown. The image of the snail climbing a *phuton* at line 571 supports this meaning. Homer uses the word for garden crops and trees, including vines (*Od.* 244–47, *Il.* 21.257–59). Since Hesiod does not specify, he could simply refer to grape vines by *phuton,* but he could certainly refer as well to orchard and garden crops not explicitly named. So in line 22, where *phuteuein* is paired with *arōmenai,* "to plow," the latter word likely includes the notion of sowing as well, making a contrast between cereal and non-cereal, "planted" crops.[33] Even at that, however, as West suggests ad loc., the most straightforward interpretation of the word is as a reference to planting vines, the only such crop mentioned explicitly in the poem. In any case it seems to me probable that tree crops and garden crops describ-

31. See Hanson 1995, 30–34, regarding Mycenean use of wild olive fruit, and Marie-Claire Amouretti 1986, 44–45, regarding the slow transition to complete reliance on domestic varieties in Greece. Isager and Skydsgaard (1992, 19–20) argue for the long presence of olive cultivation in Greece; cf. Richter 1968, 134–40; Sallares 1991, 32–34; and Sarpaki 1992, 70.

32. *Phuteuein* at 812, however, refers to propagating the farmer's progeny rather than to "planting."

33. So Hofinger s.v. *phuteuō.* The position, however, that *phuteuein* in this context is generic for all crops and so bears equally the sense of "sow" is supported by *Od.* 9.108–10, where *oute phuteuousin* (108) is glossed by *asparta* (109) and illustrated by "wheat, barley, and grapes" (110).

able as *phuta* were cultivated in Ascra.[34] Hesiod, however, hardly gives them any prominence in his agricultural year, and we must assume that they were overshadowed by cereals as the community's staple. Hesiod gives virtually no evidence at all for crops other than cereals and vines.

Livestock

The only livestock Hesiod discusses in any detail are the draft animals necessary to cultivate cereals. He does make a few generic references to husbandry, however. At *Works and Days* 120, a line rejected by West, he describes the race of gold as "wealthy in sheep" *(aphneioi mēloisi)* following upon his description of the fertility of their land. Later in a passage praising work (*W&D* 308) Hesiod explains that it is from their labor that men are "in possession of many sheep and wealthy" *(polumēloi t' aphneioi te)*. Again, this phrase occurs in a context stressing agricultural productivity. Finally in his lines on the city of justice Hesiod describes sheep weighted down with wool (*W&D* 234) as a generic mark of prosperity alongside of the bounty of the cultivated fields. But the fact that Hesiod makes general references to husbandry and associates it with wealth in itself tells us nothing about how widely or on what scale herding was practiced in Ascra.

References to husbandry in the catalogue of days have a slightly more practical ring to them. At lines 774–75 Hesiod claims the elevenths and twelfths of the month are good for shearing sheep or reaping. Hesiod specifies further (*W&D* 786, 791–92) that the sixth of the month is good for gelding goats and rams, the eighth is suited to gelding boars and bulls, and the twelfth for mules. References to clothing and food, however, provide the strongest evidence for livestock rearing. In a description of winter clothing he recommends a densely woven *chlaina* (537–38) and a felt cap, both presumably made of wool. In the same passage he describes boots made from cowhide (541–42) and a raincoat of goat's hide (543–45). Cow-

---

34. Cf. Halstead and Jones 1989, 50, regarding the combination of extensive cereal cultivation with intensive gardening. For some idea of the range of crops cultivated in Greece from the earliest times, see the tables summarizing crops evidenced at neolithic sites in Greece in Renfrew 1973, 161 and 1979, passim, where both pulses and cereals figure prominently, and in Sarpaki 1992, 64–69. Isager and Skydsgaard (1992, 41–43) list summer crops and Richter (1968, 107–46) lists Homeric crops or those attested to in the archaeological record. Cf. Burford 1993, 132–44 for lists of crops in various categories.

hide could come from draft animals but wool and goat hide must be gotten from mature herding animals. Hesiod's menu for his midsummer feast includes goat's milk and barley cakes made with milk (590), though he does not mention cheese, and both heifer and kid are listed as entrées for this special meal (591–92). The information supplied by Hesiod is too sketchy to support generalizations, but slaughter of young males would be most characteristic of a strategy aiming at maximizing milk production (see Halstead 1987, 77–81). It is possible that the unbred cow and the first-born kid are mentioned here as rarely eaten delicacies, perhaps consumed along with the first grain from the harvest. It might also be the case that it was necessary at this time of year to thin offspring in order to keep flocks within the limits of pasturage.

While Hesiod does not explicitly discuss husbandry as a part of the farmer's annual routines, he nonetheless clearly takes for granted the presence on the farm of livestock in addition to draft animals. How were these livestock integrated into the pattern of land use and how did they affect the intensity of the exploitation of the land? The reference to setting up a pen for flocks (*sēkon ... poimnēion: W&D* 787) suggests a temporary structure set up in pasture (for gelding, as West suggests ad loc.). The scene of Hesiod shepherding his flock on Mount Helicon (*Th.* 22–25), if we can use this apparently autobiographical reference from *Theogony* to illuminate *Works and Days*, may suggest a pattern: during summer, while fodder closer in to the village is in short supply, livestock are grazed in higher, outfield pastures some short distance from the village, and during winter they are grazed closer in to the village on fallow, whose soil is enriched by the dung of the grazing animals. In this case the size of flocks would be limited by the availability of winter pasture and that would be further constrained by the needs of draft animals. A more extensive scenario would place Hesiod's flocks on dedicated pasture throughout the year.

The degree to which stock-rearing and agriculture were integrated and interdependent in ancient Greek practice remains a point of controversy. Isager and Skydsgaard (1992, 99–101, Skydsgaard 1988) remain convinced that husbandry and agriculture were separate and distinct areas of economic activity for the Greeks. Halstead (1981, 1987), Hodkinson (1988), and Cherry (1988) have rejected this traditionalist position in favor of an integrated system of intensive cultivation and small-scale stock-rearing. I have already summarized my objections to Halstead's argument for intensive agriculture in a setting of low population density, but that does not rule out some level of integration between husbandry and cultivation. I suggest here that even under a fairly extensive pattern of land use and limited seasonal transhumance there could easily have been some degree of interdependence between the two.[35]

Needless to say, one must largely rely upon speculation in this matter. Hesiod's Ascra clearly enough relies upon livestock for clothing, dairy products, and occasional meat. Ascra's proximity to pasture on Helicon, moreover, would seem to make husbandry an attractive support to the agricultural economy (so *Th.* 22–23). But the absence of direct, descriptive references to herding in *Works and Days* cannot be argued away. Indeed, the very failure of additional evidence from *Works and Days* suggests that husbandry was not a central element of the subsistence economy. Based on what Hesiod does say, I would hazard the conjecture that the Ascrans kept small flocks of goats and sheep who were grazed on mountain pastures in the summer (since fields have been cleared of straw saved as fodder for draft animals) and on fallow and lowland pastures in winter. The needs of draft animals would have constituted a primary constraint on the size of such flocks. Such a pattern of land use relies upon the availability of pasture around the village, including fallow during the winter. If this is an accurate picture of Hesiod's Ascra, it suggests a fairly extensive use of the land under a short fallow regime. Certainly Hesiod does not mention transporting dung from animal pens to fields or garden as would be expected under more intensive regimes than short fallow, which require fertilizing and leave only limited pasture available.

There is a clear contrast between the livestock economy we can infer from *Works and Days* and the husbandry attributed by Homer to the house of Odysseus. His household employs three different slaves for the care, respectively, of hogs, cattle, and goats, and each of these has assistants (*Od.* 14.5–28, 96–108; 17.212–14 ff.; 20.185–225). These herds are adequate to provide the suitors with a steady supply of meat and no doubt sufficed for the entertainment of Odysseus's retainers before he left for Troy. The scale and diversity of Odysseus's herding operations reflect, however, the opportunities for enrichment available to a Homeric chieftain (*Od.* 1.389–93), but also the obligations of generosity and hospitality imposed upon this figure both by his *hetairoi* and the demos. This type of herding operation serves the requirements of a political economy.

35. Precisely the sort of integration suggested here is discussed by Boserup 1981, 18–23 and Hodkinson 1988, 42.

Storage

Storage of food is especially important for short fallow cultivation because of the widely spaced and relatively uncertain harvests. As Boserup points out (1965, 48–51), cereals, to which plow and short fallow are adapted, tend to share a common growing cycle. This circumstance prevents farmers from spreading sowing and harvesting cycles more evenly across the year and leaves them especially liable to devastating crop failures. This risk is further exacerbated by the high interannual variability of rainfall in a semi-arid region like Greece.[36] Since I have already discussed the theme of storage in detail (pp. 86–89), I can limit my comments here. Hesiod's repeated emphasis upon storage and saving throughout *Works and Days* supports the hypothesis that he describes a short fallow regime, since the greater the intensity of cultivation, the more harvests there are per year, and the less the farmer must rely upon any single crop. The consequent importance of storage to Hesiod is sufficiently attested by the opposition in *Works and Days* between storage and hunger (*W&D* 299–301 and 361–67). Hesiod's preoccupation with storage typifies an extensive regime within the parameters of short fallow cultivation.

THE AGRICULTURAL CALENDAR

Boserup presents the short fallow regime as characterized by uneven demands for labor with seasonal peaks and intervening periods of underemployment. The amount of land that a household can successfully cultivate is limited, then, by the amount of labor it can muster during the peak seasons of sowing and harvesting. At this point I would like to examine the timing of the various activities of the agricultural year in order to identify the rhythm of slack and peak seasons. Does Hesiod present a sequence of tasks that correspond to time-stress patterns characteristic of short fallow cultivation or does he present a picture more appropriate to the continuous employment required by an intensive regime of agriculture?[37]

Plowing and Sowing

The two poles organizing the agricultural year, the periods of peak time stress, are introduced in the lines commencing the agricultural calendar.

36. See Garnsey 1988, 8–16.
37. Boserup 1965, 48–51. Halstead and Jones (1989, 43–47) review the rhythm of slack and busy seasons in the agricultural calendar of the Greek islands in the modern period, and Burford (1993, 132–44) analyzes the agriculture calendar for ancient Greece.

The heliacal setting of the Pleiades marks the time for plowing and sowing in the fall and their reappearance in spring signals that harvest season is at hand (*W&D* 383–87). These same three operations of plowing, sowing, and harvest are linked again in the lines following (*W&D* 388–94) as the three most important operations of the year. West has calculated Hesiod's recommended dates for commencing the fall plowing and sowing to be October 31 and for harvest to be May 11.[38] The migration of the cranes also signals the arrival of winter rains and of plowing season (*W&D* 448–57). Hesiod warns that if the farmer has not plowed by the winter solstice, his crop will fail (*W&D* 479–84).[39] At the outside, then, plowing could be spread out from late October through late December. Hesiod's sense of haste about plowing (*W&D* 458–61) and the need to bring in extra laborers (*W&D* 441–47 with discussion below, pp. 142–43), however, suggests that the task was performed quickly once the right conditions had arrived. The injunction to plow both dry and damp soil (*W&D* 460) may refer to plowing by a specific date even if rainfall is abnormal or, perhaps more likely, to the differing conditions found in fields in different locations at the time when plowing begins. Either way, the implication is that the plowing must be done within a certain time frame even if conditions are not perfect all the way around. The advice to sow when the soil is still light (*eti kouphizousan: W&D* 463) provides a further precaution against waiting too long to commence plowing. Once the rains have started, muddy soil will make plowing difficult.[40] Plowing and sowing too soon, however, with early rains, could leave germinating seeds with too little moisture to survive. The need to time the plowing and sowing to the optimal conditions and then to complete the operation while those conditions last places heavy demands upon available labor.

Winter Work

For the roughly two months following the winter solstice Hesiod refers vaguely to tasks that can be accomplished and warns against just sitting around in the *leschē* or blacksmith's shop (*W&D* 493–503). In the following descriptions of the month of Lenaion Hesiod enumerates its hardships

38. Mazon ad loc., making slightly different assumptions about the date of composition for *W&D*, proposes November 3 and May 14.

39. Hesiod allows for a late plowing season at the time when the cuckoo first calls. West (1978, 253) times the late plowing to the winter solstice though Mazon ad loc. places the cuckoo's first call at the end of March, citing Xenophon *Oec.* 17.4, as testimony for a late plowing season towards the end of winter.

40. See West and Mazon ad loc.

(*W&D* 504–35), describes how to dress for the weather (*W&D* 536–45), and warns against getting caught out in the rain (*W&D* 546–58), but devotes only one line to a generic reference to the work to be done during this season (*W&D* 554). Mazon ad 493–503 suggests that weeding and repair of damage caused by winter weather are the farmer's occupations at this time. No doubt there was work to be done around the farm during this period, but Hesiod's lack of detail and his warning to avoid the hangouts frequented by others suggest that these months comprised a slack season for the farmer.

Pruning of the vines begins sixty days after the solstice, in late February or early March, when Arcturus rises at dusk and the swallow's appearance signals the onset of spring (*W&D* 564–70). The time for trenching the vines has passed when the Pleiades reappear and the snail begins to climb up onto plants (*W&D* 571–72). This brings us to early May, with perhaps ten weeks available for work on the vines. The fact that a farmer might consider sailing toward the end of this period (*W&D* 678–88 with West ad 678) suggests that the season's farm work required a relatively low level of effort.[41] The spring plowing of fallow (*W&D* 462) must occur during this same period since there would be no time for it during the subsequent harvest season.

Harvest and Threshing

The end of the vine trenching is marked by the arrival of the harvest (*W&D* 571–81). This commences around May 11. The advice to avoid shady siestas, to rise at dawn, and to make haste signals another period of time stress.

Before his account of the threshing Hesiod interposes a description of a summertime break from work. When the *skolumos* blossoms, the *tettix* chirps in the trees, and Sirius parches the heads and knees of men, it is time for rest. The threshing commences with the rising of Orion (*W&D* 597–608). By Mazon's calculation this pause lasts about two weeks. West, however, transposes this stage of the farmer's year, placing it *after* the threshing, and thus makes it continuous with the inactivity of the months of August and early September.[42] If we follow West, the threshing (*W&D* 597–

41. Mele (1979, 16, 93–94) overstates the conflict between time devoted to trading voyages and the demands of farm work. His argument flatly ignores the reason Hesiod supplies for a cautious attitude towards trade, namely the risks of seafaring (*W&D* 618–26, 673–88).

42. The blooming of the *skolumos* can be dated to the summer solstice on the basis of a passage in Theophrastus (West and Mazon ad 582). West (ad 417) times

608) commences on June 20, preceding the summer pause; if we accept
Mazon's calendar, threshing begins around July 5, after the summer pause.
Hesiod goes from threshing to the storage of the grain, straw, and chaff without mentioning the winnowing (597–601, 606–7). He notes a few other
tasks to be seen to after the threshing, but none that are time-consuming.
This summertime pause balances thematically the winter month of Lenaion,
at roughly the opposite time of the year, whose cold and shortage contrast
with the heat and plenty of July. Both are periods of reduced work.

Sailing Season

Hesiod next moves to the vintage (*W&D* 609–17), but, as 663–65 and
673–75 make clear, the sailing season (*W&D* 618–94) precedes the vintage
chronologically. The sailing season, Hesiod tells us, begins after the solstice
and lasts for 50 days, roughly the third week of June through the second

---

the heliacal rising of Sirius for Hesiod to July 19. There is a discrepancy of about a
month here between these two points that should, along with the chirping of the
tettix, specify the time of the summer pause. West (ad 598) dates the heliacal rising
of Orion's dominant star to June 20, roughly contemporary with the blooming of
the *skolumos* and, as he points out, a month *before* the rising of Sirius. This would
place the threshing either before the summer pause (Sirius) or simultaneous with
it *(skolumos)*, contradicting Hesiod either way. In his chart on p. 253 West (1978)
favors the astral signs over the *skolumos* and places the threshing of the grain *before* the midsummer pause even though these sections appear in the opposite order
in the poem. He also, surprisingly, shows the *skolumos* there blooming in mid-
July, a month after the solstice. Petropoulos (1994, 69–77) likewise argues that Hesiod has reversed the chronological order of the midsummer pause and the threshing (69–77). Relying upon data for the wheat harvest from Greece in the modern
period, Petropoulos (1994, 27–29) places the harvest in June, when the *tettix* is already singing. This is followed by the threshing in July, which is normally completed by the rising of Sirius on July 20. The winnowing follows, synchronized with
the onset of the Etesian winds. Petropoulos would start the harvest up to three
weeks later than the date given by Hesiod. Mazon (ad 582–96), however, who does
not discuss Sirius, specifies July 5 for the rising of Orion, about two weeks after the
solstice and thus accommodating Hesiod's account. In all fairness to Hesiod, one
must acknowledge that there is, of course, a certain imprecision in these calcula-
tions: Sirius would be in the sky at the same time as the sun, which is the issue (see
West ad 417), before the date of its heliacal rising; and it is, of course, impossible to
specify the date of the rising of an entire constellation, such as Orion, composed of
multiple stars. Although neither interpretation of the lines is satisfactory, it seems
to me best to follow Mazon here for the following reasons. (1) This is the order in
which Hesiod lists these stages of the farmer's year; (2) Mazon provides ancient testimonia for the practice of preserving an interval between harvest and threshing of
grain; (3) Hesiod does not specify the rising of Sirius but only the star's presence in
the sky; (4) West's schedule places the threshing a month before the onset of the
Etesian breezes (West ad 663), which may have been required for winnowing.

of August. As West points out (ad 663), lines 673–77, advising against staying at sea past the new wine and the rains of late summer, extend the season into late September. The sailing season overlaps either with the threshing or the midsummer break and might extend into the vintage. Presumably those farmers who did elect to export produce by sea were not absent for the entire period. Except for the possibility that it overlaps with the threshing, the sailing season extends through a period for which Hesiod specifies no activities.

The Vintage

The vintage begins with the heliacal rising of Arcturus, by which time Sirius and Orion are due south at dawn (609–10). By West's reckoning this is September 8. As, apparently, with the grain, the grapes are not processed immediately but allowed to sit in the sun and then the shade for a total of fifteen days. Allowing for time to gather in the grapes, the processing of the vintage could not be completed before the end of September and perhaps extends into October. The busy periods of the vintage itself and the pressing and bottling, however, are separated by the two weeks when the grapes are allowed to sit. This schedule allows nevertheless for some slack time before the fall plowing commences at the end of October, during which the only prescribed activity is scavenging for wood for various purposes (*W&D* 420–36).

The Annual Rhythm

Hesiod's almost maniacal preoccupation with continuous, intensive toil must be viewed within the calendar of tasks he actually details. There is a clear rhythm of periods of time stress and slack time.

> Late October—Winter Solstice: The agricultural year begins with the intensive work of plowing and sowing, lasting up to seven weeks. These tasks may not, however, occupy the entire season from October 31 through December 22, but when the right moment arrives within that period, the work must be done very quickly.

> Winter Solstice—Early March: For the following period Hesiod insists that there is work to be done, but is not able to specify anything in particular. The very warnings to avoid the *lesche* and the blacksmith's shop make it clear that many farmers are frequenting these refuges from the cold weather during this season (*W&D* 493–95). This is not a period in which high demands are made upon the household's labor.

Early March—Early May: Pruning and trenching of the vines occupies this two-month period. The amount of time available for these proce-dures suggests that they require a less intensive effort than the fall plowing, the harvest, or the vintage. This seems the most likely period for the spring plowing of fallow fields.

Early May—mid-July: The harvest season begins early in May and ex-tends through the threshing and winnowing. If we follow Mazon, these intensive activities are interrupted by an interlude of rest for about two weeks. Certainly the post-harvest tasks are complete by mid- to late July. Hesiod makes it clear that this is a time of hard work and long hours.

Mid-July—Early September: Part of July and the month of August, however, are largely devoid of farm activities. Otherwise the good sail-ing weather during this period would not be something a farmer could take advantage of. This period provides the most likely opportunity for the summer plowing, an activity that would not require the same hurry or concentration as the fall plowing.

Early September—Late October: The grape harvest begins in early Sep-tember and the processing of the grapes perhaps leaves a brief interval before plowing season returns. There is a slack period of about two weeks between the end of the vintage and the crushing of the grapes.

Hesiod's agricultural year is organized around two main peak seasons and two main slack seasons. The first period of intensive work begins with the vintage in early September and extends through plowing and planting of the cereal crops on to the winter solstice. The second peak season com-mences with the cereal harvest in early May and ends with the threshing, completed in July. This schedule leaves part of July, August, and part of September relatively free, as well as the months of January and February. The vineyard work of March, April, and early May, moreover, appears to have been less intensive than that of plowing, harvesting, and vintage. Slack seasons occur at the times of the year most inhospitable to a matur-ing annual crop, and that of the depth of winter is balanced by that of the height of summer. Hesiod appears to thematize this contrast of the two seasons in the poem through the opposition between frigid Boreas (*W&D* 505–19) and the steady Etesians (*W&D* 670–72) or refreshing Zephyr (*W&D* 594), the sheltered virgin (*W&D* 519–24) and the lustfulness of wives (*W&D* 586), short rations (559–60) and plenty (*W&D* 585, 589–

93), and between winter clothing (*W&D* 536–46) and rest beneath a shady rock (*W&D* 589, 592–93).

We can safely assume that Hesiod's sketchy calendar omits some features of the farmer's year. Notably, there is no mention of livestock, which is attested to otherwise in the poem, nor does he discuss garden crops or tree crops such as the fig. Their absence from his account, however, suggests that they did not make major demands upon the resources of the household and so were not mainstays of the agricultural economy. Hesiod's calendar clearly indicates a regular rhythm of peak and slack periods of effort—that is, a rhythm of full and partial employment over the seasons of the year. The cereal cycle comprises the core of the subsistence economy, with viticulture and perhaps gardening and husbandry filling in some of the slack periods. Hesiod's calendar of tasks does display the rhythms of slack and busy seasons characteristic of an extensive short fallow regime.

CONCLUSIONS

I take it for granted that the intensity at which agricultural land is exploited is directly related to population density and the complexity of a social formation. Under a regime of intensive cultivation we expect to find a relatively dense population as well as established institutions of social hierarchy. Conversely, the more extensive the agricultural regime, the more autonomous the subsistence economy ought to be. Does the agricultural regime described by Hesiod correspond to the degree of complexity that I attribute to the social formation described in *Works and Days*?

Hesiod is clearly not describing a long fallow regime, and I have already argued that short fallow is the most extensive regime practicable under the ecological conditions confronting Hesiod. At the same time, the narrow spectrum of crops described by Hesiod, the seasonal slack times, the importance attributed to fallowing, the omission of manuring and irrigation, and the absence of field-sown pulses as an element in a crop-rotation scheme all argue against the intensive regimes of annual or multi-cropping. His emphasis upon the importance of fallow to cultivation, the dominance of cereal crops, and the use of the plow with broadcast sowing all suggest, rather, a short fallow regime. Within this specific fallowing regime, what is the degree of intensity?

The fact that draft animals appear to be stall-fed only part of the year is a strong piece of evidence that Hesiod describes a short fallow regime practiced at a low level of intensity. More information about the extent of livestock rearing and its interaction with agriculture would illuminate further this issue of the intensity with which available land is used. Hesiod's calendar of the agricultural year, moreover, exhibits the seasonal slack times characteristic of a short fallow regime. Though it is reasonable to assume that other non-cereal crops were cultivated in Ascra, Hesiod explicitly identifies viticulture alone as a complement to the demands of the cereal cycle. Even olives were not cultivated. The central place occupied by storage likewise typifies the short fallow regime, whose heavy reliance upon cereals leaves little security against a crop failure. Land use patterns, as best we can determine them, are indicative of a relatively sparse population. Ascra was probably a place where land was still available to be cleared and brought under cultivation (indeed, this may be how Hesiod's father came into his land: *W&D* 635–40).

The pattern I sketch out here corresponds pretty closely to that attributed by Isager and Skydsgaard (1992, 21–26, 46–49, 108–14) to Hesiod as well as to ancient Greek farmers generally. That is, Hesiod appears to me to fit pretty well into the so-called traditional model, characteristic of traditional agriculture in Greece in the modern period, which Halstead and others have argued not to have been characteristic of ancient Greece (Halstead 1987, 77–79, 83–85 and Halstead and Jones 1989, 47–53). It is worth observing here that this controversy concerns itself primarily with agricultural practice in Attica in the Classical period, a time and place offering radically different circumstances from those in which Hesiod practiced an extensive form of short fallow agriculture. Indeed, the anti-traditionalists have exhibited little interest in Hesiod's somewhat inconvenient testimony. Be that as it may, in my own opinion the evidence from *Works and Days* has little to tell us about how farmers went about their business in fifth-century Attica under circumstances of a much denser population and a more complex social formation. Additionally, although evidence from *Theogony* suggests transhumance (if the five-kilometer trek onto the slopes of Helicon constitutes "transhumance"), I see no reason why Ascran farmers would not have sought to integrate small-scale husbandry with cultivation where it was possible to do so advantageously.

I have concluded that long fallow cultivation—shifting agriculture, Boserup's forest fallow and bush fallow systems—was not practicable under the ecological conditions of Greece of Hesiod's time, leaving short fallow cultivation the most extensive form of agriculture possible. This fact is significant since, even at very low population densities, it makes it advantageous to farmers to control on a permanent basis fields that they have improved for plow cultivation, and this in turn creates the conditions for the formation of hamlets or villages. I would argue, however, that the ecological conditions that impose a relatively intensive agricultural regime at low population densities do not dramatically alter the balance between the subsistence economy and the political economy. Under a long fallow regime, it is the availability of land, enabling a family to relocate really at any time, that gives settlements their impermanence and undermines the emergence of regular, self-sustaining authority. Even if the vineyards and the cleared and contoured fields of the Ascran plow-farmer tie him more closely to a specific plot than do the fire-cleared gardens and orchards of the long fallow farmer, still the plentiful supply of the basic resource for securing a livelihood, land, would foil any attempt at building hierarchy. In the first place, families dissatisfied with a domineering neighbor would simply move on. In the second, the very availability of land would make it difficult for a would-be leader to assert the control over access to this indispensable resource that could serve as the basis of power. The discussion offered here must remain rather speculative since there is too much we simply cannot know about conditions in Hesiod's Ascra. Suffice it to conclude that I find the heavy emphasis upon the self-sufficiency of the individual household and the rudimentary political economy found in *Works and Days* in keeping with the extensive agricultural regime described in the poem.

5 The Shape of Hesiod's Ascra

Donlan (1982, 1989, and 1998) has characterized the Homeric polity as a low-level chiefdom. The Homeric chieftain's ability to coerce his followers is in fact quite limited and the primary source of his authority is his generosity. The chief obliges his followers, including other chiefs where possible, within a system of generalized reciprocity, the apex of which he occupies. The *basileus* thus serves a redistributive role, at least among his followers, his *hetairoi*.[1] Donlan's analysis, however, also shows the Homeric chiefdom to be inherently unstable and its hierarchy in constant danger of disintegrating into a regime of balanced reciprocity. Homeric society— with its trade in luxury goods, its emergent aristocracy of "kings," or chieftains, its fortified settlements, its raiding parties, and its developed system of reciprocities unifying the elite across geographical boundaries and binding leaders and followers within individual communities—this system is dated by Donlan to the final stage of the Dark Age, approximately 900–800 B.C. and a bit beyond, although more recent dates have been proposed. To designate this as the dominant social formation for the Dark Age, however, does not amount to claiming that it comprises the sole mode of social organization for Greece during that period. If my arguments are correct that Hesiod represents in *Works and Days* a simpler mode of social organization than that depicted by Homer, then this emergent chiefdom establishes

---

1. Donlan and Thomas (1993, 65–66) argue that the redistributive economy in the Homeric polity as a whole was inadequately developed to support chiefly authority. The chiefly lineage did, however, control access to positions of authority, was in a position to make allocations of land, and was engaged in limited redistribution of subsistence goods (Donlan 1997, 657–63).

a threshold of complexity from which we must retreat in order to characterize the social formation presented in *Works and Days*.

While my examination of the community depicted in *Works and Days* has been largely organized as a refutation of the characterization of Ascra as a peasant village, there should nevertheless emerge out of such a project a positive description of what Hesiod's Ascra was like. Such a picture offers valuable assistance for constructing a more nuanced account of Greece at what is regarded as a transitional phase: the developments of the eighth century that catapult Greece into the dynamic world of the Archaic period. Johnson and Earle provide a good starting point. I have utilized their work to identify a range on a continuum of increasingly complex social formations within which the institutions and practices described by Hesiod can be located. Johnson and Earle themselves, regarding the status of the different evolutionary stages that they identify, make the following qualifications:

> These labels do not signify perfectly discrete levels or plateaus, to one or another of which all known cultures must be assigned; rather they designate stations along a continuum at which it is convenient to stop and make comparisons with previous stations. "Chiefdom," for example, is a convenient abstraction for a culture that is still evolving from (and contains elements of) the Big Man collectivity or the local group, and for one that may be well along the road to becoming a state. Since the evolutionary continuum represents a transformation of many variables at once, local conditions and history produce many variants that appear "more evolved" in some respects and "less evolved" in others when compared to their neighbors on the continuum. (Johnson and Earle 1987, 313–14)[2]

Ascra exhibits features characteristic of several of the social formations described by Johnson and Earle. As they acknowledge, what Johnson and Earle present at their various levels are not real societies but abstracted, synchronic models of societies. Hesiod represents his village as a community in process, in transition. It should not be expected to correspond precisely to any single model. The peculiarities of Ascra's history, moreover, as well as those of Greek history and culture, preclude an exact fit with any single generic category. Yet this evolutionary system can nevertheless enable us to locate Ascra in terms of its general level of complexity by reference to other societies. This framework will show that Hesiod's Ascra is

---

2. Cf. Morris's (1997b, 98–100) proposal of a "spectrum" of models for classification of state-level societies, focusing upon the Classical polis.

indeed a less complex community than the Homeric chiefdom described above.

The family-level society, the simplest form of community described by Johnson and Earle (1987, 19–20, 91–94, 314–16), exhibits some similarities to Hesiod's depiction of Ascra. Labor and technology are organized and provided for by the family. Inter-family cooperation is weak and occurs on a voluntary basis. Exchange partnerships are based on personal relationships unmediated by kinship structures or community hierarchy. Political identity and ceremonial are weakly developed. Characteristically, however, such societies live primarily by foraging. They are not tied to a fixed locale but congregate and disperse seasonally within a vaguely defined range. Storage does not occupy an important place in the subsistence regime. When families do congregate into hamlet-sized settlements, they are subject to splintering because of disagreements among the constituent families. Obviously, short fallow cultivation, ownership of land, sedentary habitation, storage, and many other features of life in Ascra distinguish it from the family-level society.

The local group, the next stage on Johnson's and Earle's developmental continuum (1987, 20, 152–59, 194–201, 314–20), is characterized by population density in the low-to-moderate range. Its technology is simple. Farmers cultivate domesticated foods and communities rely upon food storage. Settlements are permanent and located near resources. Field boundaries are carefully marked. The economy and technology remain under the control of individual families, which can lay claim to productive capital. Stratification in such communities is not pronounced since there is little opportunity for individuals to assert control over access to productive resources. Hierarchy does emerge in the form of the competition for status. Success in the competition for status, moreover, aids in the formation of personal networks for cooperation and exchange. In such general terms there are many features shared by the local group and Ascra.

This level distinguishes between the acephalous local group and the more complex Big Man local group. The acephalous local group may have a headman, but his influence is subordinate to the network of household-to-household relationships. The case study illustrative of this mode of organization exhibits no powerful kin structures. Subsistence insurance is managed through dyadic, voluntary relationships. Leadership, ceremony, and politics are not controlled by specialists. Again, however, similarities to Ascra are balanced by differences. This particular example represents a pastoral society, not agricultural, one that practices seasonal dispersion and aggregation. Indeed, acephalous local groups generally exhibit such elements of a political economy as segmentation into lineages or clans, a headman, and ceremony integrating the community. Thus, although the family remains the primary social unit, its behavior reflects the needs of the larger group. Such groups, moreover, exhibit a territorial sensibility.

The Big Man collectivity stands at the more complex extreme of the range of societies comprehended within the category of local group. The setting for a Big Man collectivity is characteristically one of intensive warfare over control of land and resources. The Big Man serves additionally to integrate his community internally and organizes risk management and investment in subsistence technology. This leader functions as the intermediary between his own and other communities by sponsoring trade, forming alliances, and representing it in intergroup ceremony. Through the agency of the Big Man not only are families and supra-familial structures such as clans or lineages integrated into the local group, but the local group is itself integrated into a larger system of adjacent local groups.

The features of a permanent village, privately held fields, reliance on agriculture, and food storage, all elements of the subsistence regime, are characteristic of the local-group level of organization. Yet the political economy of Ascra would more closely typify a family-group society. Ascra lacks anything resembling a Big Man seeing to its defense, organizing investments in technology, managing risk, and negotiating alliances and trade exchanges with other groups. Clearly, the presence in Ascra of a local *basileus,* someone to function at least as a village headman, would allow Hesiod's village to fit more neatly within Johnson and Earle's taxonomy. Ascra, as a permanent agrarian settlement, would be quite credible as a rudimentary Big Man collectivity, still smaller and less integrated than Thespiae but structured nevertheless by some level of political economy. Without the *basileus,* Ascra might more closely resemble the less complex form of the local group.

A further eccentricity for Ascra lies in the lack of any supra-familial kinship structures whatsoever. Yet this is not so much a stumbling block for understanding Ascra in particular as for comparative analysis of ancient Greek society generally since it is widely accepted that such corporate and extensive kin groups simply did not play an important role in Greek social organization. Even the structures of *phulon* and *phrētrē* that Donlan (1985) argues to have substituted for kinship as modes of supra-familial relation in the Dark Age play no apparent role in *Works and Days.*[3]

---

3. The authoritative discussions are those of Bourriot 1976 and of Roussel 1976. This problem for understanding the Dark Age and Archaic period is discussed by

What we see in Ascra is a community that is heterogeneous when judged against the orderly progression of institutions outlined in Johnson and Earle's evolutionary scheme. As Johnson and Earle point out in the passage quoted above, however, the local conditions and history for each specific case will produce uneven levels of development across the range of categories through which societies are conceptualized in their model.[4] Ascra exhibits traits that span the range from the family-level group to the Big Man collectivity but, significantly for my argument, not beyond. It possesses a simpler form of social organization than the communities overseen by the Homeric *basileus* and hardly qualifies as a peasant community, under the control of an outside elite.

HESIOD'S ASCRA

To sum up, then, how do I characterize Hesiod's Ascra at this point? I assume that Boeotia of the late eighth and early seventh centuries did not experience the same rapid population growth evidenced elsewhere in Greece. Ascra itself, moreover, was isolated from the early consolidations of polis communities in the lowlands, notably Thespiae's emergence from a cluster of villages as a polis. The valley in which Ascra is situated was only sparsely populated. Low population density in Ascra enabled farmers to practice an extensive agricultural regime, and plentiful resources supplied a relatively secure livelihood. Farmers practiced short fallow plow agriculture for cereal cultivation and kept vineyards as well. It seems to me highly probable that other crops were grown too, but Hesiod's silence about them suggests that they were not so significant as cereals and grapes and that they were probably therefore garden rather than field crops. Both draft animals and other livestock were fed on dedicated pasture and perhaps upon fallow. Draft animals enjoyed some stall-feeding from straw, chaff, and perhaps other waste, but not from fodder crops. Hesiod attests as well to the use of secondary products from livestock such as wool and goat's milk. Ascrans inhabited a *kōmē*, a village, which appears to have been the traditional habitation pat-

---

Whitley 1991, 352, 361–65 and by Donlan 1989, 23–24. See also the hypotheses of Morris (1987, 87–93) and Sallares (1991, 160–92).

4. In his more recent *How Chiefs Come to Power* (1997) Earle seems far more interested in tracing such discontinuities. I consider it prudent to employ a certain flexibility in working with the sort of framework constructed by Johnson and Earle. The complete "decoupling" of the social and the economic for which Upham (1990, 1–17) argues, however, strikes me as unjustified.

tern for Greece. In part this permanent settlement reflects the investment made in improving fields for plowing as well as in vineyards. *Works and Days* itself supplies no evidence for differential access to the means of gaining a livelihood—that one segment of the community has gained a monopoly over essential resources, land and water primarily, and is able to limit access to them for other members of the community. Rather the community appears to be fairly egalitarian, showing no institutional centralization or hierarchy.

Prestige and authority in the village are based upon the productivity of individual households and the possession of a surplus that can be made available to households experiencing a shortfall. Production of enough of a surplus to enable a household to extend assistance to neighbors would depend not only upon the quality of land and the age distribution within the household but also upon the family's willingness to do more work than minimally necessary to meet its own subsistence needs. Hesiod suggests that community members engaged in competition, *eris,* to achieve standing within the community through such auto-exploitation. Obligations to provide aid and claims upon that aid weaken as relationships become more distant from the immediate household. Within the household, generalized reciprocity governs sharing. Beyond the boundaries of the household, however, obligations even to close kin can be exhausted when loans are not repaid. Among non-kin, sharing on the basis of balanced reciprocity, with toleration of deferred repayment, occurs between individuals bound to each other as *philoi* or *hetairoi.* So, the propinquity of village life enables inhabitants to form voluntary associations within which obligations are traded back and forth in the form of short-term loans of food as well as draft animals or perhaps other implements or services. Hesiod views such relationships as long-term though he acknowledges that they are not always so. Through such friendships the individual is able to create a network of relationships extending beyond the kin group to secure a degree of subsistence insurance against the uncertainties that accompany short fallow cultivation in a Mediterranean climate.

The closest Ascra can come to an elite is the man of *kudos* and *aretē,* whose success at farming supplies him with a surplus that can be lent to families in need of assistance. Even if the bearers of this prestige and authority within the community might vary from year to year with the uncertainties of the agricultural economy, nevertheless the presence of such a group stands as a permanent and regular feature of life in Ascra. The *eris* among farmers to win such recognition corresponds to the competition for status said by Johnson and Earle to occur in the absence of real stratification. The result of this would have been, I would hazard, a group of men of influence within the community, of somewhat unstable composition, who were divided by infighting and one-upmanship yet who would have been able to exercise considerable guidance over the community in situations where cooperation was to their common advantage. In the absence, however, of the periodic demands of warfare or of economic integration approaching a regime of generalized reciprocity, no single man of influence would have been able to accumulate enough power to make himself preeminent in the community. The power wielded by these men of *kudos* and *aretē* is rooted in the resources of their individual households, not in access to the support and resources of other households, that is, in the resources controlled by a political economy.

I have already noted in connection with *Works and Days* 342–43 and 735–36 (pp. 94–95) that dining and sacrifice operate as a form of ceremonialism reinforcing the standing of the man of *kudos* and *aretē*. As Hesiod describes these banquets, they are organized by the individual household and do not incorporate the entire village but only neighbors on good terms with the host. While ceremony does function to construct a political economy and contributes to the prestige of the banquet-giver, still it does not enclose the entire community let alone serve to join Ascra with other communities. The ceremony that Hesiod so elliptically refers to reaches beyond the limits of the individual household of the family-level society but falls short of encompassing the entire village. The impression that Hesiod conveys of a weakly developed sense of territorial identity meshes with the embryonic hierarchy and ceremonialism of Ascra.

Hesiod does not indicate that there are extensive contacts with the world beyond the village or that Ascra is heavily dependent upon these contacts. In the case of trade, such interactions are irregular and motivated by the interests of the household. Trade on this basis could not be expected to foster long-term relations with strong mutual obligations between farmer and trader. The only clear influence exercised in Ascra by Thespiae is the kings' role as judges. Yet their authority is limited to disputes brought before them voluntarily, and there is no reason to think that they could actively enforce their decisions. Beyond that we can speculate about interactions structured within the institutions of marriage, *xeniē*, or perhaps the cult of the Muses of Helicon. In any case, Hesiod's testimony suggests that such interactions operated at the level of the individual household, outside the boundaries of a political economy. It is difficult to imagine that there were not frequent interactions between these two neighboring communities, but Thespiae's influence over Ascra was probably limited to the prestige attached to a larger, wealthier, and more highly organized community by a weaker and more backward neighbor.

Hesiod's Ascra in my view comprises a very small world. It is a world that remains unhierarchized and unregimented by the polis system, by the need to supply a *basileus* or an elite with a surplus. The desire to enjoy the benefits of cooperation is balanced against the desire to hoard the resources of the household and not share them with others. Ascra's inhabitants compete intensely for standing in the community but not for land and resources. They are unwilling, moreover, to accumulate prestige and authority or reduce subsistence risks at the cost of extending generalized reciprocity beyond the boundaries of the household.

THE CONQUEST OF ASCRA

Using a word that does not occur in Homer, Hesiod describes Ascra as a *kōmē;* a village. Hesiod knows what a polis is, with its *agorē*, walls, armed men, and ships (*W&D* 240–47), and distinguishes Ascra from that by designating it a *kōmē*. At lines 18–19 of *The Shield of Heracles* its author—the poem's attribution to Hesiod is, of course, far from certain—describes Heracles' intent to burn the *kōmai* of the Taphians and Teleboans.[5] Given Heracles' record with Troy and Oechalia, it seems unlikely that he would have spared the poleis of these peoples had there been any. Hesiod appears to attribute to them villages only. The passage suggests a familiarity with regions organized as villages unsubordinated to the centralized authority of a polis. Hesiod, however, does offer evidence for the subordination of a village to a central polis. In fr. 43a.62 (M-W) Hesiod describes Heracles' destruction of both the polis of Oechalia as well as its *kōmai*, and *Shield* 472–73 refers to the people *(laos)* dwelling around the polis of Cycnus. So, although Hesiod clearly is familiar with the relationship between a polis and its perioecic *kōmai*, a relationship also familiar to the likely later text, *Shield*, he gives no indication of such a relationship between Ascra and Thespiae in *Works and Days*.

It is not really surprising that Hesiod does not explain the difference that he presupposes between a polis and a *kōmē*. In fact, the difference appears to be rather slippery. Donlan and Thomas (1993, 65–67) refer to the

---

5. Janko (1982, 127–29, 195, 200) considers it to be in the same tradition as *Theogony* and *Works and Days* but later, dating it to around 600. *The Shield* is in any case one of the earliest texts in which the word *kōmē* occurs.

Homeric polis as a village, a designation not unjustified within a comparative frame of reference. Lévy (1986, 118–21) and Hansen (1995, 61–63, 73–75) argue that by the Classical period, their real focus, the word *kōmē* connoted both small size and political subordination to a polis. As Lévy (1986, 118) acknowledges, however, the criterion of political incorporation only emerged as a significant component of status as a *kōmē* as the process of territorial consolidation and synoecism advanced during the Archaic period and into the Classical. In any case, in the passages cited above *kōmē* refers to both dependent and autonomous settlements.

It appears likely, therefore, that the distinction between *kōmē* and polis for Hesiod is primarily one of scale. Hesiod's use of *kōmē* designates Ascra as a settlement that is small and lacking communal facilities such as walls and agora. This is not to say categorically that a *kōmē* from Hesiod's period could not have some sort of fortification wall or central open space, but investment in such public infrastructure becomes less likely as the total population of the community in question grows smaller. Such investments, moreover, serve as an index of the integration and stratification that arise directly out of growth in population density. Indeed, it is not simply walls, *agorē*, and ships that Hesiod associates with the polis, but the *basilēes* as well.[6]

Burford (1993, 18), in a discussion of land tenure and the polis, points out that the village of Mycenae was not formally incorporated into the territory of Argos until after the Persian Wars. The process of synoecism uniting villages into a single polis likewise occurred for Mantinea and Elis only in the fifth century.[7] Osborne (1985, esp. 64–92), moreover, has demonstrated the continuing vitality and administrative importance of the village even within the territory of a centralized state such as Athens. The very fact, finally, of the widespread process of synoecism in Archaic Greece attests to the ubiquity of independent and semi-independent villages in Greece as it emerged from the Dark Age pari passu with the rise of the polis system.

Although large sites were occupied continuously throughout the Dark Age and into the early Archaic period, archaeological surveys both in the Argolid and closer to home in Boeotia indicate that village and hamlet were

6. Van Effenterre (1990, 489–91) notes the link between infrastructure and hierarchy in arguing for infrastructure as a criterion for distinguishing polis from *kōmē*.

7. For Elis the original villages never entirely surrendered their autonomy or identity to a central polis. See Osborne 1987, 124–27.

the norm for settlements in the late eighth and early seventh centuries.[8] Not only is Ascra identified as the main settlement in its locale but during the period to which we would assign Hesiod's lifetime it was the only settlement in its valley (Snodgrass 1985, 90, Snodgrass 1990, 130–33). Snodgrass in fact refers to "the small village of Hesiod's lifetime" (1990, 133), and he and Bintliff (Snodgrass and Bintliff 1991, 91) speak of Ascra in its second period of habitation as embracing "the life of the poet Hesiod (circa 700 B.C.) in the village's earlier stages, when Ascra was no more than a few scattered dwellings."[9] There is some risk of putting too much weight upon such statements when the final publication of the Boeotia survey is yet to appear. These comments provide at the moment, however, our best indication of the size and situation of Ascra in the period when Hesiod is assumed to have lived, and they present a picture of a small, isolated village in a region that was sparsely populated even by Dark Age standards (cf. Bintliff and Snodgrass 1989, 287). The village, as best we can ascertain, then, represents the norm for settlements in Greece during the Dark Age

---

8. Bintliff 1982, 106–7; Bintliff and Snodgrass 1985, 137–39; Snodgrass 1990, 124–27; Jameson, Runnels, and van Andel 1994, 243–59; and van Andel and Runnels 1987, 101–9. See Coldstream 1977, 303–13; Snodgrass 1980, 29–34; and Donlan and Thomas 1993 regarding the Bronze Age and Dark Age. Whitley (1991) surveys the variety of modes of social organization and settlement pattern emerging from the Dark Age into the Archaic period. Although Hansen (1995, 52–61) argues against Aristotle's view that poleis were born from the synoecism of *kōmai*, the testimonia he collects certainly show that the *kōmē* was an important form of settlement before the polis made its appearance as a centralized "conurbation." See especially the testimony of Thuc. 1.5.1, 1.10.2, and 3.94.4, Scylax 28.32, and Plut. *Mor.* 295B, all quoted at Hansen 1995, 52–53 and 63–64.

9. Snodgrass (1985, 90), however, states of Hesiod and Ascra "that [Hesiod] lived in, or at least frequented, a substantial village." Bintliff and Snodgrass provide no specific indication of the size of Ascra in the late eighth to early seventh century. Bintliff (1989, 17) states that both the village of Ascra and the nearby polis of Haliartos reach a size of twenty to twenty-five hectares at their climax in the Classical period while Thespiae reaches one hundred and twenty-five hectares in the same period. Snodgrass and Bintliff (1991, 88) describe Ascra without time reference as a fifteen-hectare site and Haliartos and Thespiae (1991, 91) as respectively thirty hectares and one hundred and twenty hectares in reference to their maximum extent. Snodgrass (1985, 94) even states that Ascra exceeded the size of Haliartos. I assume that neither figure pertains to Ascra in the Dark Age though the difference between Ascra and Thespiae in size is quite illuminating. In the most recent discussion, Bintliff (1997b, 234–36, 243–45) presents Ascra in the Classical period as smaller than Haliartos but still large enough to exceed the category of village. In the period with which we are concerned the site of Thespiae was occupied by four distinct settlements in comparison to Ascra's one (Snodgrass 1987–89, 56–57, Bintliff and Snodgrass 1989, 287).

and was still widespread at the dawn of the Archaic period even if the polis was first beginning to appear at the same time. If independent villages could still be found as late as the fifth century, when the polis system was in full maturity and territorial boundaries had solidified, then it seems to me safe to assume that such settlements were not uncommon as Greece moved out of the Dark Age and into the Archaic period. The archaeological data produced by the Boeotia survey appear to support the picture supplied by *Works and Days* itself that Hesiod's Ascra is a small village with ample land and that it is isolated from the direct influence of the other, larger settlement in the district.

Buck (1979, 90–92) argues that by the end of the ninth century the major poleis of Boeotia have emerged, including Thespiae, but that there remained as well more or less independent districts centered around villages rather than cities. Ascra is one of these. According to Bintliff and Snodgrass Ascra's site exhibits protogeometric and geometric material, some of the earliest uncovered on any site surveyed by their team. Indeed, Ascra and Thespiae are the only occupied sites in the area during the later Geometric to the early Archaic period and Ascra is by far the largest of several villages found within what would become the territory of Thespiae. Thespiae, moreover, began to spin off secondary settlements only in the fifth and fourth centuries, so Ascra should not be looked upon as Thespiae's village from the outset.[10] Ascra was defensible from its own stronghold atop either of two neighboring hills. It was an old settlement of a large size and relatively remote from the nearest polis. It had at its disposal, moreover, a fertile valley. These qualities are certainly adequate to have supported and even encouraged a sense of common identity and a commitment to local institutions if their enjoyment were ever put in jeopardy.

These same attractions as well as the site's likely prosperity, however, would have made Ascra an obvious target for an expanding polis. An additional attraction, moreover, was Ascra's strategic value. The village's situa-

---

10. The fragment from a mythological account of the founding of Ascra supplied by Pausanias (9.29.1) makes no mention of Thespiae. On the period of earliest habitation for Ascra and Thespiae see: Bintliff and Snodgrass 1985, 139–40; Bintliff and Snodgrass 1989, 287; Snodgrass 1990, 130–32; and Snodgrass 1985, 90, 94. In Ascra's case the protogeometric settlement is a resumption of occupation lasting from Early Helladic through the Middle Bronze Age: Snodgrass 1990, 133–35. Regarding the pattern of Thespiae's development see Snodgrass 1987–89, 56–58. The implication that Ascra was founded by Thespians as a "second order" or "satellite" settlement (Snodgrass 1987–89, 62–63, Bintliff and Snodgrass 1989, 286) seems to me to be rendered quite unlikely by the antiquity of both settlements.

tion enabled it to control potential invasion routes over Helicon between Thespiae and Haliartos and, farther to the northwest, Coronea, and Lebedaea and Orchomenos beyond. Snodgrass suggests, moreover, that Ascra may have occupied the eastern extremity of the border strip separating the territories of Haliartos and Thespiae.[11] The settlement that the Ascrans viewed in terms of their fields and homes may have appeared to Thespians more as a military site significant for their city's defense. Yet incorporation into the territory of a polis can have held little attraction for the residents of Ascra. The polis system with its "kings" introduces steeper and more fixed hierarchy, greater disparities in wealth and land, unequal access to the necessities of life, a more coercive political apparatus, and more unevenly distributed political rights than what is to be found in a community like Hesiod's Ascra. What is more, it was the established pattern in Boeotia for the residents of villages and poleis annexed by neighboring cities to receive subordinate status as *perioeci* rather than equality even with the lower orders of the dominant polis.[12] As Johnson and Earle (1987, 202) observe regarding the advantages offered by a local group over a family-level society, "Yet the increase in 'efficiency' does not necessarily preserve or improve the quality of life of the individual, as 'economizing behavior' does in theory. On the contrary, the greater competitiveness, regulation, and violence that characterize the local group and the intergroup collectivity make the individual's life decidedly more tense." Ascrans might well have judged that participation in the expanding bubble of Thespiae's political economy was more expensive than it was worth.

But we know, of course, that Ascra was at some point incorporated

11. Regarding the hill Pyrgaki see Fossey 1988, 142–44; Snodgrass 1985, 91–93; and Gauvin and Morin 1992, 7. See, however, Bintliff 1996, 196 regarding settlement on the hill nearer to Ascra, designated VM4 on fig. 2, page 212. Ascra's strategic location is discussed by Kallet-Marx 1989, 301–4 and Pritchett 1985, 138–65, esp. 149 and 163–65. According to Snodgrass (1990, 133) Ascra was fortified during the Archaic and Classical periods. Both Kallet-Marx and Pritchett are concerned with events occurring considerably after Hesiod's time, but Ascra would have possessed strategic value as long as there were neighboring cities in the area. Snodgrass discusses Ascra's location in the interstices between Haliartos and Thespiae at Snodgrass 1990, 129. Burford (1993, 159–60) and Hanson (1995, 302–3) both point out the overwhelming frequency with which wars broke out over border disputes in Greece.

12. Regarding the differences between polis and village, see the interesting discussion of Bintliff 1982, 106–11. Buck (1979, 100) mentions the reduction of annexed settlements to perioecic status. The emergence of state-level communities in Archaic Greece is discussed by Qviller 1981; Donlan 1989, esp. 26–28; Morris 1991, esp. 40–43; and Runciman 1982, esp. 364–71.

within the territory of Thespiae. The scholium on *Works and Days* 631 attributes to both Plutarch and Aristotle the report that Thespiae overran and evacuated Ascra after the death of Hesiod.

Ἀοίκητον δὲ αὐτὸ ὁ Πλούταρχος ἱστορεῖ καὶ τότε εἶναι, Θεσπιέων ἀνελόντων τοὺς οἰκοῦντας, Ὀρχομενίων δὲ τοὺς σωθέντας δεξαμένων· ὅθεν καὶ τὸν θεὸν Ὀρχομενίοις προστάξαι τὰ Ἡσιόδου λείψανα λαβεῖν, καὶ θάψαι παρ' αὐτοῖς, ὡς καὶ Ἀριστοτέλης φησί, γράφων τὴν Ὀρχομενίων πολιτείαν.[13]

Plutarch recounts that it (sc. Ascra) was uninhabited at that time as well since the Thespians had slain its inhabitants and Orchomenos had taken in the survivors. On this account the god also commanded the Orchomenians to take the remains of Hesiod and to bury them in their own territory, as Aristotle also states in his *Constitution of Orchomenos.*

This notice, if it is genuine, enables us to establish termini for this Thespian attack on Ascra. It occurred after Hesiod's death but no later than Aristotle's time. Snodgrass has argued that a polis would destroy its own village only under the most extraordinary circumstances, an attempted revolt, for example. He speculates that between 386 and 364 Ascra might have attempted to win its autonomy from Thespiae, perhaps in the wake of the Theban destruction of that city, which probably took place in 373. Buck, however, offers a scenario for an earlier date, between 700 and 650, in which Ascra had sided with Orchomenos against its nearer, stronger, neighbors, Thespiae and Thebes (cf. Bintliff 1994, fig. 25). Buck argues that Orchomenos was vying with Thebes at this time for supremacy and that Ascra preferred to back the more distant Orchomenos rather than her

13. Pertusi 1955, 631bis 1 = Aristotle (*FHG* 115c), Plutarch *Moralia* fr. 82. The phrase καὶ τότε seems to me to require comment. It must be taken to mean something like "at that time as well," entailing that the author knows of at least two times when Ascra was uninhabited. Pausanias, who is close enough in time to Plutarch, confirms that Ascra was indeed abandoned in Plutarch's own time (Paus. 9.29.2), as is supported as well by the findings of the Bradford/Cambridge survey. The explanatory genitive absolutes, that the Thespians killed the inhabitants and the Orchomenians sheltered the refugees, specify the reference of τότε to the time of the Thespian evacuation of Ascra, which according to this notice had to have occurred before Aristotle's time. That is, the two periods when Ascra was uninhabited were Pausanias's own and after it was overrun by Thespiae at some earlier point. Judging again from the results of the Bradford/Cambridge survey, Ascra cannot have remained deserted long following the earlier abandonment: see Snodgrass 1985, 90 and especially 94; and Bintliff and Snodgrass 1985, 139–40, 146–47; cf. Pritchett 1985, 161–62. Strabo (9.2.25) states that Ascra was within the territory of Thespiae.

nearer neighbors. As Buck suggests, "the support of a comparatively distant Orchomenos against a nearby Thespiae or Thebes would enable these smaller towns to preserve some freedom of maneuver and a precarious liberty" (Buck 1979, 98).[14] According to both hypotheses, when Ascra loses its gamble, it is evacuated and recolonized by the victorious Thespians. Snodgrass rejects Buck's argument precisely on the grounds that it is so highly improbable that a polis would destroy its own village. Yet we must question the assumption underlying this judgment that at this early date Ascra had in fact already been incorporated within the territory of Thespiae. For, as is by now abundantly clear, I believe that Hesiod provides no support for that position.

If Ascra had not already been annexed by Thespiae early in the seventh century, then Snodgrass's objection to Buck's earlier date falls. In the context of a conflict between Orchomenos to the east and Thespiae and Thebes to the west Ascra's control of the east-west paths over Helicon and its view of the main east-west route along the shore of Lake Copais endow it with a primary strategic importance (Gauvin and Morin 1992, 7–8, and Kallet-Marx 1989, 304). Certainly if Ascra had sided with Thespiae's foes, the Thespians would have preferred to inhabit the place with their own citizens, on whom they could rely. But even outside the setting of such a large-scale confrontation Ascra's position along the border zone between Thespiae and Haliartos and its general prosperity would have made Ascra a desirable prize for Thespiae. While a land shortage closer in to Thespiae seems less likely as a motive for the conquest of Ascra during Hesiod's lifetime, the fact that Ascra was not only overcome but also evacuated suggests that Ascra's farmland could have been one attraction among others at some point after Hesiod's death. For it is likely that even if one particular issue provided the pretext for Thespiae's aggression, multiple considerations—

14. Snodgrass 1985, 94; Buck 1979, 97–99. Schachter (1989, 80) proposes a date between 650 and 500 for this conflict between Orchomenos and Thebes, still acceptable if less favorable for my hypothesis. Pritchett (1985, 156–65) argues that the site of Ceressus to which the Thespians retreated as a stronghold during the invasion of the Thessalians is none other than Ascra by another name. If Pritchett's hypothesis is correct, then Ascra would already have come into Thespiae's control before this invasion, which Buck dates between 571 and 486, arguing for 520 (Buck 1979, 107–12). Bintliff (1994, 225–26 with fig. 26) claims that Ascra was absorbed by Thespiae in the eighth century, though I infer he is relying on Hesiod's testimony from *Works and Days* for this (cf. Bintliff 1994, 220). Thespiae would probably not have been motivated to move against Ascra by the desire for more land till into the Classical period: Snodgrass 1987–89, 57 and Bintliff and Snodgrass 1989, 287–88.

strategic value, land, border disputes, conflicting alliances, for example—no doubt fueled the undertaking.

The suggestion that Ascra was destroyed and evacuated at an early date by a neighboring city that then reinhabited the site finds an interesting parallel in the nearby village of Hippotae. Fossey (1990, 207), commenting on Plutarch *Mor.* 775a, argues that the village was destroyed at an early date by the poleis neighboring to north and south, Coroneia and Thisbe, which divided the lands of Hippotae between themselves. Fossey notes that the excellent farming and grazing land of the village no doubt attracted the attentions of its neighbors. Schachter (1996, 104–5) in fact suggests that "Hippotai ought to be seen as a limitary site, marking the boundaries of Thespiai, Koroneia, and Thisbe."

There is no conclusive evidence identifying the attack recalled by Plutarch as the event bringing Ascra within Thespiae's territory, nor is there any reason to assume that Thespiae absorbed Ascra through violent means. Although this reconstruction is speculative, still it is not, I think, improbable. It sketches out a historical setting in which a yet autonomous Ascra may have experienced increasing conflict with Thespiae culminating in its conquest by its stronger neighbor and incorporation within its territory. By this scenario Ascra succumbed as so many other villages did to the process of synoecism carried forth over many centuries in Greece. At the very least our best piece of evidence for relations between Thespiae and Ascra does not require that Ascra already be incorporated within Thespiae's territory during Hesiod's time and it can easily be interpreted to indicate that Ascra was autonomous at the time. *Works and Days* may, then, bear witness to the onset of a process culminating at a later time in the destruction and annexation of Ascra by Thespiae.

ASCRA AND GREEK HISTORY

It is necessary to reevaluate the place of the community described in *Works and Days* within the history of ancient Greece. Locating Hesiod's Ascra on an evolutionary continuum leading from Homer to Solon has produced a picture of a community far more complex than what the evidence of *Works and Days* will justify. Explicit reliance upon the model of a peasantry to characterize Ascra, or its implicit introduction through the paradigm of Solonian Athens, must be rejected. In particular, the conflict between village and city, far from being central to the political and economic reality depicted in *Works and Days*, is rather a side effect of a dispute otherwise confined entirely to the village. As I will discuss in the next chapter, more-over, it is the overall rhetorical purpose of *Works and Days* to eliminate the city's presence even in that limited capacity and in effect to restore the in-tegrity and isolation of the village as a self-sufficient universe.

Towards the end of his discussion of the "forces of constraint," the su-perior power exercised by a supra-local elite over a peasant community, Magagna generalizes (1991, 45–46):

> Throughout much of human history powerful elites have attempted to capture the countryside through institutions of subjugation and sur-veillance. . . . Agriculture is too important to be abandoned to fortune, and throughout history we can find instances of an elite project that denies popular autonomy in the name of privilege and power.
>
> What I propose, therefore, is that we see the peasantry as a mode of domination that is always contested and incomplete. Peasants do not exist in some "natural" state; they are created through mechanisms of political subordination that lie at the interface of popular institutions and translocal authority.

In my view this "interface of popular institutions and translocal authority" has yet to be established between Ascra and Thespiae. It is at best incipient. Either the Ascrans have been equal to the task of contesting the domina-tion that would make of them peasants, or no outside elite has yet made a concerted attempt to dominate them. Ascra has not yet been captured and incorporated into the countryside of Thespiae, its agricultural poten-tial subjugated to external power. Yet the constellation of interests that might propel Ascra into such a relationship can be discerned within *Works and Days*.

Through the discourse of its persona, "Hesiod," *Works and Days* sup-plies us with a figure whose outlook identifies him with a local hierarchy. He is interested in protecting his own power and influence—especially when it comes to his land—against encroachments by an outside elite. In Perses we discern a dependent kinsman who in seeking further assistance threatens to circumvent that same local hierarchy in order to gain leverage over his more prosperous brother, who is becoming progressively less will-ing to continue helping him. The "kings" represent an external elite pos-sessing no formal and direct authority in Ascra but ready to build relation-ships of patronage within the village by trading upon their role as judges in disputes brought to them. This array of forces and interests may mark an early stage in a campaign by the kings of Thespiae to extend their influ-ence into the village of Ascra. It may be that we discern in Hesiod's Ascra a community evolving towards a regime of generalized reciprocity, able to instigate greater interdependence and a steeper hierarchy. That is, Ascra may be moving towards a greater complexity under which its boundaries will be defined and its membership fixed by the limits of a local *basileus*'s generosity, the expanding bubble of a political economy. Or, again, the triangle of conflicting interests and objectives defined by Perses, the kings, and Hesiod may comprise a relatively stable status quo of ongoing, low-level confrontation between a local hierarchy and an external elite.

In either case *Works and Days* records Hesiod's reaction to a perceived encroachment upon Ascra's autonomy by Thespiae. Around the specific and limited flash point of Perses' threat to take his complaint to the kings we witness the condensation in a primitive form of attitudes, yet to become formal expectations or claims, that are indicative of a peasant mentality. Hesiod's appeal strives to create a sense of territoriality, of a village boundary within which a certain solidarity is expected and certain norms of behavior can be enforced. From the other side, however, Perses' behavior can be seen as a complementary assertion of an obligation to share, to acknowledge need in the distribution of community resources. If Hesiod wishes to close off his community to outside intervention and to exercise within its boundary a more far-reaching authority, the price will be a more generalized reciprocity among the community's inhabitants. Hesiod and Perses can be seen here as in effect negotiating where the boundary between the subsistence economy and the political economy will be set, how far beyond the limits of the household the line between generalized reciprocity and balanced reciprocity will fall. Both brothers put forth demands that would make of Ascra a more stratified and integrated community. We perhaps observe in *Works and Days* the onset in embryonic form of a distinctively "peasant" sensibility about the integrity of the village boundary and the obligations interconnecting those living within that boundary, a sensibility that has arisen in direct response to the pressure exerted upon Ascra by the kings of Thespiae.

6 Persuading Perses

Readers of *Works and Days* have recognized the importance of the contrast Hesiod builds up in the poem between the village and the polis. In fact, it is the weight given this topos in *Works and Days* that has, in my view, led astray most attempts to reconstruct its historical context. My own argument that this opposition is not primary but is governed by that between the prosperous and the needy within the village should in no way, moreover, be understood as denying to the village/polis contrast its prominence. In analyzing the relationship between these two topoi—poor/prosperous and village/polis—one confronts the difference between the historical and the rhetorical. From the perspective of the poem's historical setting animosity towards the city only enters the poem as a side effect of the more central conflict between a successful and a failing farmer within the village. It is Perses' threat to take the brothers' preexisting dispute to the kings in the town square that precipitates all of Hesiod's vitriol against the city. Yet from the perspective of persuasion, in terms of Hesiod's rhetorical program, this connection between the village and the city is unmistakably at the heart of *Works and Days*, even providing the immediate impetus for the poem. As a representation of a historical setting *Works and Days* is enfolded within a rhetorical strategy whose effects on that representation must be acknowledged.

Works and Days cannot be regarded as a window onto its historical context. The extent to which it is fictionalized remains a mystery, and Hesiod clearly leaves out much detail that he assumes his audience will already know. The poem is rather a literary representation of a historical setting, and as a representation *Works and Days* presents itself as functioning within that historical setting as a piece of persuasion. Persuasion, of course, never operates objectively, in a disinterested fashion, as it works to achieve its ends. Its appeal, moreover, is generally grounded in some sense of values, a morality, even if that boils down to something so narrow as self-interest alone. Although Hesiod's position may be dictated by his own self-interest, he strives to formulate his appeal to Perses in the language of values that held the respect and guided the behavior of members of the community. So that even if the poem's scenario is fictitious, *Works and Days* stands nevertheless as a condensation and celebratory assertion of the values of the audience for whom it was composed, men of *kudos* and *aretē* themselves and those striving to emulate that model of virtue.

If we think of persuasion as a process that works its effects over the course of the poem, it becomes clear that Hesiod is not attempting in *Works and Days* to open up the issue of relations between Ascra and the polis but rather to shut it down and to banish the city beyond the poem's horizon. This treatment of the village/polis opposition is in keeping with Hesiod's own interests in the dispute and it expresses simultaneously the outlook of the village. Hesiod's rhetorical goal is to collapse the village/city contrast, that opens the possibility for Perses of taking his complaint to the kings, back within the limits of the village alone, the *authi*—"here and now"— of line 35. This *authi*, the village, defines a social universe where Perses will be compelled to settle his dispute with Hesiod within the confines of the moral framework built up over the course of *Works and Days* as a whole to portray village life. The effect of this rhetorical movement in the poem is to shed the polis term of the village/polis contrast, which is enunciated with such emphasis at the beginning of the poem, and constrain Perses within the boundaries of the village, harmonizing the rhetorical and the historical.

Hesiod constructs his opening appeal to Perses (27–41) out of a series of restatements of the basic opposition of the village and the city. He begins (27–29) by urging Perses not to be attracted from his farm/work *(ergou)* to the town square *(agorēs)*. Lines 30–32 focus this contrast between the farm and the town square upon the year's worth of livelihood *(bios . . . epēetanos)* won from toil on the farm and the quarrels *(neikeōn)* and speeches *(agoreōn)*, the litigation, of the town square. Hesiod repeats this opposition for a third time in the slightly different terms of livelihood won through one's own labor and the possessions of others seized through quarreling and wrangling (33–34). In the remaining lines Hesiod again reiterates the geographical opposition established at the beginning of the section between farm and town square through the emphatic *authi* (35),"right here," offered as an alternative location for the quarrel (*neikos:* 35) to that of the town square of the "kings" (*basileas:* 38).[1] Within this spatial contrast Hesiod opposes both the straight judgments (*itheiēisi dikēis:* 36) sanctioned by Zeus to those provided by the gift-eating kings (*basileas / dōrophagous:* 38–39), and the family plot (*klēron:* 37), which Perses desires as a source of wealth, to the town square, where litigation and deceit bring gain. Hesiod allies himself with the farm, the locus of toil, with livelihood, with what is one's own, and with justice (Zeus's *itheiēisi dikēis:* 35–36), and ties Perses to the kings and the town square, to indolence, want, the property of others, and crooked justice.

The series of harangues and myths following the poem's introductory passage and extending up to the transition to the agricultural calendar at 293–97 all serve in varying degrees to elaborate elements of this contrast and to reinforce the ethical geography established by Hesiod in his initial address to Perses. The etiologies of labor provided in the Pandora and the Ages of Man segments, the fable of the Hawk and Nightingale, the speeches on justice addressed variously to Perses and the kings, and the paths of wickedness and virtue deepen and unfold the terms in which the respective worlds of village and city contrast with each other. The village is founded upon the values of justice, labor, and plenty while the city, with its *agorē* and kings, embodies those of *hubris*, indolence, and ill-gotten wealth. Over the course of this first major division of the poem Hesiod heaps up an ethical barrier between village and city, he succeeds in converting the geographical distance between the two settlements into a moral distance. Perses, as the primary addressee of the poem, is suspended between the village that he inhabits and the city where he seeks an advantage in his quarrel with Hesiod. The rhetorical challenge faced by Hesiod is to reenclose Perses within the limits of the village both spatially and morally while simultaneously eliminating the city from the landscape.

I regard the various segments that Hesiod wove together to create *Works and Days* as traditional. Prometheus and Pandora, the Ages of Man, the Hawk and the Nightingale, the goddess Justice, the cities of justice and violence, the road of virtue, the agricultural calendar, and the catalogue of days all represent inherited commonplaces that Hesiod adapted and colored to

1. See West 1978, ad 35 for the spatial reference of *authi*. Verdenius, however, argues for "at once," summarizing the debate over spatial vs. temporal references. The sense is "here and now," but the centrality of the geographical contrast to the passage gives the spatial reference primacy. For the association of the *basileus* with the *agorē* see pp. 64–67.

serve the purposes of his appeal. Hesiod exploits a rich store of traditional wisdom rooted in the mores and lived experience of his community. The persuasive power itself of *Works and Days* relies upon the prestige of poetry as a privileged mode of discourse, upon the august language of the epos, and upon the authority of mythic narratives that are seen as constitutive of the order of things. These provide Hesiod with the preexisting forms within which he attempts to mold both the collective judgment of his community as well as the shame felt by Perses in the face of such a rhetorical performance. Hesiod shapes the topoi he selects, focuses them, and marshals them within *Works and Days* in order to alter Perses' behavior by altering the way Perses perceives his social world. As an attempt to persuade, *Works and Days* comprises a rhetorical enactment of privileged topoi mobilized to impose a specific moral construction on events. *Works and Days* viewed in this way, as an attempt to persuade through the manipulation of collectively held, culturally salient commonplaces, assumes an almost incantational force.[2]

The rhetorical purpose of *Works and Days* is clearly expressed in the passage initiating the transition from the series of harangues composing the first major segment of the poem to the agricultural calendar that is its heart. Looking back at all the precepts and examples he has offered Perses so far as well as ahead to the instruction to follow, Hesiod asserts at lines 293–97:

> οὗτος μὲν πανάριστος, ὃς αὐτὸς πάντα νοήσει
> φρασσάμενος τά κ' ἔπειτα καὶ ἐς τέλος ᾖσιν ἀμείνω·
> ἐσθλὸς δ' αὖ καὶ κεῖνος, ὃς εὖ εἰπόντι πίθηται·
> ὃς δέ κε μήτ' αὐτὸς νοέῃ μήτ' ἄλλου ἀκούων
> ἐν θυμῷ βάλληται, ὁ δ' αὖτ' ἀχρήιος ἀνήρ.

> Best of all *(panaristos)* is the one who on his own understands all things, recognizing what will be best later, in the end.
> Good *(esthlos)* too is the man who trusts in another who gives good counsel.
> But the one who neither knows for himself nor listens to another and takes his advice to heart, that one is a useless *(achrēios)* man.

This passage stands as the culmination of the numerous injunctions to listen and learn issued by Hesiod to Perses over the course of the poem. In what might be described as an inverted priamel Hesiod ranks the relative

2. See Pucci 1996, 191–94 and Peabody 1975, 207–8, 256, 268–72. "The song does not tell; it does. A world is realized in which the singer is unchallengeable, because the singer's world becomes the real world" (Peabody 1975, 272).

esteem accorded to the good counselor, to the one following the good counsel of another, and finally to the man who neither knows for himself nor listens to anyone else. The specific references of this generic passage are obvious enough in any case but can be filled in explicitly from the line opening the preceding section (σοὶ δ' ἐγὼ ἐσθλὰ νοέων ἐρέω, μέγα νήπιε Πέρση [But I, Perses, you big fool, know what is right and will tell it to you]: 286) and from the line serving as a transition into the harangue that 293–97 introduce (ἀλλὰ σύ γ' ἡμετέρης μεμνημένος αἰὲν ἐφετμῆς [But you being ever mindful of my injunction . . .]: 298). The *panaristos* here is of course Hesiod himself, the speaker, and the *achrēios* is Perses, the addressee. So Hesiod triumphantly proclaims in the final lines of the poem (at least as we have them) that the man who knows and puts into practice all that he has said, probably referring specifically to the catalogue of days, is both *olbios* and *eudaimōn*, "prosperous" and "fortunate."[3]

Up to this point the overall project of *Works & Days* has been precisely to transform Perses from an *achrēios* into an *esthlos*, from a man who keeps no counsel to a man who follows the good counsel of another. It is in this sense that *Works and Days* is a didactic poem and offers instruction.[4] Heath (1985, 253–63), I believe, misses the point in his discussion of *Works and Days* as a didactic poem by failing to consider precisely what it is that Hesiod is intending to teach, or persuade. Hesiod does not intend to instruct Perses in farming technique but to exhort him to lead a moral life by glorifying labor and its benefits. In concrete terms this means convincing him to abandon the town square, with its kings and litigation, as the course of *hubris* and to return to toil on his farm as the only source of a secure livelihood because it is in accordance with justice. What leads up to this generic and formal assertion of Hesiod's authority is the series of mythic topoi, beginning with his opening harangue and extending to the parable of the paths of virtue and wickedness, all meant to illustrate the virtues of labor and urging Perses to adopt that course. An encomiastic rendition of the agricultural calendar, the works of the cultivator according to their season, follows these transitional lines. This movement from protreptic harangue to celebration, marked by the announcement of his own authority as counselor at 293–97, presupposes that within the logic of *Works and Days* Hesiod has by this point indeed succeeded in winning

---

3. Cf. Marsilio 2000, 3–4 on this passage.
4. The didactic or persuasive purpose of the poem is announced at the outset at line 10 where Hesiod asserts that he is about to tell Perses the truth. See Pucci 1996, 197–200; Liebermann 1981, 400–401; and Detienne 1963, 42–48.

Perses over to the path of justice and away from *hubris*.[5] Since Perses has at last been convinced at least in principle of the rightness of Hesiod's advice, Hesiod can begin to recount how to achieve prosperity within the limits of the village before an addressee now willing to be reminded of the age-old rhythms of the agricultural cycle. The remainder of the poem, at the same time as it reminds and instructs Perses, simultaneously comprises an encomiastic expression of the shared ideals of Ascra's community of farmers, the audience for Hesiod's poetic performance. The rhetorical trajectory of the poem and the psychological transformation it effects in Perses, then, moves away from the moral conflicts sparked by contact between country and city and towards the rhythms of justice and prosperity epitomized in the agricultural cycle, the idealized cadence of village life.

Strictly speaking, the agricultural calendar does not commence until line 381, just over 80 lines after the transitional passage at 293–97. In these intervening lines Hesiod continues to reformulate the thematic focus of the poem as part of a gradual transition typical of *Works and Days*. In lines 298–319 Hesiod contrasts the famine afflicting the shiftless with the prosperity and prestige of the diligent. Begging, seeking a handout from neighbors, replaces the kings and their crooked judgments in the town square as an escape from hunger for the indolent. The substitution of begging for litigation effectively reincorporates Perses' dilemma within the boundaries of the village—its ethics, institutions, and hierarchy. Lines 320–80 comprise a catalogue of precepts on how to get along with neighbors and family and be a success (ill-gotten gains, transgressions against kin, piety towards the gods, neighbors and reciprocity, saving and self-reliance, pilfering, and children). From the perspective of the poet in the process of oral composition, these lines enable him to begin to refocus thematically, as I will discuss momentarily. As regards persuasion, they serve to draw Perses further into the reality of life within a rural community and further remove him from the world of the *agorē*. Finally, the passage provides verification for Hesiod's claim to authority through a virtuoso display of his command of traditional wisdom.

I think that it can be taken for granted that in *Works and Days* Hesiod praises the life of the countryside while condemning along the way the institutions of the city. This regional bias is fundamental to his attempt to

---

5. This implicit transition has been noted by Wilamowitz (1962, 133–34, 144), van Groningen (1957, 11–12), Heath (1985, 250–51), and Nagy (1990, 63–67), though van Groningen and Heath imagine that it represents a change of heart taking place over a period of weeks or months.

divert Perses from the town square and back to his farm. At this point, however, I am less interested in the specific interpretation of individual passages than in the evolution of the poem's argument, its direction insofar as that can be gauged by tracking the distribution of salient topics across its whole length. This distribution reveals both the itinerary of Hesiod's persuasive strategy and the direction in which he intends to move Perses.

Lines 293–97 mark the abandonment of the themes that dominate the first section of the poem, where Hesiod struggles to turn Perses from the city and back towards village and farm, and their consequent replacement by a new set of themes expressive of the circumscribed world of the countryside. Out of 82 attestations of words related to litigation, justice, and the city (ἀγορή, ἄδικος, ἄτη, βασιλεύς, βίη, δῆρις, δικάζω, δίκαιος, δίκη, ἔρις, ζῆλος, νεῖκος, πόλις, ὕβρις) only 12 occur after the transition introduced at 293. There are 11 references to wealth or livelihood (ἄφενος, ἀφνειός, βίος, βίοτος, ὄλβος, πλοῦτος) before line 293 but 25 instances after. Of the 46 occurrences of "labor" (ἔργον, ἐργάζομαι) 13 occur before line 293 and 33 after. Out of 41 attestations of words having to do with shiftlessness, need, or begging (forms of ἀεργός, ἀνολβίη, ἀχρήιος, ζητεύω, λιμός, πενίη, πτώσσω, πτωχός, χατίζω, χράομαι, χρέος, χρηίζω) only 8 occur before line 293. Such statistics provide a clear indication of a general change in orientation marked by the transition at 293–97. Following those lines Hesiod abandons his preoccupation with justice and the related issues of litigation and judgments, the kings are forgotten, and the polis disappears from the horizon. In the wake of Hesiod's emphatic assertion of his role as Perses' guide, the controlling themes of how to succeed at farming and avoid ruin emerge into full prominence. In the world of the village the only outcomes of shiftlessness are either hunger or begging, and labor is the path to prosperity; litigation is not an option. The shift to an exclusive focus upon the countryside gives new prominence to the overarching contrast of prosperity and poverty. Peabody (1975, 254–56), noting this same transition in the poem's orientation in terms of the replacement of *eris* by *ergon*, comments, "This gradual shift may effect the magical transformation of a hostile competitor into a constructive laborer. Seen in this way, *Works and Days* is more than a contest song; it is active, transformational conjuring" (256).[6]

6. Hamilton (1989, 53–65) argues that the transition occurs rather at *W&D* 286. What comes before that is ruled by the wicked *eris* and what comes after is expressive of the good *eris*. His surveys of the distribution of vocabulary overlap with and corroborate my own. See also Griffith 1983, 57–60.

Hesiod's concern with the city is triggered by Perses' threat to resort to the kings of Thespiae for a settlement of their quarrel. It intrudes into the affairs of Hesiod and Perses, then, as the side effect of their dispute, and Hesiod reacts by moving as quickly as possible to forestall Perses' maneuver. To this end he strives to turn Perses from a course of action that will undermine his own power within the village of Ascra while enhancing the prestige and influence of the kings of Thespiae. Hesiod does so by establishing a moral barrier along the spatial frontier dividing city from village. Hesiod accomplishes this task through mythic examples, moral precepts, and threats of divine retribution that stress the moral perspective of the countryside, above all the necessity and benefits of work and the autonomy and self-reliance of rural life. This separation of inside from outside and of friend from foe along a spatial axis is intended to convince Perses that piety, justice, and self-interest point him back towards the village, and so to dissuade him from enlisting the aid of an outside elite in his struggle against Ascra's local hierarchy as represented by his (big?) brother.

Within the poem's dramatic scenario our persona, Hesiod, hopes through his performance of *Works and Days* to efface the city, simply to purge it from Perses' consciousness, and thereby to reenclose him within the boundaries of the village and fields. There is in effect an exorcism played out over the course of *Works and Days* in which the city is simply wiped from the map. For Hesiod the unifying force of the villages' shared geographic space masks the divisiveness of the opposition of prosperous and poor. By realizing in his discourse the values of farm and village, Hesiod attempts to reenclose Perses, as he hesitates between the two zones, within Ascra's perimeter, where he will be constrained to solve his problems through remedies available there. Perses must either return to his plot and get back to work or else make do by begging, a solution implemented within the village, relying upon the ethics of the neighborhood, and reinforcing the local hierarchy in the same way that recourse to the kings undermines it. These are the options which decisively replace litigation and the city as the poem's persuasive strategy unfolds. For, once Hesiod is satisfied that he has attracted Perses back into the orbit of the village and persuaded him to pursue the solutions which it provides for his problems, we hear no more of the city.

But what stand as badly needed warnings and advice for the likes of Perses boil down to preaching to the choir for the villagers who, I believe, would have composed the audience for *Works and Days*. For men of *kudos* and *aretē* Hesiod's defense of the village in the face of encroachments by the polis amounts to an encomium of a way of life. Hesiod realizes his appeal within the moral rhetoric of the village, the values of labor, accumulation, self-sufficiency, piety, parsimony, and success, among others—the values which serve to rationalize the prestige and authority of village leaders and which command the respect of villagers who either aspire to that status or hope for assistance from such men. As a representation of a social world and an event Hesiod's poem is clearly slanted. His persuasion offers praise to his peers, successful farmers, and chastisement to those who fail to toe the line. The spatial boundary conjured up in the poetry of *Works and Days* stands as a both a bulwark and a monument for the man of *kudos* and *aretē*.

Works Cited

Amouretti, M.-C. 1986. *Le pain et l'huile dans la Grèce antique.* Paris.

Andel, T. H. van, and C. Runnels. 1987. *Beyond the Acropolis. A Rural Greek Past.* Stanford.

Aston, T. H., and C. H. E. Philpin, eds. 1985. *The Brenner Debate: Agrarian class structure and economic development in pre-industrial Europe.* Cambridge.

Austin, M. M., and P. Vidal-Naquet. 1977. *Economic and Social History of Ancient Greece.* Berkeley.

Barker, G. 1985. *Prehistoric Farming in Europe.* Cambridge.

Bintliff, J. L. 1982. Settlement patterns, land tenure and social structure: A diachronic model. In *Ranking, Resource and Exchange. Aspects of the Archaeology of Early European Society,* edited by C. Renfrew and S. Shennan, 106–11. Cambridge.

———. 1989. Reflections on Nine Years with the Bradford-Cambridge Boiotia Project. In *Boeotia Antiqua I. Papers on Recent Work in Boiotian Archaeology and History,* edited by J. M. Fossey, 13–20. Amsterdam.

———. 1994. Territorial Behavior and the Natural History of the Greek Polis. In *Stuttgarter Kolloquium zur historischen Geographie des Altertums 4, 1990,* 207–49 and tables XIX–LXXIII. Geographica Historica, Bd. 7. Bonn.

———. 1996. The archaeological survey of the Valley of the Muses and its significance for Boeotian history. In *La Montagne des Muses,* edited by A. Hurst and A. Schachter, 193–224. Genève.

———. 1997. Regional Survey, Demography, and the Rise of Complex Societies in the Ancient Aegean: Core-Periphery, Neo-Malthusian, and Other Interpretive Models. *Journal of Field Archaeology* 24: 1–38.

———. 1997b. Further Considerations on the Population of Ancient Boeotia. In *Recent Developments in the History and Archaeology of Central Greece,* edited by J. Bintliff. Proceedings of the Sixth International Boeotian Conference. Oxford.

Bintliff, J. L., and A. M. Snodgrass. 1985. The Cambridge/Bradford Boeotian Expedition: The First Four Years. *Journal of Field Archaeology* 12: 123–61.

———. 1988. Mediterranean Survey and the City. *Antiquity* 62: 57–71.

———. 1989. From Polis to Chorion in South-West Boeotia. In *Boiotika. Vorträge vom 5. Internationalen Böotien-Kolloquium zu Ehren von Professor Dr. Siegfried Lauffer*, 285–99. München.

Boserup, E. 1965. *The Conditions of Agricultural Growth. The Economics of Agrarian Change under Population Pressure*. Chicago.

———. 1981. *Population and Technological Change*. Chicago.

Bourriot, F. 1976. *Recherches sur la nature du genos: Étude d'histoire sociale Athénienne, périodes archaïque et classique*. Paris.

Braun, T. 1995. Barley Cakes and Emmer Bread. In *Food in Antiquity*, edited by J. Wilkins, D. Harvey, and M. Dobson, 25–37. Exeter.

Bravo, B. 1977. Remarques sur les assises sociales, les formes d'organisation et la terminologie du commerce maritime Grec à l'époque archaïque. *Dialogues d'histoire ancienne* 4: 1–59.

Buck, R. J. 1979. *A History of Boeotia*. Edmonton.

Burford, A. 1960. Heavy Transport in Classical Antiquity. *The Economic History Review* n.s. 13.1: 1–18.

———. 1993. *Land and Labor in the Greek World*. Baltimore.

Cartledge, P. 1983. "Trade and Politics" revisited: Archaic Greece. In *Trade in the Ancient Economy*, edited by P. Garnsey, K. Hopkins, and C. R. Whittaker, 1–15. London.

Chantraine, P. 1970–80. *Dictionnaire étymologique de la langue grecque*. 4 vols. Paris.

Cherry, J. E. 1988. Pastoralism and the Role of Animals in the Pre- and Proto-historical Economies of the Aegean. In *Pastoral Economies in Classical Antiquity*, edited by C. R. Whittaker, 6–34. Cambridge.

Cohen, M. N. 1977. *The Food Crisis in Prehistory. Overpopulation and the Origins of Agriculture*. New Haven.

Coldstream, J. N. 1977. *Geometric Greece*. New York.

Cunliffe, R. J. 1963. *A Lexicon of the Homeric Dialect*. Norman, Okla.

Davies, K. J. 1998. Ancient Economies: Models and Muddles. In *Trade, Traders, and the Ancient City*, edited by H. Parkins and C. Smith, 225–56. London and New York.

Denniston, J. D. 1959. *The Greek Particles*. 2nd ed. Oxford.

Detienne, M. 1963. *Crise agraire et attitude religieuse chez Hésiode. Collection Latomus* 68. Bruxelles.

Donlan, W. 1973. The Tradition of Anti-Aristocratic Thought in Early Greek Poetry. *Historia* 22: 145–54.

———. 1982. Reciprocities in Homer. *Classical World* 75: 137–76.

———. 1985. The Social Groups of Dark Age Greece. *Classical Philology* 80: 293–308.

———. 1989. The Pre-State Community in Greece. *Symbolae Osloenses* 64: 5–29.

———. 1993. Dueling with Gifts in the *Iliad:* As the Audience Saw It. *Colby Quarterly* 29: 125–72.

————. 1997. The Homeric Economy. In *A New Companion to Homer*, edited by I. Morris and B. Powell, 649–67. Leiden.

————. 1998. Political Reciprocity in Dark Age Greece: Odysseus and his *hetairoi*. In *Reciprocity in Ancient Greece*, edited by C. Gill, N. Postlethwaite, and R. Seaford, 51–71. Oxford.

Donlan, W., and C. G. Thomas. 1993. The Village Community of Dark Age Greece: Neolithic, Bronze, and Dark Ages. *Studi miceni ed egeo-anatolici* 31: 61–71.

Drews, R. 1983. *Basileus. The Evidence for Kingship in Geometric Greece*. Yale.

Earle, T. 1997. *How Chiefs Come to Power. The Political Economy in Prehistory*. Stanford.

Edwards, A. 1993. Historicizing the Popular Grotesque: Bakhtin's *Rabelais* and Attic Old Comedy. In *Theater and Society in the Classical World*, edited by R. Scodel, 88–117. Ann Arbor.

————. 1993b. Homer's Ethical Geography: Country and City in the *Odyssey*. *Transactions of the American Philological Association* 123: 27–78.

Edwards, G. P. 1971. *The Language of Hesiod in its Traditional Context*. Oxford.

Effenterre, H. van. 1990. La notion de ville dans la préhistoire égéenne. In *L'Habitat Égéenne Préhistorique*, edited by P. Darcque and R. Treuil. *Bulletin de Corréspondence Hellénique Supp. XIX*: 485–91.

Ellis, F. 1993. *Peasant Economics. Farm Households and Agrarian Development*. Cambridge.

Finley, M. I. 1979. *World of Odysseus*. 2nd ed. Middlesex.

————. 1980. *Ancient Slavery and Modern Ideology*. New York.

Forbes, H., and L. Foxhall. 1995. Ethnoarchaeology and Storage in the Ancient Mediterranean: Beyond Risk and Survival. In *Food in Antiquity*, edited by J. Wilkins, D. Harvey, and M. Dobson, 69–86. Exeter.

Fossey, J. M. 1988. *Topography and Population of Ancient Boiotia*. Vol. I. Chicago.

————. 1990. *Papers in Boiotian Topography and History*. Amsterdam.

Foxhall, L. 1998. Cargoes of the Heart's Desire. The Character of Trade in the Archaic Mediterranean World. In *Archaic Greece: New Approaches and New Evidence*, edited by N. Fisher and H. van Wees, 295–309. London.

Francis, E. K. L. 1945. The Personality Type of the Peasant According to Hesiod's *Works and Days*. *Rural Sociology* 10: 275–95.

Gagarin, M. 1973. *DIKE* in the *Works and Days*. *Classical Philology* 68: 81–94.

————. 1974. Hesiod's Dispute with Perses. *Transactions of the American Philological Association* 104: 103–11.

————. 1986. *Early Greek Law*. Berkeley.

————. 1992. The Poetry of Justice: Hesiod and the Origins of Greek Law. *Ramus* 21: 61–78.

Gallant, T. W. 1982. Agricultural Systems, Land Tenure, and the Reforms of Solon. *Annual of the British School at Athens* 77: 111–24.

————. 1991. *Risk and Survival in Ancient Greece. Reconstructing the Rural Domestic Economy.* Stanford.

Garlan, Y. 1988. *Slavery in Ancient Greece.* Rev. and exp. ed. Translated by J. Lloyd. Ithaca and London.

Garnsey, P. 1988. *Famine and Food Supply in the Graeco-Roman World. Responses to Risk and Crisis.* Cambridge.

Garnsey, P., and I. Morris. 1989. Risk and the *polis:* The evolution of institutionalized responses to food supply problems in the ancient Greek state. In *Bad Year Economics. Cultural Responses to Risk and Uncertainty,* edited by P. Halstead and J. O'Shea, 98–105. Cambridge.

Gauvin, G., and J. Morin. 1992. Le site d'Ascra et ses carrières. In *Boeotia Antiqua II. Papers on Recent Work in Boeotian Archaeology and Epigraphy,* edited by J. M. Fossey, 7–15. Amsterdam.

Griffith, M. 1983. Personality in Hesiod. *Classical Antiquity* 2: 37–65.

Groningen, B. A. van. 1957. *Hésiode et Perse.* Mededelingen der koninklijke Nederlandse Akademie van Wetenschappen, Afd. Letterkunde, Nieuwe Reeks, Deel 20, no. 6. Amsterdam.

Halstead, P. 1981. Counting sheep in Neolithic and Bronze Age Greece. In *Pattern of the past. Studies in honour of David Clarke,* edited by I. Hodder, G. Isaac, and N. Hammond, 307–39. Cambridge.

————. 1987. Man and Other Animals in Later Greek Prehistory. *Annual of the British School at Athens* 82: 71–83.

————. 1989. The economy has a normal surplus: Economic stability and social change among early farming communities of Thessaly, Greece. *Bad Year Economics: Cultural Responses to Risk and Uncertainly,* edited by P. Halstead and J. O'Shea, 68–80. Cambridge.

Halstead, P., and G. Jones. 1989. Agrarian Ecology in the Greek Islands: Time Stress, Scale and Risk. *Journal of Hellenic Studies* 109: 41–55.

Halstead, P., and J. O'Shea. 1982. A friend in need is a friend in deed: Social storage and the origins of social ranking. In *Ranking, Resource, and Exchange. Aspects of the Archaeology of Early European Society,* edited by C. Renfrew and S. Shennan, 92–99. Cambridge.

Hamilton, R. 1989. *The Architecture of Hesiodic Poetry.* Baltimore.

Hansen, M. H. 1995. *Kome.* A Study in How the Greeks Designated and Classified Settlements Which Were Not *Poleis.* In *Studies in the Ancient Greek Polis,* edited by M. H. Hansen and K. Raaflaub, 45–81. Historia Einzelschriften 95. Stuttgart.

Hanson, V. D. 1995. *The Other Greeks. The Family Farm and the Agrarian Roots of Western Civilization.* New York.

Heath, M. 1985. Hesiod's Didactic Poetry. *Classical Quarterly* 35: 245–63.

Hodkinson, S. 1988. Animal Husbandry in the Greek Polis. In *Pastoral Economies in Classical Antiquity,* edited by C. R. Whittaker, 35–74. Cambridge.

Hofinger, M. 1978. *Lexicon Hesiodeum cum Indice Inverso.* Leiden.

Isager, S., and J. Skydsgaard. 1992. *Ancient Greek Agriculture.* London and New York.

Jajlenko, V. P. 1988. Die sozialstrukturelle Charakteristik der hesiodischen Polis im Epos "Werke und Tage." *Jahrbuch für Wirtschaftsgeschichte*, 95–111.

Jameson, M. H., C. N. Runnels, and T. H. van Andel. 1994. *A Greek Countryside. The Southern Argolid from Prehistory to the Present Day.* Stanford.

Jarman M. R., G. N. Bailey, and H. N. Jarman, eds. 1982. *Early European Agriculture. Its Foundation and Development.* Cambridge.

Johnson, A. W., and T. Earle. 1987. *The Evolution of Human Societies. From Foraging Group to Agrarian State.* Stanford.

Jones, G. 1987. Agricultural Practice in Greek Prehistory. *Annual of the British School at Athens* 82: 115–23.

Jones, N. F. 1984. Work "In Season" in the *Works and Days. Classical Journal* 79: 307–23.

Kallet-Marx, R. M. 1989. The Evangelistria Watchtower and the Defense of the Zagara Pass. In *Boiotika. Vorträge vom 5. Internationalen Böotien-Kolloquium zu Ehren von Professor Dr. Siegfried Lauffer*, edited by H. Beister and J. Buckler, 301–11. München.

Lamberton, R. 1988. *Hesiod.* New Haven.

Latte, K. 1968. Beiträge zum griechischen Strafrechte. In K. Latte, *Kleine Schriften*, edited by O. Gigon, W. Buchwald, W. Kunkel, 252–93. München.

Lee, R. D. 1986. Malthus and Boserup: A Dynamic Synthesis. *The State of Population Theory*, edited by C. Coleman and R. Schofield, 96–130. Oxford.

Lele, U., and S. W. Stone. 1989. *Population Pressure, the Environment and Agricultural Intensification. Variations on the Boserup Hypothesis.* MADIA Discussion Paper 4. Washington, D.C.

Lévy, E. 1986. Apparition en Grèce de l'idée de village. *Ktéma: Civilisation de l'orient, de la Grèce et de Rome antiques* 11: 117–27.

Liebermann, W.-L. 1981. Die Hälfte mehr als das Ganze. Zu Hesiods Rechtfertigung der "Werte." *Hermes* 109: 385–409.

Livi-Bacci, M. 1997. *A Concise History of World Population.* 2nd ed. Translated by C. Ipsen. Oxford.

Magagna, V. 1991. *Communities of Grain. Rural Rebellion in Comparative Perspective.* Ithaca and London.

Marsilio, M. 2000. *Farming and Poetry in Hesiod's Works and Days.* Lanham, Md.

Martin, R. P. 1992. Hesiod's Metanastic Poetics. *Ramus* 21: 11–33.

Mazarakis Ainian, A. 1997. *From Rulers' Dwellings to Temples. Architecture, Religion and Society in Early Iron Age Greece (1100–700 B.C.).* Studies in Mediterranean Archaeology, vol. 121. Jonsered.

Mazon, P. 1914. *Hésiode. Les Travaux et les jours.* Paris.

Meillassoux, C. 1991. *The Anthropology of Slavery. The Womb of Iron and Gold.* Translated by A. Dasnois. London.

Mele, A. 1979. *Il Commercio Greco Arcaico. Prexis ed Emporie.* Naples.

Merkelbach, R., and M. West, eds. 1967. *Fragmenta Hesiodea.* Oxford.

Millett, P. 1984. Hesiod and his World. *Proceedings of the Cambridge Philological Society* n.s. 30: 84–115.

Morris, I. 1986. The Use and Abuse of Homer. *Classical Antiquity* 5: 81–138.

———. 1987. *Burial and Greek Society*. Cambridge.

———. 1991. The Early Polis as City and State. In *City and Country in the Ancient World*, edited by J. Rich and A. Wallace-Hadrill, 26–57. London and New York.

———. 1997. Homer and the Iron Age. In *A New Companion to Homer*, edited by I. Morris and B. Powell, 536–59. Leiden, New York, and Köln.

———. 1997b. An Archaeology of Equalities? The Greek City States. In *The Archaeology of City-States. Cross-Cultural Approaches*, edited by D. L. Nichols and T. H. Charlton, 91–105. Washington, D.C.

———. 1998. Archaeology as a Kind of Anthropology: A Response to David B. Small. In *Democracy 2500? Questions and Challenges*, edited by I. Morris and K. A. Raaflaub, 229–39. Archaeological Institute of America Colloquia and Conference Papers No. 2, 1997. Dubuque, Iowa.

———. 2000. *Archaeology as Cultural History. Words and Things in Iron Age Greece*. Oxford.

Nagy, G. 1982. Hesiod. In *Ancient Writers*, edited by T. J. Luce. Vol. I: 43–73. New York.

———. 1990. *Greek Mythology and Poetics*. Ithaca and London.

———. 1996. *Poetry as Performance*. Cambridge.

Nelson, S. 1996. The Drama of Hesiod's Farm. *Classical Philology* 91: 45–53.

———. 1998. *God and the Land. The Metaphysics of Farming in Hesiod and Vergil*. Oxford.

Osborne, R. 1985. *Demos: The Discovery of Classical Attika*. Cambridge.

———. 1987. *Classical Landscape with Figures: The Ancient Greek City and its Countryside*. London.

———. 1996. *Greece in the Making: 1200–479 B.C.* London and New York.

———. 1996b. Pots, Trade, and the Archaic Greek Economy. *Antiquity* 70: 31–44.

Palmer, R. 2001. Bridging the Gap: The Continuity of Greek Agriculture from the Mycenaean to the Historical Period. In *Prehistory and History. Ethnicity, Class, and Political Economy*, edited by D. Tandy, 41–84. Montréal, and New York, London.

Parkins, H. 1998. Shaping the Future of the Ancient Economy. In *Trade, Traders, and the Ancient City*, edited by H. Parkins and C. Smith, 1–15. London and New York.

Peabody, B. 1975. *The Winged Word*. Albany.

Pertusi, A., ed. 1955. *Scholia vetera in Hesiodi opera et dies*. Milano.

Petropoulos, J. C. B. 1994. *Heat and Lust. Hesiod's Midsummer Festival Scene Revisited*. Lanham, Md.

Polignac, Francis de. 1995. *Cults, Territory, and the Origins of the Greek City-State*. Chicago and London.

Pritchett, W. K. 1985. *Studies in Ancient Greek Topography.* Part V. Berkeley.

Pucci, P. 1996. Auteur et destinataires dans les *Travaux* d'Hésiode. In *Le Metier du mythe. Lectures d'Hésiode,* edited by F. Blaise, P. J. de la Combe, and Ph. Rousseau, 191–210. Lille.

Qviller, B. 1981. The Dynamics of Homeric Society. *Symbolae Osloenses* 56: 109–56.

Raaflaub, K. A. 1998. A Historian's Headache. In *Archaic Greece: New Approaches and New Evidence,* edited by N. Fisher and H. van Wees, 169–93. London.

Rackham, O. 1983. Observations on the Historical Ecology of Boeotia. *Annual of the British School at Athens* 78: 291–351.

Radermacher, L. 1918. *Beiträge zur Volkskunde aus dem Gebiet der Antike.* Wien.

Redfield, R. 1953. *The Primitive World and its Transformations.* Ithaca.

———. 1956. *Peasant Society and Culture.* Chicago.

Renfrew, J. 1973. Agriculture. In *Neolithic Greece,* edited by D. R. Theocharis, 147–64. Athens.

———. 1979. The First Farmers in South East Europe. *Festschrift Maria Hopf. Archaeo-Physika,* Band 8: 243–65. Köln.

Richter, W. 1968. *Die Landwirtschaft im homerischen Zeitalter. Archaeologia Homerica,* Band II, Kapitel H. Göttingen.

Roussel, D. 1976. *Tribu et cité: Études sur les groupes sociaux dans les cités grecques aux époques archaïque et classique.* Paris.

Rowe, C. J., ed. 1978. *Essential Hesiod.* Bristol.

Runciman, W. G. 1982. Origins of States: The Case of Archaic Greece. *Comparative Studies in Society and History* 24: 351–77.

Sahlins, M. 1972. *Stone Age Economics.* New York.

Sallares, R. 1991. *Ecology of the Ancient Greek World.* Ithaca.

Sanderson, S. 1990. *Social Evolutionism.* Cambridge, Mass., and Oxford.

———. 1995. *Social Transformations. A General Theory of Historical Development.* Cambridge, Mass., and Oxford.

Sarpaki, A. 1992. The Palaeoethnobotanical Approach. The Mediterranean Triad or Is It a Quartet? In *Agriculture in Ancient Greece,* edited by B. Wells, 61–79. Proceedings of the Seventh International Symposium at the Swedish Institute at Athens, 16–17 May, 1990. Stockholm.

Schachter, A. 1986. *Cults of Boiotia.* Vol. 2. BICS Supplement 38.2. London.

———. 1989. Boiotia in the Sixth Century B.C. In *Boiotika. Vorträge vom 5. Internationalen Böotien-Kolloquium zu Ehren von Professor Dr. Siegfried Lauffer,* edited by H. Beister and J. Buckler, 73–86. München.

———. 1996. Reconstructing Thespiai. In *La Montagne des Muses,* edited by A. Hurst and A. Schachter, 99–126. Genève.

Schusky, E. L. 1989. *Culture and Agriculture. An Ecological Introduction to Traditional and Modern Farming Systems.* New York.

Scott, J. C. 1976. *The Moral Economy of the Peasant.* New Haven.

Shanin, T. 1987. Introduction: Peasantry as a Concept. In *Peasants and Peasant Societies,* edited by T. Shanin, 1–11. 2nd ed. Oxford.

Sheratt, A. 1981. Plough and pastoralism: Aspects of the secondary products revolution. In *Pattern of the past. Studies in honour of David Clarke,* edited by I. Hodder, G. Isaac, and N. Hammond, 261–305. Cambridge.

Sihvola, J. 1989. *Decay, Progress, and the Good Life?* Commentationes Humanarum Litterarum 89. Helsinki.

Sinclair, T. A., ed. 1966. *Hesiod. Works and Days.* Hildesheim.

Skydsgaard, J. E. 1988. Transhumance in Ancient Greece. In *Pastoral Economies in Classical Greece,* edited by C. R. Whittaker, 75–86. Cambridge.

Small, D. B. 1997. City-State Dynamics through a Greek Lens. In *The Archaeology of City-States. Cross-Cultural Approaches,* edited by D. L. Nichols and T. H. Charlton, 107–18. Washington, D.C.

———. 1998. An Archaeology of Democracy? In *Democracy 2500? Questions and Challenges,* edited by I. Morris and K. A. Raaflaub, 217–27. Archaeological Institute of America Colloquia and Conference Papers No. 2, 1997. Dubuque, Iowa.

———. 1998b. A Democracy of Archaeologies. A Response to Ian Morris. In *Democracy 2500? Questions and Challenges,* edited by I. Morris and K. A. Raaflaub, 241–46. Archaeological Institute of America Colloquia and Conference Papers No. 2, 1997. Dubuque, Iowa.

Snodgrass, A. M. 1980. *Archaic Greece. The Age of Experiment.* Berkeley.

———. 1983. Heavy Freight in Archaic Greece. In *Trade in the Ancient Economy,* edited by P. Garnsey, K. Hopkins, and C. R. Whittaker, 16–26. London.

———. 1985. The site of Ascra. In *La Béotie Antique,* edited by P. Roesch and G. Argoud, 87–95. Actes du Colloque International "La Béotie Antique" à Lyons et à Saint-Étienne du 16 au 20 mai 1983. Paris.

———. 1987–89. The Rural Landscape and its Political Significance. *Opus* 6–8: 53–70.

———. 1990. Survey Archaeology and the Rural Landscape. In *The Greek City from Homer to Alexander,* edited by O. Murray and S. Price, 113–36. Oxford.

———. 1993. The Rise of the Polis. The Archaeological Evidence. In *The Ancient Greek City State,* edited by M. H. Hansen, 30–40. Symposium on the occasion of the 250th Anniversary of the Royal Danish Academy of Sciences and Letters, July 1–4, 1992. Historisk-filosofisk Meddeleser 67. Copenhagen.

Snodgrass, A. M., and J. L. Bintliff. 1991. Surveying Ancient Cities. *Scientific American* 264 (March): 88–93.

Solmsen, F., ed. 1970. *Hesiodi Theogonia Opera et Dies Scutum.* Oxford.

Spahn, P. 1980. Oikos und Polis. Beobachtungen zum Prozess der Polisbildung bei Hesiod, Solon und Aischylos. *Historische Zeitschrift* 231: 529–64.

Ste. Croix, G. E. M. de. 1981. *The Class Struggle in the Ancient Greek World.* Ithaca.

Stone, G. D., and C. E. Downum. 1999. Non-Boserupian Ecology and Agricultural Risk: Ethnic Politics and Land Control in the Arid Southwest. *American Anthropologist* 101: 113–28.

Tainter, J. A. 1988. *The Collapse of Complex Societies.* Cambridge.

Tandy, D. 1997. *Warriors into Traders. The Power of the Market in Early Greece.* Berkeley.

―――. 2001. Agroskopia: Material Centripetalism and the Contingent Nature of Early Greek Economic Development. In *Prehistory and History: Ethnicity, Class and Political Economy,* edited by D. Tandy, 159–78. Montréal, New York, and London.

Thalmann, W. G. 1998. *The Swineherd and the Bow. Representations of Class in the Odyssey.* Ithaca and London.

Thomas, C. G., and C. Conant. 1999. *Citadel to City-State: The Transformation of Greece, 1200–700 B.C.E.* Bloomington.

Thorner, D. 1987. Peasant Economy as a Category in History. In *Peasants and Peasant Societies,* edited by T. Shanin, 62–68. 2nd ed. Oxford.

Trever, A. A. 1924. The Age of Hesiod: A Study in Economic History. *Classical Philology* 19: 157–68.

Trigger, B. 1998. *Sociocultural Evolution.* Oxford and Malden, Mass.

Tsetskhladze, G. 1998. Trade on the Black Sea in the Archaic and Classical Periods: Some Observations. In *Trade, Traders, and the City,* edited by H. Parkins and C. Smith, 52–74. London and New York.

Upham, S., ed. 1990. *The Evolution of Political Systems.* Cambridge.

Verdenius, W. J. 1985. *A Commentary on Hesiod Works and Days, vv. 1–382.* Leiden.

Walcot, P. 1970. *Greek Peasants, Ancient and Modern.* New York.

Weber, M. 1978. *Economy and Society.* Berkeley.

Wees, H. van. 1998. The Law of Gratitude: Reciprocity in Anthropological Theory. In *Reciprocity in Ancient Greece,* edited by C. Gill, N. Postlethwaite, and R. Seaford, 13–48. Oxford.

West, M. L., ed. 1966. *Hesiod. Theogony.* Oxford.

―――, ed. 1978. *Hesiod. Works and Days.* Oxford.

―――, ed. 1998. *Iambi et Elegi Graeci ante Alexandrum Cantati.* 2nd ed. Oxford.

Whitley, J. 1991. Social Diversity in Dark Age Greece. *Annual of the British School at Athens* 86: 341–65.

Whittle, A. 1996. *Europe in the Neolithic. The Creation of New Worlds.* Cambridge.

Wilamowitz-Moellendorff, U. von, ed. 1962. *Hesiodos Erga.* Berlin.

Wilk, R. R. 1996. *Economies and Cultures.* Boulder and Oxford.

Will, Édouard. 1957. Aux origines du régime foncier grec. Homère, Hésiode et l'arrière-plan Mycénien. *Révue des Études Anciennes* 59: 5–50.

Will, Ernest. 1965. Hésiode: Crise Agraire? Ou recul de l'aristocratie? *Revue des Études Grecques* 78: 542–56.

Wolf, E. R. 1966. *Peasants.* Englewood Cliffs, N.J.

Wood, J. W. 1998. A Theory of Preindustrial Population Dynamics. Demography, Economy, and Well-Being in Malthusian Systems. *Current Anthropology* 39: 99–135.

Zanker, G. 1986. The *Works and Days:* Hesiod's *Beggar's Opera? Bulletin of the Institute of Classical Studies* 33: 26–36.

Index

Achilles, spoils of, 43
Aegyptus *(Odyssey)*, 121
Aeolis, trade with Ascra, 46
Agamemnon, spoils of, 43
agathoi, in *Works and Days*, 102
Age of Iron, children in, 84, 88
aggos (storage vessel), 87n9
agorāe: dispute settlement at, 64–65, 66, 69–70, 178; Hesiod's knowledge of, 166; as market, 48; in *Odyssey*, 121–22
agrarian crises, 11n13; in Ascra, 8, 30–31, 33; inheritance system in, 31; in peasant society, 5, 7–8
agricultural calendar, 24, 150–56, 178, 179, 180–81; annual rhythm in, 154–56; crops in, 134; harvest and threshing in, 152–53, 155; livestock in, 147; omissions from, 156; Pleiades in, 151, 152; plowing in, 150–51, 155; sailing season in, 153–54, 155; sowing in, 150–51; trade in, 51; vintage in, 154, 155; winds in, 155; winter work in, 151–52
agricultural regimes: and animal husbandry, 148; annual cropping in, 130; of Classical Greece, 157; intensification of, 127–28, 132–35, 140n21; livestock in, 148, 157; marginal returns in, 128n2; plowing in, 84–85, 109, 130n9, 131, 139–40,

142n25, 150–51, 155; of small holders, 135; and social organization, 128n2; swidden, 129, 130, 157; traditional, 157; in *Works and Days*, 18–19, 132–50. *See also* crops; cultivation; fallowing regimes
aidāos (shame), 112
Ainian, Mazarakis, 119
aktāe (crop), 141
Al Mina, trade relations of, 46
animal husbandry. *See* draft animals; livestock
Arcturus, rising of, 154
aretāe: in Ascra, 114, 118, 164, 177, 183–84; of farmers, 115; reinforcement of, 165; role of *eris* in, 116; as social standing, 112n34; in *Works and Days*, 102, 111–12
Argolid: archaeological surveys of, 167; land ownership in, 33n2; material culture of, 47
Argos, rate of development in , 77
aristocracy. *See basilāees*; elites
Aristophanes: farmers in, 26; *Peace*, 44n9
Aristotle: on Ascra, 171; on *kāomai*, 168n8
Ascra: abandonment of, 171–73; access to markets, 49; agrarian crisis model of, 8, 30–31, 33; agricultural regime of, 39–41, 127, 143, 161,

Compositor:	G & S Typesetters, Inc.
Text:	10/13 Aldus
Display:	Aldus
Printer and binder:	Thomson-Shore, Inc.